ADAMS THE PILOT

To Sonoe, Edward and Rosa

Adams the Pilot

The Life and Times of

Captain William Adams: 1564–1620

WILLIAM CORR

JAPAN
LIBRARY

ADAMS THE PILOT

JAPAN LIBRARY
Knoll House, 35 The Crescent
Sandgate, Folkestone, Kent CT20 3EE

Japan Library is an imprint of Curzon Press Ltd
St John's Studios, Church Road, Richmond, Surrey TW9 2QA

First published 1995

British Library Cataloguing in Publication Data

A CIP catalogue record for this book
is available from the British Library

ISBN 1–873410–44–1

Typeset by Bookman, Slough, in Bembo 12 on 12½pt
Printed and bound in England by Bookcraft, Midsomer Norton, Avon

CONTENTS

The destruction of Osaka Castle in the summer campaign of 1615 made it evident to all, Japanese and foreigners alike,that Toyotomi Hideyoshi's heritage had been annihilated. It was in this mighty fortress that William Adams first met Tokugawa Ieyasu following the arrival of the *Liefde* in 1600.

PREFACE

The present work had its genesis in the reading which preceded the writing of *Miura Anjin: The Story of Captain William Adams*, published by Dawn Press of Nara in 1989. To John Terry of Dawn Press due thanks are offered. Others assisted at various stages. Michael Cooper, Charles Boxer, Derek Massarella and Anthony Farrington were kind enough to suggest helpful clues. The errors and omissions are not to be laid at their doors, however.

Adams himself wrote little; his letters and logs, while vivid and valuable, would convey too little about the eventful years between 1600 and 1620 on their own. Other sources, such as the various writings of other Europeans in Japan, complete the tale. The researches of Derek Massarella and Anthony Farrington provide much detail which was not available to P.G. Rogers or Richard Blaker earlier this century. As Michael Cooper has said, eventually a full biography of the redoubtable and ill-fated Richard Cocks will be written; it will be worth reading because Cocks, an immensely likeable man if an indifferent merchant and chief, lived in interesting times. The Adams legend, which continues sporadically to the present day, is not the least astonishing aspect of a remarkable career and an eventful life. Those who have perpetuated Adams' memory, whether Japanese or British, deserve congratulation. It is remarkable but true that the names of only two Europeans of the era of the *Christian Century* are widely known in contemporary Japan; one is Francis Xavier, the other is, predictably, William Adams.

Finally, thanks are due to Sonoe Kurimoto Corr for unfailing tolerance, encouragement, forbearance and love.

William Corr
Lhasa
June 1995

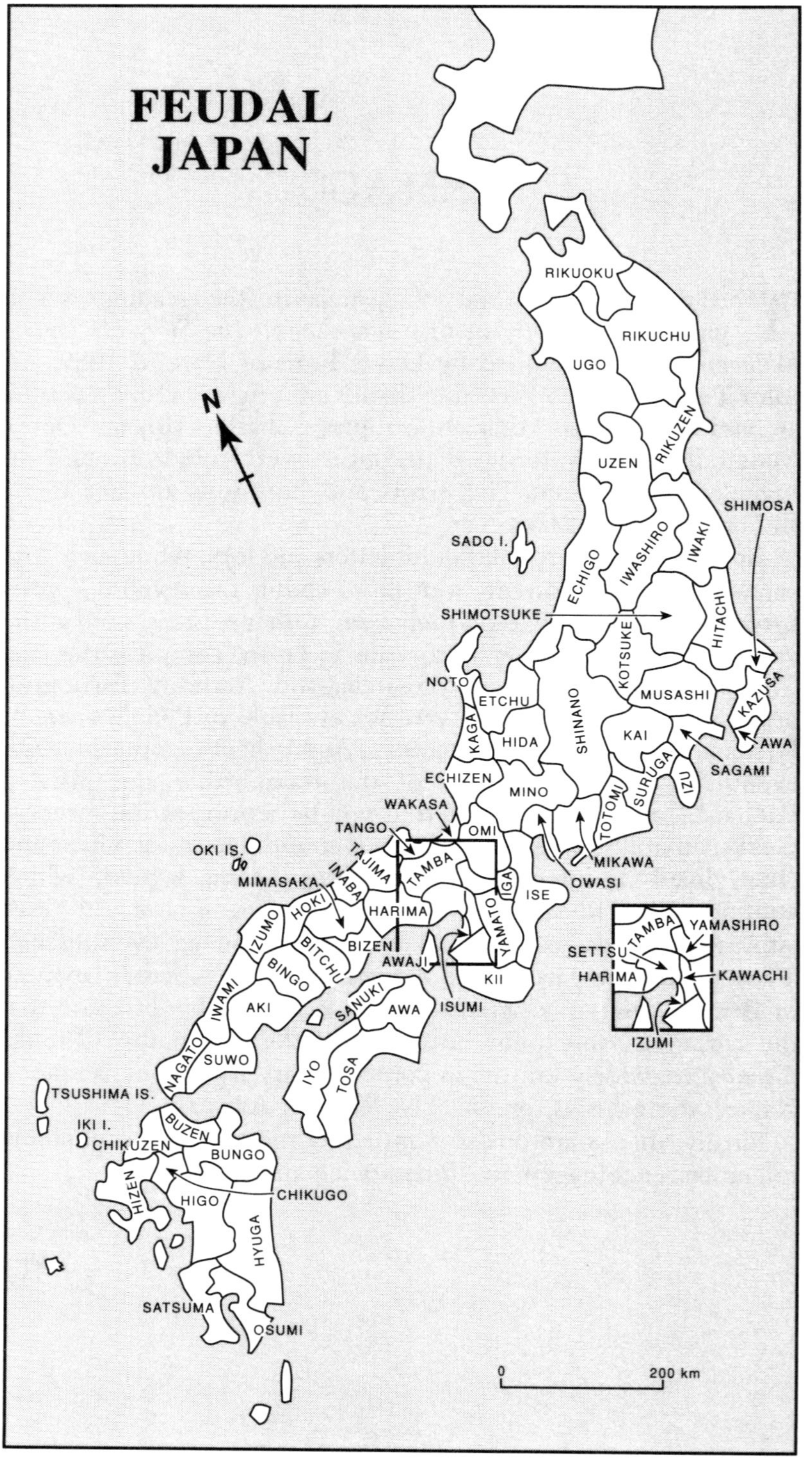
FEUDAL JAPAN
N
RIKUOKU
RIKUCHU
UGO
RIKUZEN
UZEN
SHIMOSA
SADO I.
ECHIGO
IWASHIRO
IWAKI
SHIMOTSUKE
HITACHI
KOTSUKE
NOTO
ETCHU
SHINANO
MUSASHI
KAZUSA
KAGA
HIDA
KAI
AWA
SAGAMI
ECHIZEN
MINO
SURUGA
IZU
TOTOMI
WAKASA
TANGO
OMI
MIKAWA
OKI IS.
TAJIMA
TAMBA
OWASI
MIMASAKA
INABA
IGA
ISE
HOKI
HARIMA
YAMATO
IZUMO
BITCHU
BIZEN
AWAJI
KII
BINGO
IWAMI
AKI
SANUKI
AWA
ISUMI
TAMBA
YAMASHIRO
SETTSU
HARIMA
KAWACHI
IZUMI
NAGATO
SUWO
IYO
TOSA
TSUSHIMA IS.
IKI I.
BUZEN
CHIKUZEN
BUNGO
HIZEN
HIGO
CHIKUGO
HYUGA
SATSUMA
OSUMI
0
200 km

CHRONOLOGY

1543 The first Portuguese traders arrive in Japan aboard a Chinese junk
1549 Francis Xavier arrives in Japan; inception of Christian mission
1550 The first European ships, Portuguese vessels, anchor at Hirado, an island off the coast of Kyushu. Portuguese trade with Japan becomes a royal monopoly, known as *The Japan Voyage*
1559 Padre Gaspar Vilela founds the mission of the Kyoto area
1560 Beginnings of Oda Nobunaga's rise to prominence
1562 Omura Sumitada gives the Jesuits license to preach in his domains, and privileges in the port of Yokoseura
1563 Omura Sumitada is baptized (Dom Bartolomé): first of the Christian *daimyo*
1564 William Adams is born in Gillingham, England.
1565 The *shogun* Ashikaga Yoshiteru is destroyed by Matsunaga Hisahide (June); Matsunaga expels the Christian missionaries from Kyoto (July)
1568 Oda Nobunaga occupies Kyoto and installs Ashikaga Yoshiaki as *shogun*
1569 Nobunaga interviews Padre Luís Frois and permits the missionaries to return to Kyoto
1570 Francisco Cabral becomes Japan Mission Superior
1571 Nagasaki becomes the terminal of the Portuguese trade with Japan
Nobunaga destroys the warrior monks of the Tendai Sect on Mount Hiei
1573 Nobunaga expels Yoshiaki from Kyoto: end of the Ashikaga *shogunate*
1576 The Jesuit Church dedicated to the Assumption of Our Lady (the *Nambanji*) is built in Miyako with the permission of Oda Nobunaga
1577 João Rodrigues, aged 16 or 17, arrives in Japan

1578 Completion of the Kyoto *Nanbanji* (spring)
Otomo Sorin baptized (August)
Araki Murashige turns against Nobunaga; Takayama Ukon betrays Araki and hands over the castle of Takatsuki to Nobunaga (November-December)
Battle of Mimigawa: beginning of the Otomo eclipse and the Shimazu ascendancy over Kyushu (December)

1579 Alexandro Valignano arrives in Japan on his first visit (to 1582)

1580 Omura Sumitada cedes Nagasaki to the Society of Jesus (9 June)
The Jesuit Order's first formal educational institutions begin to operate in Japan (October-December)
Death of Henry of Aviz; Portugal ruled by Spain until 1640

1581 Firm guidelines for a Japanese mission policy are set down by Valignano

1582 Honnoji Affair: Akechi Mitsuhide attacks and kills Nobunaga
Battle of Yamazaki: Toyotomi Hideyoshi eliminates Akechi and begins his rise to hegemony over Japan.
150,000 Christians in Japan

1584 The Shimazu destroy Ryzoji Takanobu at Okitanawate and rise to prominence in Kyushu

1585 Tokugawa Ieyasu sends hostages to Hideyoshi, concluding a peace agreement (January); Hideyoshi defeats the Shingon sectarians of Negoro (April) and Chosogabe Motochika of Tosa (July)
Dirk Gerritszoon Pompe, later to be Linschoten's informant about Japan and the way thither, arrives in Japan aboard the Macau-Nagasaki *naó Santa Cruz*, (July), remaining in Japan until March 1586

1586 Vice-Provincial Coelho requests Hideyoshi's intervention against the Shimazu and promises Christian support in his invasion plans (Osaka Audience; 4 May); Hideyoshi orders Shimazu Yoshihisa to make peace in Kyushu (19 May)

1587 The Shimazu forces occupy Funai in Bungo (January)
Hideyoshi sets out from Osaka to invade Kyushu (April)
Shimazu Yoshihisa capitulates to Hideyoshi (June)

Hideyoshi issues decrees restricting the practice of Christianity (23 July) and expelling the missionaries from Japan (24 July)

1588 William Adams commands a supply ship, the *Richard Dyffylde*, at the time of Philip II of Spain's attempted invasion of England, the *Enterprise of England* (the Spanish Armada)

The Jesuit Church, the *Nambanji*, in Miyako is destroyed on the orders of Toyotomi Hideyoshi. The donation of Nagasaki to the Jesuits is revoked by Hideyoshi

1590 Valignano arrives in Japan on his second visit (to 1592)

Hideyoshi defeats the Hojo of Odawara and is supreme in Japan (12 August)

1591 Suppression of the rebellion of Kokonoe Masazane in Mutsu: all Japan is reunified under Hideyoshi's hegemony

1592 Hideyoshi's armies invade Korea

Hideyoshi issues the first *shuinjo* to merchants from Nagasaki, Miyako and Sakai, authorising voyages to Qui-nam (in Annam), Cambodia, Tongking, Patani, Ligor (now Nakhorn Si Thammarat in Thailand), Taiwan, Luzon, Macau and Ayuthia

1593 Spanish Franciscans are permitted to remain in Japan: the Jesuit mission monopoly is broken

1596 The Spanish galleon *San Felipe* is wrecked on Shikoku and its cargo confiscated; the Jesuit-Franciscan quarrel exacerbates the situation

Jan Huyghen van Linschoten's *Discourse of voyages, Itinerario and Navigation* is published in Holland, greatly stimulating north European maritime endeavour.

1597 Martyrdom of the Twenty-Six Saints of Japan: first instance of bloody persecution of Christianity (5 February)

137 Jesuits resident in Japan

1598 Valignano arrives in Japan on his third visit (to 1603)

The fleet commanded by Jacques Mahu and Simon de Cordes leaves Holland (June)

Death of Toyotomi Hideyoshi; the Japanese armies are withdrawn from Korea

1599 Tokugawa Ieyasu permits the Franciscans to settle in Edo

1600 The first Dutch ship (*Liefde*) arrives in Japan. William Adams is taken before Tokugawa Ieyasu and questioned; he explains that Holland and England are at war with Spain and Portugal. Ieyasu declines the Portuguese suggestion that he execute the *Liefde*'s crew
The Jesuits resume their public mission in Kyoto
Battle of Sekigahara: Tokugawa Ieyasu becomes the paramount power in Japan (21 October)
The first two Japanese are ordained to the priesthood
1601 Jacob van Neck attacks Portuguese-held Tidore in an unsuccessful attempt to recapture the *Trouwe*, one of the vessels which had left Holland with the *Liefde* in 1598
1603 Ieyasu acquires the title of *shogun*: establishment of the Tokugawa *Bakufu* (24 March)
The Dominicans begin mission activities in Japan
1605 Ieyasu passes on the *shogunal* title to his son Hidetada, retires to Suruga. The Dutch seize, loot and burn the great *naó* in Macau harbour, temporarily impoverishing the commerce of Macau (July/August)
Adams is offered a safe-conduct to leave Japan aboard Portuguese shipping by a Jesuit, probably João Rodrigues; he declines the offer
1606 Jacob Jansz Quaeckernaeck, formerly Captain of the *Liefde*, is killed in a naval battle with the Portuguese near Malacca (October)
1609 The Dutch establish a trading factory at Hirado
222,000 Christians under the care of the Society of Jesus in Japan. Don Rodrigo Vivero y Velasco, former governor of the Philippines, survives the shipwreck of the *San Francisco* on the Japanese coast. In conversation with Tokugawa Ieyasu, Don Rodrigo offers Spanish trade to supplant the Portuguese monopoly of the Macau-Nagasaki Trade Route
1610 The Macau-Nagasaki *naó*, *Nossa Senhora de Graça*, also known as the *Madre de Dios*, and commanded by André Pessoa, is destroyed in Nagasaki Bay after a four-day fight with the *daimyo* of Arima
João Rodrigues, grammarian, linguist, historian and interpreter to Ieyasu, is expelled from Japan after 33 years' residence; Adams succeeds him as Ieyasu's

unofficial interpreter and trade negotiator
Don Rodrigo Vivero y Velasco leaves Japan aboard the larger of the two ships Adams built in Japan; the ship, called the *Santa Buenaventura*, remains in Spanish service for many years

1612 The *Bakufu* issues decrees prohibiting Christianity and takes steps against the mission in its immediate domains

1613 The English establish a trading factory at Hirado

1614 *Statement on the Expulsion of the Bateren*: beginning of the general persecution (1 February)
Osaka Winter Campaign (November; armistice 19 January 1615)
Adams' first attempted Siam voyage, in company with Wickham and Sayers of the E.I.C. Hirado factory, proves abortive. The junk *Sea Adventure* is obliged to spend five months in Okinawa

1615 Fall of Osaka Castle, death of Toyotomi Hideyori and end of Hideyoshi's heritage (4 June)
The *Sea Adventure*, commanded by Adams, sails to Siam, trading with fair success

1616 Death of Ieyasu (1 June)
The *Bakufu* restricts foreign trade to Nagasaki and Hirado (September)

1617 Adams' third voyage from Japan, to Cochin-China

1618 Adams sails for Cochin-China but only reaches Okinawa. The *Attendance*, a British ship, is brought into Hirado harbour as 'lawful prize' after capture at sea by the Dutch. Macau-Nagasaki trade is carried aboard fleets of galliots for the first the first time, a measure to frustrate Dutch interception

1619 Two more captured British ships are brought into Hirado harbour after capture by the Dutch. Richard Cocks, the E.I.C. factor at Hirado, witnesses the martyrdom of fifty Miyako Christians while visiting the capital (October 7)
Adams' fifth, and last, voyage: to Tonking. William Wright's English translation of Pedro Morejón's book, first published in Mexico in 1616, *A Briefe Relation of the Persecution Lately Made Against the Catholike Christians in the Kingdome of Iaponia*, is published in Saint-Omer; Adams is mentioned obliquely as an enemy of 'religious

men' and Spaniards
The Treaty of Defence is signed between the British and the Dutch, agreeing '. . .*to make Spoile and Havock of all Portingalls and Spaniards wheresoever we meet them'*

1620 Adams' death at Hirado, 16 May

1622 The Great Martyrdom in Nagasaki
The Dutch attack on Macau, with nominal E.I.C. support, in the combined *'Fleet of Defence'*, is a failure (June)

1623 Hidetada passes on the shogunal title to his son Iemitsu (August)
The Great Martyrdom in Edo (December)
The E.I.C. factory at Hirado closes after trading for 10 years, 6 months (December)

1624 Spanish traders compelled to leave Japan
Richard Cocks dies while aboard the E.I.C. ship, the *Bull*, in the Indian Ocean (March)

1633 *Sakoku* Edict I severely restricts Japanese trade and travel overseas, and prohibits the return of Japanese who had settled abroad (7 April)

1634 *Sakoku* Edict II (23 June)

1635 *Sakoku* Edict III puts an end to Japanese shipping overseas and prohibits under pain of death, the return of any Japanese who had settled abroad (7 April)

1636 *Sakoku* Edict IV (22 June)
The Portuguese traders are restricted to the artificial island of Deshima in Nagasaki harbour

1637 Shimabara Christian Rebellion (11 December–12 April 1638)

1639 Final *Sakoku* Edict: end of the Portuguese trade and of all Japanese traffic with Catholic lands (4 August)

1640 The city of Macau sends an embassy to Japan; 61 members of the crew and embassy are executed. Thirteen survivors are returned to Macau

1641 The Dutch V.O.C. traders are compelled to move to Deshima, an artificial island in Nagasaki harbour; they remain there for more than two centuries.

(After Elison, 1973, and Matsuda, 1991)

I

ADAMS AND HIS AGE

William Adams was born in England in 1564 and died in Japan in 1620. Believed to have been the first English-speaker to reside in Japan, he became an adviser to the founder of the Tokugawa *shogunate*, Ieyasu, and was, briefly, an influential figure in Japan. William Adams' life is of interest for a number of reasons; his upbringing in Elizabethan England and his command of a supply ship at the time of Philip II of Spain's attempted invasion and subjugation of England in 1588, the *Enterprise of England*, known subsequently in English-speaking countries as the Spanish Armada, shaped his attitude towards Catholicism and Spanish power. Despite this, during his prolonged residence in Japan, he never lacked either Catholic or Spanish friends.

Adams, like many of his contemporaries, spent some time in Dutch service, most notably aboard the five-vessel Mahu and De Cordes fleet of 1598-1600. Whether he served aboard one or more Dutch ships attempting to discover the non-existent North-West passage to Asia is uncertain; the Catholic missionaries in Japan later wrote that he did but the evidence beyond this second-hand assertion is non-existent.

The voyage which took Adams to Japan was a signal disaster, both in terms of human life and as a commercial enterprise. Only one of the five ships returned to Europe and that bore no rich cargo of the kind the expedition's backers had desired. Of the remaining four, one surrendered to the Spanish at Valparaiso, another to the Portuguese in the Moluccas and one foundered with all hands in the Pacific Ocean. The *Liefde,* to which Adams had fortunately transferred, reached Japan in wretched condition. As Adams recorded, at the time, the *Liefde* came to anchor in Bungo Strait there were but twenty-four living men aboard. Of these, three died the following day and another three not long afterwards. Adams' career in Japan is the aspect of his life which has proven most attractive to novelists and historians. He was an unofficial advisor to Togukawa Ieyasu, a shipwright and almost certainly, a cartographer. He traded on his own account as well as acting as a commercial agent for Japanese merchants and Europeans. The period of his residence in Japan saw many changes in the political life of the country. At the time of his arrival, he was, as he recorded, in danger of death by crucifixion and impalement at the instigation of the Jesuits. By the time of his death in 1620, the Jesuits together with the other missionary orders then active in Japan were in no position to influence affairs. Indeed, Adams briefly supplanted the erudite Jesuit, João Rodrigues as Ieyasu's interpreter and advisor.

Adams' influence on Japan's rulers was short-lived. The two ships he built in the European style were not the forerunners of an immense seagoing fleet, although nothing but Tokugawa policy prevented the construction of such a fleet, armed with European-style artillery and manned by seafarers equal to any in Pacific waters. Although Adams did what he could to facilitate the trade of his fellow-countrymen of the East India Company in Japan, the E.I.C's venture was unsuccessful, lasting a mere decade (1613-1623), yet in 1673 the E.I.C tried to return, unsuccessfully.

While it is true that the British trading settlement established in Japan in the first quarter of the seventeenth century proved to be, ultimately, a failure, the history of what chroniclers have called 'the English factory' remains a fascinating if relatively unimportant footnote in the long story of relations between two great maritime and mercantile powers.

In retrospect, it is evident that while the East India Company's trading venture in Japan was of marginal importance to the British, the presence of European traders in Japan was of no greater real significance to the Tokugawa *shogunate*. At the time, however, things were perceived differently; in December 1615, Richard Cocks, the Cape Merchant of the Hirado factory (as trading stations were then known) recorded that Ieyasu graciously offered to give the English anything that might be for the benefit of their nation, '. . .esteeming us above all other Christian nations whatsoever.' (Murakami and Murakawa, 1973, 163).

Within less than a decade, the I.E.C's Japanese venture was

abandoned, the entire endeavour apparently a total loss. Upon the expulsion of the Spanish and Portuguese a few years later, the chief rivals of the English, the Dutch became the unchallenged monopolists of what little trade and intercourse survived between Japan and the exterior world, other than a relatively insignificant volume of foreign trade in the hands of a small, closely supervised, Chinese mercantile community permitted, like the Dutch, to reside at Nagasaki. (Plutschow, 1983, 77)

From the earliest days of the English factory at Hirado, it was clearly understood that the acquisition of the right to trade into China was a highly desirable objective. In retrospect, it seems probable that the successful establishment of secure trading relations between the Britons at Hirado and one or more ports in China, would have made the East India Company's venture a success rather than a failure. There were, however, a number of difficulties which stood in the way of attaining so desirable an end. The Chinese, who had a well-founded apprehension of Japanese piracy and raiding, refused to permit Japanese vessels to enter their ports and the indirect trade, funnelled through Okinawa, Macau and (illegally) Tsushima, was jealously guarded. It was enormously profitable and far too highly coveted to permit the English a share of it. Much has been made of Cocks' reliance on the *China Captain*; 'Desperately hoping a profit from the Chinese trade, Cocks entrusted 6,636 taels of silver to the *China Captain* a junk skipper called Li Tan (or Li Han Kok) who wished to act as an intermediary for trading but was cheated by him.' (Makino, 1983, 78). Whether Cocks was deliberately cheated or not is open to question; Cocks was a shrewd judge of character and knew the individual concerned for a considerable period of time. In any case, the 'China Captain' and his brother were not unsuccessful as merchants; 'The Chinas of late time, within these 2 or 3 years, have begun a trade into certain islands called by them Tacca Sanga and is named in our sea cards Isla Fermosa near to the coast of China. The place the shipping enters into is called Las Islas Piscadores, but none but small shipping can enter, neither will they suffer any shipping or trade with any people but Chinas. It is within 30 leagues (as they say) of the main of China, so that they make 2 or 3 voyages in small shipping each monsoon. Andrea Dittis (*Li Tan*) and Captain Whaw, his brother, are the greatest adventures for that place. They sent 2 small junks the last year and bought silk for the one half they pay either at Cochin-China or Bantam.' (Thompson, 1883, II, 298)

Li Tan, the *China Captain* or head of the Chinese community at Hirado, was a remarkable figure in his own right. A native of Chuanchow (Quanzhou) in Fujian, he traded to the Philippines early in his career and was sentenced to the galleys by the Spaniards for some unknown offence. He escaped and fled to Hirado. There, he prospered. By the time he had dealings with the Dutch and English, he was married and, not unusually for a wealthy Chinese, possessed concubines. Captain Whaw, his brother, acted as his agent at Nagasaki. Another brother, Niquan, lived in Hirado and a third brother remained in China. Captain Whaw was issued *shuinjo* to trade to Annam and Tonking between 1614 and 1618. (Boxer, 1941, 402-3). Li Tan was evidently a Christian convert, baptised as Andrea or Andreas; one of his daughters, to whom Richard Cocks was godfather, was named Ignacia.

The following year, Cocks wrote to his employer of the East India Company; 'I am of your Worships opinion that, except we procure trade into China, it will not quite cost to maintain a factory in Japan. . .' (Thompson, 1883, II, 297). Three years later, it seemed that success was at hand at last; 'I am now informed by a messenger we sent into China that the old Emperor hath resigned the government unto one of his sons; and that the new Emperor hath granted our nation, trade into China for 2 ships a year, and the place appointed near to Foochow and that there wanted but the fermes (*seals*) of 2 viceroys of 2 provinces to confirm it and that the *goshon* or passport will be sent us by the next monsoon and had been here before now had it not been letted (delayed) per the wars of Tartary. Thus, much our China friends tell us and I hop it will prove true.' (Thompson, 1883, II, 324).

Despite the closure of the E.I.C. factory at Hirado, luxuries from Japan continued to be highly esteemed by the wealthiest classes in England. On 12 December 1663, a Mr. Abrahall, a contractor supplying chandlery to the Royal Navy, sent the wife of Samuel Pepys 'a fine Japanese gown.' Since this was forty years since the Hirado factory closed and nearly ten years prior to the

Return's attempt to reopen direct trade between Britain and Japan, the gown can only have been purchased from the Dutch. (Taylor, 1967, 56)

At the time of Charles II's death in 1685, the Duchess of Portsmouth, one of his mistresses, possessed cabinets described as 'masterpieces of Japanese art.' (Macauley, 1966, I, 324). Unless these had been purchased prior to 1623, which is inherently improbable, they were almost certainly purchased through the Dutch.

That the E.I.C's venture might have prospered more had the factory, as trading posts were then called, been established at Uraga, as Adams suggested, rather than at Hirado, is debatable.

Adams was familiar with Uraga, the port he told Saris would be an excellent place for the British E.I.C. to establish a factory. At the time the two men visited Uraga, Saris enquired about the purchase of a ship the Spanish had for sale but concluded that the price asked, £100, was too dear. He did, however, purchase some Kyoto ceramic ware which Adams kept at Uraga to sell to the Spaniards. (Murdoch, 1949, 588)

Captain Saris observed, in September 1613: 'Note that Oringgaw (*Uraga*) is a very good harbour for shipping, where ships may ride as safely as in the River of Thames before London, and the passage thereto by sea very safe and good: so that it will be much better for our ships to sail thither than to Firando (*Hirado*). . .Oringgaw is for all other matters to be preferred before Firando.' (Satow, 1900, 136).

Adams said much the same in his letter to Augustine Spalding in 1613, making the telling point that good harbours were to be found near Edo (Tokyo), the new capital city under the *Pax Tokugawa*:

> The charges in Japan are not great: only a pressent for ye Emperour and a pressent for ye Kinge, and 2 or 3 other pressents for the Secretaris. Other coustoumes here be nonn. Now, once, yf a ship do coum, lett her coum for the esterly part of Japan, lying in 35d. 10m. whear the Kinge and ye Emperour court is: for coum our ships to Ferando whear the Hollanders bee, it is farr to ye court, about 230L, a wery soum way and foul. The citti of Edo lyeth in 36, and about this esterly part of the land thear be the best harbors and a cost so cleer as theayr is no sholdes nor rokes ½ a myll from the mayn land. It is good also for sale of marchandis and security for ships, forr which cass I haue sent a pattron

> [? *pattern, card, or chart*] of Japan, for which my self I hau been all about the cost in the shipping that I haue made for ye Emperour, that I hau experyence of all yt part of ye cost that lyeth in 36d., etc.
>
> (Rundall, 1850, 43)

It is regrettable that Adams' *pattron* has not survived.

Richard Cocks evidently shared Adams' estimate of Hirado. Long before the proximity of the V.O.C. factory made Hirado a hazardous place he wrote '. . .it were as good for the Emperor to banish us all out of Japan as to shut us up in Hirado, it being a place of no sales.' (Thompson, 1883, I, 187)

Cocks had strong opinions on the relative merits of Hirado and Nagasaki as harbours: '. . .the harbour at Nagasaki is the best in all Japan, where there may 1,000 sail of ships ride land locked, and the greatest ships or carricks in the world may go in and out at pleasure and ride before the town within a cables length of the shore in 7 or 8 fathom of water at least, it being a great city and many rich merchants dwelling in it, where to the contrary, Hirado is a fisher town and a very small and bad harbour, wherein not above 8 or 10 ships can ride at a time without great danger to spoil one other in stormy weather; and that which is worst, no shipping can enter in or out of that harbour, but they must have both tide and wind as also 8 or 10 pinnaces or barks to tow them in and out, the current runneth so swift that otherwise they cannot escape running ashore; where to the contrary, there is no such matter at Nagasaki, it being one of the fairest and largest harbours that ever I saw, whereinto a man may enter in and go out with shipping at all times, the wind serving without help of boat or pinnace.' (Thompson, 1883, II, 313–314)

That Cocks bitterly regretted Saris' decision to establish the English factory at Hirado is plain: '. . .(we) settled ourselves at Hirado when we might as well have made choice of any other province of Japan, and now to be so misused to have some of our people killed and others extremely misused; and, lastly, others carried away captives to be sold to our enemies; which if it were not remedied, there was no staying for us in Japan.' (Thompson, 1883, II, 244)

Adams knew the eastern and southern coasts of Japan as well as any contemporary Japanese coastal trader or pilot and his recommendation of Uraga, a port close to present-day Yokosuka, as a suitable situation for the East India Company should have been heeded. As well as offering a far better harbour for large ships than did Hirado, Uraga was conveniently close to the *shogun*'s court at Edo and a long way from Dutch and Iberian influence at Hirado and Nagasaki. It had been Uraga for which the *Liefde*, the Dutch vessel aboard which Adams arrived in Japan, had been making in April 1600 and it was, significantly, near Uraga that Commodore Matthew Perry's squadron anchored in July 1853. In addition to Uraga's other advantages as a site for the East India Company's station, it was conveniently close to Adams' home and estate at Hemi.

In disdaining to accept Adams' advice on so crucial a matter, Saris chose to ignore the written instructions of his employers: '. . .to consult and take good advice with the rest of the factors and especially with William Adams, an Englishman now resident there (*Japan*) and in great favour with the king as we hear. . .' (Satow, 1900, xiii-xiv)

Adams lived in an era of astonishing individuals, such as Fray Juan Pobre of Zamora, whose remarkable career has been described by Professor Boxer in terms of suitable awe (Boxer, 1951, 480-1). Nor were these remarkable men all Europeans; the first Japanese to visit Moscow, Brother Nicolão of the Order of St. Augustine, arrived in that city from Goa in 1599 and was martyred there in 1611.

The posthumous cult of William Adams, which continues unabated to the present day, is not the least singular aspect of a singular life. There remains the enigma of William Adams the man; William Adams the staunch Protestant and former 'Master and Pilott in her Maiesties ships', who married a Japanese Catholic woman, knowingly committing bigamy by so doing and who refused offers to return to his own country on at least four occasions; Adams, the man to whom the Jesuit chroniclers ascribed malign influences little short of diabolical; Adams, the man who never lacked Catholic friends and associates during a sojourn in Japan lasting two decades; Adams, the man who fathered a fifth child by an unknown woman in Hirado and who died wealthy yet neglected to make any provision for either this third mother or her child in his will, who referred to the Christian deity not infrequently in his letters and who was given a posthumous Buddhist name. Adams was neither wholly admirable nor contemptible. A man of modest formal education, he was for a short span of years, undeniably the most influential foreigner in Japan, supplanting one of the most learned foreigners in contemporary Japan, João Rodrigues Tçuzzi.

Any consideration of Adams' life in Japan necessarily involves an understanding of the *Christian Century*, the remarkable period between 1543, the year of the arrival of the first Europeans, and 1639, the year in which it was decreed that Japan was virtually closing her doors to the outside world.

In the century following 1543, the year in which the first Portuguese mariners, António da Mota, Francisco Zeimoto and António Peixoto, arrived in Japan and, by an uncanny coincidence, the year after that which Tokugawa Ieyasu was born, Japanese official policy made a complete circle.

Although official policies and the direction of events in Japan, as elsewhere, are not infrequently notoriously difficult to discern at the time, seven quite clear periods are apparent in retrospect:

Firstly, the ready receptivity to, and acceptance of, Europeans after the first arrival of the Portuguese at Tanegashima in 1543.

Secondly, apparent encouragement of the Jesuit missionaries in the time of Oda Nobunaga.

Thirdly, encouragement and continuation of the Portuguese trade between Macau and Nagasaki on the one hand, and, on the other, the first bloody repression and martyrdom of Christians in the time of Toyotomi Hideyoshi.

Fourthly, far-flung overseas trade by Japanese traders and mariners in officially sanctioned 'vermilion-seal ships' (*shuinsen*), commencing in the days of Toyotomi Hideyoshi.

Fifthly, invasion of the Korean Peninsula, on the mainland of Asia, intended as the prelude to the conquest of all China, followed by ignominious withdrawal after Hideyoshi's death in 1598.

Sixthly, intensifying and systematic persecution of Christianity from 1614 onwards, in the time of Tokugawa Ieyasu.

Seventhly, total prohibition of Japanese travel abroad in the 1630s, followed by the expulsion of the Portuguese and the adoption of *Sakoku*, a policy of national isolation, in 1639.

Events which occurred prior to Adams' arrival in Japan aboard the *Liefde* affected his life in Japan greatly. It is with the period in which Adams lived in Japan, the years 1600 to 1620, no less than with the life of Adams the man *per se*, with which this work deals.

At the time of the first Europeans' arrival, independent warlords governed, or misgoverned, their territories as they pleased, without paying heed to the authority of Emperor in Miyako to whom all were nominally subject. On various occasions, Miyako was raided and burned by marauding bands of soldiers and even wayward monks, whom court officials acting in the Emperor's name were powerless to control.

This lawless state of affairs – *Sengoku Jidai* (the country at war) – lasted until the middle of the sixteenth century. The first of three ruthless and remarkable men, Oda Nobunaga (1534-82) began his career as an insignificant baron governing a single province, yet his military skill and utter ruthlessness enabled him to gain control of no fewer than thirty-two of the sixty-six provinces before his assassination in 1582. His achievements were defended and consolidated by his able lieutenant Toyotomi Hideyoshi (1536-98), who subdued the southern provinces and launched an invasion of Korea during his rule of sixteen years. His successor, Tokugawa Ieyasu (1542-1616), completed the work of national unification under a strong central government independent in all but name from the Imperial Court in Miyako. Ieyasu's successors instituted a policy of national isolation, *Sakoku*, which kept Japan aloof from the rest of the world until the middle of the nineteenth century.

The ludicrous and apparently ineradicable practice of referring to Adams by a folksy diminutive of his name was begun by William Dalton, the British Victorian novelist, in his book *Will Adams: The First Englishman in Japan*, published in 1861. As Dr. Michael Cooper of Sophia University has observed, Adams was referred to in his lifetime as William Adams, Captain Adams and Master Adams. (Cooper, 1982, 121) Cocks referred to him as 'Adames' on at least one occasion and it is interesting to note that Adams signed himself as '*Addames*'. Even John Saris, the 'General' of the first British expedition to Japan – described, ridiculously by Papinot as a 'Salesman of the English factory of Bantam' (Papinot, 1988, 784) – referred to Adams in reasonably respectful terms, although there was little affection between the two men:

> And if you think it good to appoynt Mr. Addames Captain of the business, it will stir up his sperrits, who hath laine frutles there a longe tyme. (Satow, 1900, 209)

That Saris could assert that Adams, a pilot known all along the coast, an advisor to Tokugawa Ieyasu, a cartographer and shipbuilder to the *Bakufu*, had *laine frutles* in Japan is a measure of how little of Adams' position in Japan Saris grasped.

Adams built two ships for Tokugawa Ieyasu. The larger of these conveyed Don Rodrigo Vivero y Velasco to Acapulco after the *San Francisco* foundered on the Japanese coast in 1609. Named the *Santa Buenaventura,* it remained in Spanish service for many years.

Japanese gunsmiths could cast guns comparable to European weapons; the financing, construction and manning of a Japanese fleet greatly superior to the combined fleets of all European powers in Pacific waters would have been well within the power of Tokugawa Japan early in the seventeenth century.

Had the *Bakufu* made the construction of an ocean-going fleet of large, well-armed European-style ships a major policy objective there can be no doubt that the conquest of the Philippines and probably, the Indonesian archipelago would have been perfectly feasible. (Storry, 1985, 65) Subsequent voyages would have brought them to the immense island known today as Australia, already known to the Portuguese from 1542 at the latest and probably from an unascertainable date between 1511 and 1529. (Stevens, 1930, 5) Two Portuguese cannon of the period 1475-1525 were recovered from Broom Bay in North-West Australia. It is presumed that they came from a single, wrecked vessel rather than having been used as ballast on a Dutch vessel at a later date; the Portuguese knew far more about the vast southern continent than they were willing to disclose, being justifiably apprehensive that the Dutch, ever eager and ready to exploit Portuguese knowledge for their own ends, would somehow turn Portuguese discoveries to their own advantage. (Major, 1859, v)

Recent linguistic research carried out in the north-west of Western Australia was established that the Ngarluma and Karriera tribes have a great many Portuguese loan-words in their vocabulary; only the presence of Portuguese residents or sojourners, voluntary or otherwise, can be presumed to be adequate explanation of this. (Von Brandenstein, 1989, 195–9).

Beyond the immense island now known as Australia are the two islands now known as New Zealand. Had the Japanese been resolute oceanic sailors in the early Tokugawa period, nothing would have stood between them and the discovery and settlement of an area far larger than that temporarily conquered in 1942.

II

WILLIAM ADAMS' EARLY LIFE

As Adams recorded in a letter written some years after his arrival in Japan, he was born in Gillingham, a town in Kent not far from the castle town of Rochester and the port of Chatham.

The parish register of the Anglican Parish Church of St. Mary Magdalen, Gillingham, covering the years 1558, the year of Elizabeth Tudor's accession to the throne, to 1650, the year following the establishment of the Commonwealth under Oliver Cromwell, records: WILL. ADAMS SONNE OF JOHN ADAMS BAPTISED THE 4 AND 20TH OF SEPTEMBER 1564.

He had at least one brother, Thomas, who served on the Mahu and De Cordes fleet and who perished on the South American Pacific coast. From the age of twelve until the age of twenty-four, Adams served an apprenticeship to Nicholas Diggens, a shipbuilder whose business was situated on the Thames at Limehouse. Diggens was a shipwright of considerable reputation, a person of some note in the local Anglican parish of Stepney and sufficiently reputable to be entrusted with considerable amount of repair work for ships of the East India Company. (Massarella, 1990, 72)

Adams was married to Mary Hyn in the Parish of Stepney in August 1589. His wife bore him two children of whom his daughter, Deliverance, outlived him, as did both his English and Japanese wives, Mary and Oyuki.

The fact that his daughter was given a decidedly puritan name was probably of less significance than might be suspected; such names were common in Adams' era and the choice of the name may well reflect nothing more than relief on the part of Deliverance's parents that she had entered the world safely after a difficult delivery.

Adams commanded the *Richard Dyffylde,* or *Richard Duffield,* a small supply ship of 120 tons, during the brief but sanguinary naval struggle against the Armada in 1588. While the services performed by the supply vessels was strongly criticised by contemporaries who served aboard the fighting vessels which constituted Elizabeth's fleet, their existence was essential and the role they performed, however many shortcomings they may have displayed, invaluable (Martin and Parker, 1988; 207, 210). It is interesting to recall that Cervantes served aboard a supply vessel at the same time, on the Spanish side.

The years between the struggle against Philip II's Armada in 1588 and the departure of the Mahu and De Cordes fleet in 1598 offer few clues as to Adams' activities. Beyond his claim, which would certainly not have been fraudulently made, that he had served 'for Master and Pilott in her Maiesties ships', there is the puzzling claim made immediately thereafter that he spent 'eleven or twelve years' in what he described as 'the Worshipful Companie of the Barbarie Marchants'. This can only have been a lapse of memory; Adams was writing thirteen years after his departure from Europe; barely a decade elapsed between the defeat of the Armada and Adams' last view of Europe.

The Barbary Company had been established in 1585 with a charter for twelve years (which was not, as events turned out, renewed.) The Company's stated purpose being to trade with Morocco, it is likely that Adams served aboard one or more of the Barbary Company's ships plying between the British Isles and the Atlantic and Mediterranean ports of Morocco. These vessels, usually of a modest 100 tons, not infrequently took advantage of their course to engage in privateering, intercepting Iberian vessels homeward bound from the East Indies, in the case of Portuguese, and from the New World in the case of the Spanish.

As Professor Massarella has observed, few captains of armed vessels could resist the opportunity to engage in privateering if a tempting opportunity presented itself, Francis Drake even disobeying explicit orders to engage in privateering during the struggle against the Armada. (Massarella, 1990, 72; Martin and Parker, 1988, 169).

According to Diogo do Couto, writing in 1611, Adams was believed by the Jesuits resident in Japan to have served on one or more Dutch voyages in search of the elusive north-west passage during the years 1593-1595. This would have been impossible had Adams spent a decade in the service of the Barbary Company, as he claimed in his letter to the Englishmen resident in Java, but it is certain that Adams showed an active interest in the discovery of the north-west passage while resident in Japan. In his 'vearey Larg Letter wrot from Japan. . .and sent home in the Clove 1614', he wrote: 'Now in my sympel iudgment, yf the northwest passag be ever discovered, it wilbe discovered by this way of Jappan' (Rundall, 1850, 67). Somewhat later in the same letter he referred to Ieyasu's 'frindship to the countri of Yedzoo and Matesmaye, whear his subiects are ressident', a reference to present-day Hokkaido, then barely known even to the Japanese themselves, except for a few hardy settlers established on the southern coast and mainly engaged in trading with the indigenous Ainu.

The north-west passage was eventually navigated by Roald Amundsen in 1903, but it has never been utilised as a commercial waterway. It is of course, possible that Adams was referring to what Europeans knew as the equally elusive north-east passage since, from Japan, a voyage bearing in a north-westerly direction after passing through the Bering Straits would take a vessel parallel to the Siberian Coast. As Adams was well aware, many Englishmen had lost their lives in unavailing attempts to open this short cut to the fabled riches of the Indies, by-passing the Portuguese altogether. As late as 1611, the East India Company voted an annual grant of £300 for encouraging attempts to discover a northern passage. (Murdoch, 1949, 616). In 1580, for example, Charles Jackman and his crew perished in the ice of the Kara Sea, the Muscovy Company having sent two vessels furnished with buoyantly optimistic advice written by Dr. John Dee, one of the most learned cosmographers of the age:

> The '*Brief advises given by Master John Dee unto Arthur Pet and Charles Jackman, for a voyage by them to be made, for discovery of Cathay, 1580,*' had held out the illusory hope of a speedy and effortless voyage to Quinsay (*Hangchou*) by way of the North-East passage: 'When you are past Tabin, or come to the longitude of 142 degrees as your chart sheweth, or two, three, foure, or five degrees further Easterly, it is probable you shall finde the land on your right hand runne much Southerly and Eastward, in which course you are likely either to fall into the mouth of the famous river Oechardes, or some other, which yet I conjecture to

> passe by the renowned Citie of Cambalu and the mouth to be in latitude about 50 or 52 degrees and within 300 or 400 miles of Cambalu it selfe, being in the latitude of 45 degrees Southerly of the saide rivers mouth, or els that you shall trend about the very Northerne and most Easterly point of all Asia, passing by the province Ania and then to the latitude of 46 degrees, keeping still the land in view on your right hand (as neere as you may with safetie) you may enter into Quinsay haven, being the chiefe citie in the Northern China, as I terme it for distinctions sake, from the other better knowen.
>
> And in or about either or both of these two warme places, you may to great good purpose bee occupied the whole winter, after your arrivall in those quarters, as sometime by sea, sometime in notable fresh rivers, sometime in discreet view and noting downe the situation of the Cities within land, &c. and ever assaying to come by some charts or maps of the countrey, made and printed in Cathay or China and by some of their bookes likewise for language, &c. You may also have opportunitie to saile over to Japan Island, where you shall finde Christian men, Jesuits of many countreys of Christendome some, and perhaps some Englishmen, at whose handes you may have great instruction and advice for your affaires in hand.' (Hakluyt, 1973: II 213-4)

Just as there are rival claims advanced as to who 'discovered' the American continent, so there are splendidly extravagant claims concerning the north-east and north-west passages: 'In 1660, David Melgueiro from Japan sailed northwards and skirting the coasts of Kamchatka crosses the Behring Strait, turned westwards along the coasts of Siberia, reaches Spitzbergen, proceeds to the northern tip of Ireland and contouring the western coast of that Island ends his unprecedented voyage in the harbour of the City of Oporto, in Northern Portugal'. (Graça, 1984, 10). The same work assures the reader that João Martins, in 1585, sailed from the coast of Greenland to the Behring Strait – 'named by him Anian Strait' – before icebergs compelled him to return to Lisbon, arriving safely in 1586. One glaring flaw in the Melgueiro claim is that no Portuguese vessels sailed, or could have sailed, from Japan in 1660; Portuguese commerce with Japan ended drastically in 1639.

Adams certainly never sailed northwards while in Japan; such a voyage would have been amply recorded. Instead, his voyages were commercial ventures to Siam and Cochin-China as well as, by force of circumstances, Okinawa.

Did William Adams sail to Arctic waters prior to enlisting on the Mahu and De Cordes fleet? The evidence is inconclusive but the balance of probability suggests that this was unlikely. Adams was not given to hiding his light under a bushel; none of the Europeans who knew him well in Japan recorded that he had spoken of such a voyage. Despite the uncertainty, several responsible chroniclers have recorded that Adams sailed to inhospitable northern seas as though this was a fact established beyond doubt: *1593: Adams took part in the expedition into the north-western seas, at the age of 30* (Makino, 1983, 209).

Thomas Rundall's book *Narrative of Voyages towards the North-West in search of a passage to Cathay and India*, published by the Hakluyt Society in London in 1849, discusses the supposition that Adams sailed to Spitzbergen with the Dutch boldly advanced by John Barrow in *A Chronological History of Voyages into the Arctic Regions* (1818). Barrow having stated that it was 'very probable' that Adams had accompanied Cornelis Ryp to Spitzbergen in 1596, there being no doubt of his having lived in Holland and of his having piloted Dutch vessels and that a passage in the *Decadas* of Diogo do Couto to the effect that Adams had 'averred to the Jesuits at Meaco, the capital of the empire, that he had been employed on various services of importance by the Prince of Orange, particularly in 1593-94 and 1595, in the discovery of a 'route above Biarmia and Finnmarchia' to Japan, China and the Moluccas; and that on the last occasion,he reached 'eighty-two degrees north'. . .' (Rundall, 1849, xii-xiii). Rundall dismisses Barrow's hypothesis briskly, observing that according to Do Couto, the fathers 'alleged that the pilot asserted he went up to 82°N in 1595: which the advocate for Adams declares was 'probably 1596',' concluding as we can only conclude today, 'without deciding whether the voyage attributed to Adams were performed by him, or not, it cannot be considered that sufficient evidence has been adduced to prove the fact.' (Rundall, 1849, xx) If indeed, Adams had ventured to the Arctic prior to sailing to Japan, there is an element of irony in the fact.

The brave but ill-fated attempts to force a north-east or a north-west passage, in which such navigators as Cabot, Frobisher, Willoughby, Chancellor, Gilbert, Cartier and Hudson played a leading part, were chiefly designed to break through icy wastes into warm tropical waters. There is, indeed, a tragic irony in the fate of some of those seamen who, after years spent in struggling against the hazards of arctic exploration, ended their careers in southern seas while engaged in efforts to loosen the Portuguese hold on trade in the Indian Ocean and beyond the Strait of Malacca, which consisted largely in traffic in spices. Among them were John Davis, who was killed by Japanese pirates off Singapore in 1605 and William Baffin, another famous polar navigator, who was killed by a Portuguese shot during fighting in the Persian Gulf. (Sansom, 1987, 44)

III

THE MAHU AND DE CORDES FLEET

The circumstances which led Adams to enter Dutch service stemmed from political events in Europe.

Within thirty years of the outbreak of Holland's revolt from Spain which began in 1556, the burghers of the United Provinces had created a bustling commercial economy and along with it, an ever-increasing navy and merchant marine. This spurt of Dutch maritime activity was given added impetus when, in 1594, Philip II (1527-98), King of Spain and Portugal, closed the port of Lisbon to his 'rebel subjects' in an attempt to cut them off from the then lucrative Portuguese commerce. As an immediate and unforeseen result of this ban, the pioneer expedition of Dutch ships to Java and Sumatra was formed and Cornelius de Houtman, an escapee from a Portuguese prison, was given command of it. De Houtman's return to Holland with his ships richly laden with the rare commodities of the Indies aroused tremendous enthusiasm for further voyages.

Between 1598 and 1603, no fewer than thirteen Dutch fleets, financed by nearly as many separate and rival companies, sailed to the East to try their luck. Many ships were lost, countless sailors lost their lives, but a fortunate expedition made a profit of 200 per cent or more. The Dutch commanders were, initially at least, instructed to keep clear of the Portuguese and Spaniards, but greed, always a far stronger factor than religious enthusiasm where the Dutch were concerned, soon led them to active piracy. The rewards of this were, according to Grotius, the learned advocate of the freedom of the seas, '*the most beautiful and worthiest fruit of voyaging to the Indies*'. [Masselman 1963: 131]

The English were relative laggards in sending ships to the Indies, despite Drake's shining example. Whereas the English despatched a paltry fourteen ships to the East Indies and beyond before 1609, the Vereenigde Ost-Indische Compagnie alone sent roughly the same number every twenty-four months. Nor was this ratio to change for a long time; between 1613 and 1622 the East India Company of London sent only 82 ships to Asia, compared to the 201 of the V.O.C. (Scammell, 1981, 480)

That the Dutch in the east and the officers of the V.O.C. in particular sought the expulsion of the English, along with that of the Iberians, from the whole of Eastern Asia cannot be reasonably disputed; the strident propaganda war which exposed and proclaimed grievances hitherto unknown to the literate English public [*The Hollanders Declaration etc.*, of 1622 (1971); *An Answer to the Hollanders etc.*, of 1622 (1971); *A Courante of News*, of 1622 (1975); *A Second Courante etc.*, of 1622 (1975)] did, however, little or nothing to shake the firm conviction held by the majority of thinking Englishmen that Holland, in her role as the heroic rebel against Catholic oppression in the age of the counter-reformation and the Inquisition was the true incarnation and personification of all the political and spiritual virtues. For an Englishman of the period to speak harshly of the Dutch was regarded as a major breach of good manners. Had not even the frugal Elizabethan court aided the embattled Dutch in their noble struggle against Spain to the tune of 1,419,596 pounds sterling? This vast expenditure can be compared with the trifling outlay required to fund the assembly of troops at Tilbury and the marshalling of warships and supply vessels required to defeat Philip II's great *Enterprise of England*, the Armada of 1588: 161, 185 pounds sterling! (Trevelyan, 1973, 420).

The government's assessment of the total costs incurred in the struggle of 1588 came to nearly £400,000. Of this, 'rewards to the injured' amounted to £180. By comparison, the cargo of the Portuguese carrack *São Felipe*, captured in summer 1587, was worth £140,000. (Martin and Parker, 1988, 131)

Adams, although an Englishman, continued to feel affection for Holland during his years in Japan, carefully staying out of the open warfare which eventually erupted between the British and the Dutch at Hirado, for example. This attitude was noted, with no little approval, by the Dutch. In 1608, Victor Sprinkel, the Dutch factor at Patani, wrote to Adams commenting that it was especially pleasing to hear of 'the good favour, love, inclination which Your Honour, with some others, show towards the Fatherland.' (Massarella, 1990, 83)

The phenomenon of large numbers of men accepting service with foreign employers was well established long before Adams' birth; a Portuguese report written at Ternate in the Moluccas in February 1544 refers to a Scottish pilot in Portuguese service going to 'China and the Lequeos', (*Okinawa*) and by the time Adams entered Dutch service, large numbers of Europeans were in the service of Asian monarchs, mainly as gunners. Japanese, too, served outside Japan as mariners and armed retainers in the service of foreigners. In 1603, the City Council of Goa appealed against the emancipation decree of the Portuguese crown, maintaining that 'Golden Goa' would be desperately imperilled were their Japanese slaves to be freed, '. . .since the Portuguese do not suffice to garrison the smallest bulwark of this island; and, in time of war, a Portuguese with five or six such lads with their muskets at his side counts for much; the more so since this people (*i.e., the Japanese*) is a warlike one. . .' (Boxer, 1986, V, 20).

Armed Japanese, fighting alongside the Portuguese, saved Malacca from capture by the Dutch on at least one occasion, while armed Japanese and Malays were conspicuous in the abortive Dutch attempt to seize Macau in 1622. In the Amboina Massacre of 1623, nine Japanese, ten Englishmen and a lone Portuguese were executed by the Dutch after 'confessing', under torture, that they had conspired to seize the Dutch fort on the island, an incident which created lasting ill-will between Britain and Holland. (Meilink-Roelofsz, 1988, 186).

During the Amboina Massacre of 1623, nine Japanese were executed by the Dutch in addition to the Englishmen under Towerson. Three were from Hirado, three from Nagasaki and the remainder from Karatsu and other places in Kyushu. The two spared execution, those who had 'confessed both to have been privie to this pretented 'treason'' were also from Hirado. The names of the majority of the Japanese named in *Unjust, Cruell and Barbarous Proceedings against the English at Amboina*, published by the East India Company in London in 1624, suggest that most were known by their Japanese names while three, Sidney Migiel, Pedro Congie and Thomé Corea, bore decidedly Christian names and were presumably, Catholics. [E.I.C., 1971 (1624), 29]. Sidney Migiel (or Miguel) is known to have been in the service of the English House at Hirado at an earlier period of his life.

Long before the Dutch or the British employed Japanese as soldiers or sailors, the Portuguese had been accustomed to the services of both Japanese freemen and slaves in both capacities. Among those shipwrecked on the South-Eastern African coast in May 1593, were 4 slaves; 2 were kaffirs (black Africans), 1 was Javanese, the fourth was Japanese.

In Adams' surviving letter of 1613 to Spalding of the Bantam E.I.C. factory, he refers to the Dutch recruiting mariners and soldiers in Japan to serve them in their struggle against the Spanish in the Moluccas. (Rundall, 1850, 42). This practice was forbidden by the *Bakufu* in 1621 but the edict was frequently circumvented.

Enterprising Europeans, mainly Portuguese, were to be found in the service of many non-European sovereigns; a great number of them took employment as mercenaries in the armies of the warring Kings of Arakan, Burma and Siam. Thus, in the wars of the Burmese with Arakanese to the west, Shans to the north and Siamese to the east, Portuguese soldiers of fortune played an important part, fighting on any side that offered an attractive reward. It often happened that Portuguese fought against Portuguese in this endemic warfare, which by the end of the sixteenth century had brought great areas of Lower Burma to famine and desolation. The Portuguese *Decadas* relate, for instance, that a well-known captain, Diogo Soares de Mello, in 1548 led an attack on Ayuthia, the Siamese capital, which was successfully resisted by mercenaries under another Portuguese, Diogo Pereira. On another occasion, de Mello was employed by a Burmese king to crush rebels in his own dominions who in their turn were assisted by Portuguese soldiers. Some of these adventurers, not content with paid military service, attempted to hold cities for themselves, as when Felipe de Brito took, and retained for several years, the town of Syriam, then the chief port of Pegu.

In 1607, the King of Arakan, in what is now coastal Burma, killed 600 Portuguese – most of whom were probably Goans of mixed race but culturally Portuguese to a greater or lesser extent – claiming to be disturbed by their growing power and lawlessness. The careers of such individual mercenaries, freebooters and adventurers could be 'romantic' – to use the term in its nineteenth-century sense – in the extreme. Diogo Soares de Mello, a fidalgo and evidently, a man of some standing, had been involved in several homicides in Galicia and was banished to India. In 1540, his patron and another fidalgo quarrelled over an unmarried woman. Soares' leader killed his rival and was executed by the local Portuguese governor. Soares fled to Goa and later set up in business with twenty followers off Melinde, on the East African coast. In 1542, he was pardoned but between 1548 and 1553, he was a leader of Portuguese mercenaries fighting for the Burmese against the Siamese. Finally, he was executed by the Burmese (Pearson, 1987, 86).

It has been claimed that there were perhaps 5,000 Portuguese in the service of local rulers or trading independently in just three extra-Portuguese areas at this time; Bengal, Siam and Macassar.

IV

THE VOYAGE

The Dutch at the dawn of the seventeenth century were the most daring and enterprising of Europe's maritime nations, venturing to challenge the Iberians in every sea and ocean. In 1598 alone, the year in which Adams sailed from Rotterdam, some twenty-two Dutch vessels set sail for the Far East. (Goodman, 1986, 9)

It was aboard one of these ships that Adams sailed. His entry into the service of a Rotterdam *voorcompagnie* voyage, that funded by Pieter van der Hagen and Johan van der Veeke, came through one Hans Broers, a Dutchman who traded with Morocco. The Dutch were ready and willing to employ competent English navigators at this time; the distinguished navigator John Davis sailed with Cornelis de Houtman's second voyage round the Cape of Good Hope to Achin in Sumatra. This same John Davis perished at the hands of Japanese *wo'k'uo* or *wako*, pirates, in a sanguinary struggle between peninsular Malaya and Sumatra in 1605, probably one of the first Englishman to die at Japanese hands. (Wild, 1937, 77-80)

Thirteen other English mariners, including Adams' brother Thomas, thirty English musicians and at least one Scotsman, William Lyon, sailed aboard the fleet. The fleet, commanded by Jacques Mahu and Simon de Cordes, consisted of five vessels. Of these, the flagship was the *Hoop* (Hope), 250 tons and 130 men, the others were as follows:

Geloof (Faith) 160 tons; 109 men
Liefde (Charity)150 tons; 110 men
Trouw (Fidelity)110 tons; 86 men
Blijde Boodschap (Good Tidings) 75 tons; 56 men.

The intended *modus operandi* of this fleet, which left Holland inexplicably late in the year, was to repeat Drake's success by sailing through the Straits of Magellan, then believed to separate

South America from the vast, inhospitable Southern Continent, *Terra Australis*. Thereafter, Spanish settlements on the coast of Chile and Peru would be raided, treasure ships captured if opportunity arose and successful trade conducted in the Moluccas and nearby islands of the East Indies before heading homewards around the Cape of Good Hope. Drake's voyage of 1577-1580 had returned a miraculous £47 for every pound invested in it, as van der Hagen and van der Veek knew.

As events turned out, the Mahu and de Cordes expedition became a disaster which bankrupted its backers. Having departed late, in June rather than in March, the five ships were further delayed by a counter-productive visit to one of the Cape Verde islands:

> And the one and twentieth of *August*, we came to one of the isles of *Capo Verde*, where we abode foure and twentie dayes. In which time, many of our men fell sicke, through the vnwholsomenesse of the aire, and our generall among the rest. Now the reason that we abode so long at these ilands was, that one of the captaines of our fleet made our generall beleeue that at these ilands we should find great store of refreshing, as goats and other things, which was vntrue.
>
> Here I and all the pilots of the fleet were called to a councell; in which wee all shewed our iudgements of disliking the place; which were by all the captaines taken so ill, that afterward it was agreed by them all, that the pilots should be no more in the councell, the which was executed. The fifteenth day of September we departed from the isle of *Sant' Iago*, and passed the equinoctiall line. And in the latitude of three degrees to the south, our generall dyed; where, with many contrarie windes and raine, the season of the yeare being very much past, wee were forced vpon the coast of *Guiney*, falling vpon an head-land called *Cabo de Spirito Sancto*. The new generall comanded to bear vp with *Cape de Lopo Consalues*, there to seeke refreshing for our men, the which we did. In which place, we landed all our sicke men, where they did not much better, for wee could find no store of victuals.

Cape Lopez is now part of the territory of the Republic of Gabon, a place with a notoriously unhealthy climate. Adams' letter to his wife is somewhat less critical in tone, however:

> So that to fulfill our voyage, wee set our course for the coast of *Brasill*, beinge determined to passe the Streigtes of *Magilanus*; and by the way cam to an Iland called *Annabona*, which island we landed at, and tooke the towne, in which was about eightie houses. In which Iland we

> refreshed ourselues, hauing oxen, oranges, and diuers fruites, etc. But the vnwholesomenesse of the aire was very bad, that as one bettered, an other fell sicke: spending vpon the coast vp the cape *Gonsalues* and vp *Annabona*, a two moneths tyme, till the twelfth or thirteenth Nouember. At which time, wee set sayle from Annabona, finding the windes still at the south and south by east, and south south-east, till wee got into foure degrees to the southwards of the line: at which time the winde did fauour vs comming to the south-east, and east south-east, and so that we were vp betweene the Iland of *Annabona*, and the Streightes of *Magilano*, about a fiue monethes. (Rundall, 1850, 19)

In December, the crews burned a Portuguese settlement on the island of Annobon, now part of the Republic of Equatorial Guinea, after being refused permission to land and care for their sick. From Annobon to the Straits took five months; it is probable that the water and fruit laden aboard the ships of the fleet at Annobon were contaminated with amoebic dysentery. Adams, a laconically straightforward chronicler, did not mention this probability in his letter to the Englishmen resident in Java. Since Adams had hopes of assisting the Java Britons to trade in Japan, the difference in the tone between the two letters is self-explanatory. It would have been improper for Adams to be openly critical of former commanders while entertaining the express hope of being of service to his fellow-countrymen at some future time. That this was the case is certain. Adams wrote:

> 'I told him (*Tokugawa Ieyasu*), if he would permit me to depart, I would bee a meanes, that both the English and Hollanders should come and traffic there (*Japan*).' (Rundall, 1850, 29)

Due to the delays at Cape Verde, the African mainland and Annobon, as well as the impediment of contrary winds, food ran short soon after the fleet left Annobon, as Adams explained in the letter to his wife:

> Hauing refreshed our men, we set saile againe. At which time our generall commanded, that a man for foure dayes should haue but one pound of bread, that was a quarter of a pound a day; with a like proportion of wine and water. Which scarcitie of victuals brought such feeblenesse, that our men fell into so great weaknesse and sicknesse for hunger, that they did eate the calves' skinnes wherewith our ropes were couered. (Rundall, 1850, 34).

For men aboard a fleet intending to circumnavigate the globe to be reduced to gnawing ship's leather before the intended voyage was a quarter completed was a sign that worse lay ahead. It did. Once in the Straits of Magellan, Simon de Cordes displayed a unique talent for needless procrastination:

> And the eighth day we passed the second narrow with a good wind, where we came to an anchor, and landed on *Penguin* Island, where we laded our boate ful of penguins, which are fowles greater then a ducke, wherewith we were geratly refreshed. The tenth, we weighed anchor, hauing much wind, which was good for vs to goe thorow. But our generall would water and take in prouision of wood for all our fleet. (Rundall, 1850, 34)

The penguins proved insufficient refreshment. Men continued to die and Simon de Cordes continued to procrastinate. As Adams baldly wrote years later:

> 'Many times in the winter, we had the wind good to go through the straights, but our generall would not.' (Rundall, 1850, 34–5)

This hideous period evidently affected Adams deeply. His letter to the Java Britons, although written in measured terms, expressed outrage at being so poorly commanded:

> Hauing at that time the wind at the north-east, six or seven dayes, in which time wee might haue past through the Streightes. But for refreshing of our men we waited, watering and taking in of wood, and setting vp of a pynnas of fifteene or twentie tonnes in burthen. So at length, wee would haue passed through, but could not by reason of the sotherly windes: the weather being very cold, with aboundance of snowe and yce. Wherefore, we were forced to winter and to stay in the Streightes from the sixt of Aprill, till the foure and twentieth of September, in which time our victualles was for the most part of spent and for lacke of the same, many of our men dyed of hunger. (Rundall, 1850, 1920)

Once out of the Straits, the five ships encountered severe weather, the storms which made Cape Horn a mariner's nightmare. A rendezvous had been agreed upon beforehand in the expectation of just such an eventuality, however. Only two ships managed to reach the agreed rendezvous. One was the *Hoop*, the other the *Liefde*.

The *Geloof* struggled back through the Straits and returned to

Europe. It can be surmised that her crew were in a state of virtually open mutiny by this time.

The *Trouw* attempted to navigate the Straits of Magellan once more, too, but was unsuccessful. Astonishingly, the *Trouw* succeeded in crossing the Pacific with her crew reduced to twenty-four including the Scotsman William Lyon and four South American Indians coerced or tricked into coming aboard off the South American coast. (Massarella, 1990, 73). All were arrested by the Portuguese when the ship made landfall at Tidore in the Moluccas and only three or four subsequently returned to Europe, the others being executed. (Boxer, 1951, 286) Lyon was still a prisoner in Goa, the capital of Portuguese India, in 1608.

The *Blijde Boodschap*, with Jan Huyghen van Linschoten's informant, Dirk Gerritz, aboard, surrendered to the Spanish at Valparaiso in Chile. Eleven men, including Gerritz, eventually made it back to the Netherlands.

Further trials awaited Adams, who had begun the voyage aboard the *Hoop*, as had Gerritz, but had transferred to the *Liefde*. While awaiting the arrival of the *Hoop* the crew of Adams' ship traded peaceably with the local people for 'five or sixe dayes' before the latter inexplicably decamped. The vessel then sailed to the mainland near the island of St Maria. The local Indians hurt eight or nine of the crew in an affray on the beach, according to Adams' letter to his wife, 'but in the ende, they made a false composition of friendship, which our men did beleeve. . .' The following day a landing party which included the *Liefde*'s captain, Thomas Adams and twenty-one of the crew went ashore, only to be ambushed by over a thousand Mapuche Amerindians, who slew them all. As Adams tersely recorded:

> By this losse, we had scarse so many men whole as could weigh our anchor. So the third day, in great distresse, we set our course for the Island of *Santa Maria*, where we found our admirall; whom when we saw, our hearts were some-what comforted: we went aboord them, and found them in as great distresse as we, having lost their Generall, with seven and twentie of their men, slaine at the Island of Mocha. . . (Rundall, 1850, 36)

There were insufficient men aboard the two remaining ships to obtain food by force, it was agreed. However, by a stroke of good fortune, they obtained supplies in a manner which would have met with the approval of Jason or Ulysses:

> There came a Spaniard by composition to see our shippe. And so the next day he came againe, and we let him depart quietly. The third day came two Spaniards aboord vs without pawne, to see if they could betray vs. When they had seene our shippe, they would haue gone on land againe, but we would not let them, shewing that they came without leaue, and we would not let them goe on land againe without our leaue; whereat they were greatly offended. We shewed them that we had extreame neede of victualls and that if they would giue vs so many sheepe and so many beeues, they should goe on land. So, against their wils, they made composition with vs, which, within the time appointed, they did accomplish. Hauing so much refreshing as we could get, we made all things well againe, our men beeing for the most part recouered of their sickenesse. (Rundall, 1850, 36)

This was the best that could be hoped for, given the circumstances in which the crews of the two ships found themselves.

A young man with the singular name of Hudcopee, 'which knew nothing, but had served the admirall', as Adams drily observed, became the admiral,or commander of the two remaining ships. The captain of the *Liefde*, Jacob Jansz van Quaeckernack of Rotterdam, became the vice-admiral. Adams and the pilot of the *Hoope*, Timothy Shotten, a veteran of Thomas Cavendish's circumnavigation of the globe, were, at long last, taken into the commanders' counsels once again, reversing the foolish policy adopted at the Cape Verde islands. The fateful decision was taken to sail across the immensity of the Pacific Ocean for Japan. Adams, writing many years later, gave two slightly different accounts of this decision. Both merit quotation:

> Being at the island of St. Maria, which lieth in the lattetude to the sward of the line of thirtie seuen degrees twelue minutes on the cost of *Chili*, wee tooke counsell to take all things out of one ship, and to burne the other; but that the captens that were made newe, the one nor the other, would not, so that we could not agree to leave the one or the other; and having much cloth in our ships, it was agreed that wee should leaue the coast of *Perow*, and direct our course for *Iapon*, having understood that cloth was good marchandiz there; and also how vpon that coast of *Perow*, the king's ships were out seeking vs, hauing knowledge of our being there, vnderstanding that wee were weake of men, which was

> certaine; for one of our fleet, for hunger, was forced to seeke reliefe at the enemies hand in *Saint Ago*. For which reason, hauing refreshed ourselues in this Iland of *St. Maria*, more by policie then by force, we departed the twentie seuen of Nouember, from the Iland of *St. Maria* with our two ships; and for the rest of our fleete we had no newes of them. (Rundall, 1850, 22-3)

The note of criticism of 'the captens that were made newe' is veiled, but still discernable. It is evident that Adams then, and subsequently, believed that the most rational course would have been to transfer all the surviving crewmen, together with both ships' cargoes, into a single ship. In the light of the mortality rate aboard the *Liefde* on its oceanic crossing, Adams was almost certainly right.

The death toll aboard the *Liefde*, while catastrophic enough, was by no means unusual in Adams' era. Aboard the great Portuguese vessels plying between Europe and Goa it was quite common for two, three or even four hundred men to die before Goa was reached. (Cooper, 1974, 29-30). Worse could happen: in the mid-seventeenth century sailors aboard a ship cruising off the coast of Acapulco sighted a galleon drifting off the Mexican coast, sails slatted in the wind. This proved to be the *San José*, which had departed Manila for Acapulco over a year before. Every last soul aboard had perished from starvation or disease; the ship was a floating bier of silks and corpses.

Concerning the identity of the commander of the doomed *Hoope*, Adams may well have been in error. It is possible that Adams confused the new commander with Jacob Jansz Huydecoper, who had sailed as a midshipman under Oliver van Noort in the first Dutch expedition of 1595. Spanish sources record that the Admiral at this stage was Simon de Cordes jun., a young man of 19 or 20 years. (Farrington, 1991, 55)

> So the generall and vice-admirall called me and the other pilote, beeing an Englishman, called *Timothy Shotten* (which had been with *M. Thomas Candish*, in his voyage about the world), to take counsell what we should doe to make our voyage for the best of our marchants
>
> At last, it was resolued to goe for *Iapon*. For by report of one *Dirrick Gerritson*, which had been there with the Portugals, woollen cloth was in great estimation in that Iland. And we gathered by reason, that the *Malucos*, and the most part of the East Indies, were hot countreyes, where woollen cloth would not be much accepted: wherefore, we all

> agreed to goe for *Iapon*. So, leauing the coast of *Chili* from thirtie-sixe degrees of south-latitude, the seuen and twentieth of Nouember 1599, we tooke our course directly for *Iapon* and passed the line equinoctiall with a faire wind, which continued for diuerse moneths. (Rundall, 1850, 37)

There remains the question why it was the Spaniards, who knew that their Protestant enemies knew the way through the Straits of Magellan, left the narrow gateway so negligently unguarded.

Nobody at this time was aware that Cape Horn existed or that there was any other way into the Pacific from the Atlantic, other than by crossing the notoriously unhealthy Isthmus on Panama on foot and constructing a privateering vessel on the Pacific shore. This was what the crew of the English corsair John Oxenham did in 1575. Hiding their ship on the Caribbean coast, they crossed the Isthmus on foot, constructed a small sailing ship on the coast below Panama and soon successfully intercepted two unarmed Spanish treasure ships sailing from Peru to Panama. Unluckily for Oxenham and his men, their party was intercepted by the Spanish as they attempted to recross the isthmus. Oxenham and five of his officers were tried and executed by the Inquisition in Lima. Drake sailed through the Strait of Magellan in 1578, capturing the *Concepción,* a Spanish vessel laden with plate, together with its charts showing the route of the Manila galleon. He was followed by Thomas Cavendish, aboard whose fleet Timothy Shotten sailed.

The first Dutch expedition to the Pacific Coast of America was that of Mahu and Simon de Cordes, that aboard which William Adams sailed.

It may be argued that the Spanish authorities, alerted by Drake's successful piracy in the Pacific, should have ensured that the Straits of Magellan were firmly closed to all but friendly shipping. A glance at an historical atlas of South America shows the presence of what were clearly intended to be strong fortresses closing the Straits. Nombre de Jesús was at the Easternmost gate of the Straits, while Rey Don Felipe effectively barred the narrow channel leading to the Pacific. Both were founded by Pedro Sarmiento de Gamboa in 1583 but were evidently abandoned shortly thereafter, probably due to the bitter winter cold, isolation, scurvy and – in all probability – actual or incipient mutiny. Nombre de Jesús stood close to Pta. Dungeness at the

Eastern mouth of the Straits. Rey Don Felipe stood close to Pta. Santa Ana. Neither settlement was large. (Rioseco, Henriquez and Errazuriz, 1983, 10)

At the time Adams and his companions sailed through the Straits, it was thought that Tierra del Fuego was merely part of *Terra Australis*, the vast but unknown Southern Continent known to lie south of New Guinea; the existence of a sea passage south of Cape Horn was a discovery which lay many years in the future; it would have made excellent sense for the Spanish crown to have maintained at least one adequate fortress with a naval squadron in a strategic position guarding the Straits. In any event, there appears to be no record of either settlement having prevented interlopers sailing through the Straits. Substantial fortresses with ample provisions, large garrisons and a naval interdiction force would have been needed to prevent the passage of a well-armed fleet such as that aboard which Adams sailed.

The story of the establishment of the two settlements in the Straits of Magellan may be found in an excellent English translation taken from contemporary accounts. Mutiny was an ever-present danger in the course of such endeavours. (Markham, 1895, 296)

It may be wondered why the captains and pilots of the two Dutch ships were so confident that their cargoes would find a ready market in Japan. Dirk Gerritz had spent seven months in Japan and had no small reputation as Linschoten's informant, the *Itinerario* having been published in Dutch in 1596 and in English in 1598, the same year as that in which the Mahu and de Cordes fleet sailed. It is improbable that Gerritz ventured far from Nagasaki, the trading city established by the Jesuits in 1571 or thereabouts. Nonetheless, Nagasaki winters can be cold, if generally milder than those of Edo (Tokyo) or Miyako (Kyoto). Gerritz, presumably not a taciturn man, would have agreed readily if asked whether a market for woollen cloth existed in Japan. The evidence in Linschoten's magnum opus was so vague as to be positively delphic.

> The countrie is cold, (proceeding) of much rayne, snow and ice, (that falleth therein), it hath some Corne lande, but their common Corne is Ryce. (Burnell, 1885, II, 152)

At a glance, this seems nonsensical, few Europeans who had not spent some time in North China or Japan would have readily credited that a country could grow rice in one season and be subject to snow a few months later, although many parts of the Mediterranean littoral are equally subject to similar extremes of climate. The Dutch, however, never shared Richard Hakluyt's unshakable obsession that there was a ready market for cloth in Japan or the countries to the west and north of it. (Massarella, 1990, 94-5)

As it transpired, the market for English cloth in Japan was never as profitable as the English hoped it would be. Writing to Augustine Spalding, in Bantam, early in 1613, Adams observed:

> I feear yt theer wilbe no profitt, which is principall: for ye coumodeties of our countri are heer good cheep, yt is clloth; for by reason of the ship that comes from Noveo Spaynia of the on party and the Hollanders on the other party, hath made the priss of cloth so good chep as in Ingland. An 8 or 9 years ago cloth was very deer, but now verry chep. (Rundall, 1850, 41-2)

The Japanese observed that the English in Japan disdained to wear English cloth themselves, preferring silks and fustian, noted that the cloth brought from England was all too frequently worm-eaten and on the rare occasions that English cloth could be sold in any quantity, it was used to line armour-cases rather than tailored into everyday apparel.

Asia did not need foreign goods and Europe did not wish to spend gold in the purchase of Asiatic produce which was so important to her. The Portuguese used their earnings as carriers for the purchase of Indian and Chinese goods; the Dutch and the English followed their example, but did not succeed in capturing the interport trade from them. The history of English commercial enterprise in the Far East shows a continuous but abortive effort to find a 'vent' for English woollens; and it was a failure to establish markets for English manufacturers that led in the long run to the sale of opium for the purpose of redressing the adverse balance of which Roman writers had complained.

By the time the shattered *Liefde* arrived in Japan, the Portuguese had been trading there, with gradually increasing success, for over 50 years. It was not until the establishment of the Dutch and British factories on the small island of Hirado, in 1609 and 1613 respectively that Holland and Britain began trade with Japan. Neither venture was greatly successful; the Dutch endeavour was most profitable when their Hirado factory was offering silks seized at sea from Manila-bound Chinese vessels. The British factory, situated dangerously close to its Dutch rival, was a commercial disaster until the period of joint Anglo-Dutch piracy, preying on Iberian shipping and intercepting junks trading to Manila.

V

LANDFALL IN HAWAII

Whether the two captains and their pilots assumed that crossing the Pacific from the coast of Chile to Japan would be an easy undertaking after the hardships the crews had already suffered is unknown. In the event, the *Hoop* foundered with all hands not long after one, or both, of the ships made landfall in the Hawaiian Islands, the first sailors from Protestant Europe to do so.

If one takes a map and draws a line from the island of Mocha (a small island close to Concepción on the Chilean coast) one strikes the Hawaiian Islands. Adams kept this course between 'three and four months' (sailing some five thousand miles) and as the record states, they 'encountered a group of Islands about sixteen degrees north latitude.'

With the imperfect observations of the day that is near enough for the southern part of Hawaii; that the islands were the Hawaiian group seems certain from what follows. North of the course which the *Liefde* was taking (and which it continued to follow until it reached twenty-seven degrees north latitude) there are no islands north of 'about sixteen degrees north latitude' until you reach the Aleutians over two thousand miles distant. To the east there are none until you near the coast of Mexico and to the west there is no group of inhabited islands for a very long distance, while to the south the Fanning group is but a little north of the equator.

If the Islands sighted by Adams were the Ladrones (Marianas) he would have seen many other islands between Chile and Japan whereas on this hypothesis he would sail over a sea clear of islands. (Wieder, 1925, 149)

William Ellis, an English missionary who resided in Hawaii, then known as the Sandwich Islands, for approximately two years after 1822, collected an oral tradition which probably throws light on a neglected aspect of the *Liefde*'s voyage from Chile to Japan.

Ellis said that in interesting conversations with the local people, they told him of three distinct traditions regarding the coming of white men prior to the time when Captain Cook arrived off Niihau and Kauai.

It appears quite certain that the Spaniard Gaetano, in one of the yearly voyages of his countrymen from Acapulco to the Philippines in the middle of the sixteenth century, discovered these islands and that perhaps on one, or perhaps two occasions, white men, presumably Spaniards, had been wrecked on the south-west of Hawaii.

Ellis stated that the third account of the landing of foreigners is more 'recent and precise'. The story he heard was that seven men arrived at Kelakekua Bay 'in white or yellow' and one of them had a *pahi* or sword. These men remained in Hawaii, married natives and were made chiefs. (Wieder, 1925, 147)

If becoming a chief in the Hawaiian islands may be considered a fortunate outcome, as one may suppose to be the case, these men did well enough. The oral tradition collected by the missionary agrees with Adams' account in all particulars but one; the number of deserters from the *Liefde* who preferred to take their chances ashore than continuing to sail onward into the unknown.

> In our way, we fell with certain islands in sixeteene degrees of north latitude, the inhabitants whereof are men-eaters. Comming neere these islands, and hauing a great pinnesse with vs, eight of our men beeing in the pinnesse, ranne from vs with the pinnesse, and (as we suppose) were eaten of the wild men, of which people we tooke one; which afterward generall sent for to come into his shippe. when wee came into the latitude of seuen and twentie and eight and twentie degrees, we found very variable winds and stormy weather. The foure and twentieth of February, we lost sight of our admirall, which afterward we saw no more: Neuerthelesse, we still did our best, directing our course for *Iapon*. (Rundall, 1850, 37)

The abducted Hawaiian, being aboard the doomed *Hoope,* perished with that vessel when it foundered, an event which Adams described with characteristic brevity in his letter to the Java Britons:

> Wee had a wonderous storme of wind, as euer I was in, with much raine, in which storme wee lost our consort, whereof we were very sorry: nevertheless, with hope that in *Iapon* we should meet the one the other, we proceeded on our former intention for *Iapon* and in the height of thirtie degrees, sought the northermost [?] Cape of the forenamed Iland; but found it not, by reason that it lieth faulce in all cardes and maps, and globes; for the Cape lieth in thirti-fiue degrees ½ which is a great difference. In the end, in thirtie-two degrees ½, we were foure moneths and twentie-two daies; at which time were no more than sixe besides my selfe that could stand vpon his feet. (Rundall, 1850, 23)

Alone on the bosom of the immense ocean, the stricken *Liefde* sought the coast of Japan in vain. The maps and rutters they possessed were of no use, having been drawn up by mariners accustomed to approaching Japan from Macau and the Philippines.

In setting their course for Japan the ships were relying on what turned out to be a false latitude for the position of Japan. All available maps and globes were wrong. Even Linschoten's *Itinerario* gave the southern point of the archipelago as 30° 31'. (Massarella, 1990, 74)

At some point in time, Adams' letter to the Java merchants was incorrectly copied; *southernmost* mysteriously turned into *northernmost.*

VI

ARRIVAL IN JAPAN

The arrival of the stricken *Liefde* on the shores of Japan came not a day too soon; there were barely sufficient men capable of working the ship:

> Great was the miserie we were in, hauing no more but nine or tenne able men to goe or creepe vpon their knees; our captaine, and all the rest, looking euery houre to die. The eleuenth of Aprill 1600, we saw the land of *Iapon*, neere vnto *Bungo*: at which time there were no more but fiue men of vs able to goe. The twelfth of Aprill, we came hard to *Bungo* where many barkes came aboord vs, the people whereof wee willingly let come, hauing no force to resist them; at which place, we came to an anchor. The people offered vs no hurt, but stole all things they could steale; for which some paid deare afterward. The next day, the king of that land sent souldiers aboord to see that none of the marchants goods were stolen. Two or three dayes after, our shippe was brought into a good harbour, there to abide till the principall king of the whole island had newes of vs, and vntill it was knowne what his will was to doe with vs. In the meane time we got fauour of the king of that place, to get our captaine and sicke men on land, which was granted. And wee had an house appointed vs, in which all our men were laid and had refreshing giuen them. (Rundall, 1850, 38)

Three men died the day after the ship anchored and a further three clung to life for a while before death claimed them. The arrival of the *Liefde* cannot be dated with precision; it is certain that it was around mid-April 1600, the *Hoop* having foundered about 23 February (Old Style, or Julian Calendar).

Adams gives conflicting dates for the day the vessel arrived in Japan, 19 April (New Style, or Gregorian Calendar, then ten days 'ahead' of the Julian Calender, or Old Style) according to his letter of 23 October 1611. His letter to his wife, presumably written later, gives 12 April (NS). If as Adams suggests, all his books and instruments were confiscated by the Japanese authorities he was necessarily writing from memory or piecing together facts from the recollections of others. As Massarella notes, in the two letters some dates are accurate while others, such as the date of departure from Rotterdam are not. (Massarella, 1990, 385). The precise location of the landfall is a matter of mild controversy in contemporary Japan; although the place has been claimed confidently as Sashibu (or *Sashio*), Usuki-shi, there are those who claim that the true landfall was Saiki Bay, Oita. A group of local historians, *Saimi Shindankai*, have vociferously advanced the claims of the latter locality. Neither the precise location nor the precise date are of a great deal of consequence, except as fascinating *minutiae* of history. The significant fact was that the first non-Iberian ship had reached Japan, an event which was to have far-reaching consequences in the years ahead

> After wee had beene there fiue or sixe dayes, came a Portugall Iesuite, with other Portugals, who reported of vs, that we were pirats, and were not in the way of marchandizing. Which report caused the gouernours and common people to thinke euill of vs: In such manner, that we looked always when we should be set vpon crosses; which is the execution in this land for theeuery and some other crimes. Thus daily more and more the Portugalls incensed the justices and people against vs. And two of our men, as traytors, gaue themselves in seruice to the king, beeing all in all with the Portuggals hauing by them their liues warranted. The one was called *Gilbert de Conning*, whose mother dwelleth at *Middleborough*, who gaue himselfe out to be marchant of all the goods in the shippe. The other was called *Iohn Abelson Van Owater*. These traitours sought all manner of wayes to get the goods into their hands, and knowne vnto them all things that had passed in our voyage. Nine dayes after our arriuall, the great king of the land sent for me to come vnto him. So, taking one man with me, I went to him, taking my leaue captaine and all the others that were sicke, commeding my self into His hands that had preserued me from so many perils on the sea. (Rundall, 1850, 38-9)

One of the two 'traitors', Gilbert de Conning, to give his name in Adams' spelling, living in Japan for many years, entering the service of the E.I.C. factory at Hirado in 1614 and dying sometime before February 1616. (Massarella, 1990; 148, 173)

The precise identity of the man who accompanied Adams to Osaka is uncertain. Adams was the only officer sufficiently fit to make the journey safely; had Melchior van Sandvoort been well enough, he would probably have accompanied Adams. The clue lies in his letter written to the Britons in Bantam:

> And for that time I was commanded to prisson, being well vsed, with one of our mariners that cam with me to serue me. (Rundall, 1850, 24)

Adams would not have written about Sandvoort in such terms; he would have done so, however, had he been writing about Jan Joosten van Lodensteyn.

Diogo do Couto, writing of the arrival of the *Liefde* some years after the event, noted:

> In this year 1600, of which we are treating, about this same time there arrived a Dutch ship at the Islands of *Japão*, that time it was not the monsoon for ships to come from China, nor from the Filippinas, it appeared to the fathers of the Company, who reside there, that it might be some ship going from New Spain to the Lusoes, that through some storm had been driven out of her course. They sent word to king of Bungo, in order that he might send help, lest some disaster should befall her; which he at once did. And at this same time, two fathers of the Company who resided near Xativai, seeing the ship, went with some boats to assist her; and coming near to her, and discovering that were in Naganzaque, as soon as they heard of the ship, sent advice by letters to Tirazava, governor-general of those realms on the western side, of how that ship was one of the Lutheran corsairs, enemies of the Portuguese and of all Christians. On receiving this message, and having already had letters from the king, Tirazava hastened to the kingdom of Bungo, and ordered the ship to be brought into port, and laid hold of the Hollanders, and their goods, of which an inventory was made, and what was found therein was the following: Eleven great chests of coarse woollen cloths, a box with four hundred branches of coral and as many of amber, a great chest of glass beads of divers colours, some mirrors and spectacles, many children's pipes, two thousand cruzados in reals, nineteen large bronze pieces of ordnance and other small ones, five hundred muskets, and five thousand balls of cast-iron, three hundred chain-shot, fifty quintals of powder, three great chests of coats of mail, three-fourths of powder, three great chests of coats of mail, three-fourths having breastplates and pectorals of steel, three hundred and fifty-five darts, a great quantity of nails, iron, hammers, scythes and mattocks and other various kinds of implements, with which it would seem they were coming to conquer and inhabit. (Sinclair, 1892, lxxvi-lxxvii)

Couto's loyalties as a Catholic and a Portuguese evidently overcame his judgement; even had the *Liefde* been fully manned by an adequate complement of healthy mariners, so small a crew would have been ill-equipped to 'conquer and inhabit' any but the most primitive and ill-organised society.

The Tirazava of this account was Terasawa Hirotaka, the *daimyo* of Karatsu in Hizen. Whether Terasawa Hirotaka came to the *Liefde*'s mooring in person may be doubted. Ohta Kazuyoshi, also known as Shigemasa, was the man to whom Adams referred as the King of Bungo (Makino, 1983, 35).

Fernão Guerreiro, in his *Relaçam Annual* of the *Cousas do Japão* which described the work of the Jesuits in Bungo, wrote:

> . . .there came to land at this *Bungo* this ship of which I have spoken much shattered. She brought only five and twenty men alive and these sick and prostrated by the cold and hunger that they suffered on such a long voyage, of whom two died on arrival. She carried some woollen cloths and scarlets, raxas (coarse cloths of little value), mirrors, glass beads, corals, and other curiosities of Flanders; and they had much and large ordnance. The Father, speaking with them, understood that they were heretics. On arriving in port and coming ashore they said that they came to carry on trade in *Japão*, but the Tono soon discovered that they were going to another part, and that they came to *Japão* only through the storm, since they did not carry goods in such quantity or of the same quality as brought by the other ships that came to *Japão*, nor did they come well dressed and splendid with the pomp of servants and attendants, as the other merchants were accustomed to come, but only as soldiers and sailors and beside this with much ordnance and arms: by all of which they were known to be people not of good title; and *Dayfuçama*, having been advised to this effect, at once sent a captain of his to *Bungo* to have the ship brought to *Meaco* or to *Sacay*, where he took possession of her as a wreck, according to the laws of *Japão* and sent her to a port in his kingdoms of *Quantò*, with the Hollanders that came in her, and eighteen or twenty pieces of ordnance; and all the rest that she carried he retained, the greater part of which was arms and a large quantity of powder. (Sinclair, 1892, lxxix-lxxx)

These two accounts of the *Liefde*'s crew and cargo are in broad agreement and this assessment is upheld in Massarella's magisterial and definitive work *A World Elsewhere*. (Massarella, 1990, 75)

It is significant that the Jesuits possessed sufficient powers of persuasion at this time as to gain access to the crew of the *Liefde* without undue difficulty. William Adams' own account of the

Liefde's arrival makes interesting reading when compared with the two Portuguese versions:

> So that betweene the Cape of *St. Maria* and *Iapon*, we were foure moneths and twentie-two daies; at which time, there no more then sixe besides my selfe that could stand upon his feet. So we in safetie let fall our anchor about a league from a place called *Bungo*. At which time cam to us many boats, and we suffred them to come abord, being not able to resist them, which people did us no harme; neither of understanding the one the other. Within a 2 or 3 daies after our arivall, ther cam a Iesuit from a place called *Langasacke*, to which place the Carake of *Amakau* is yeerely wont to come, which with our Iaponers that were Christians, were our interpreters, which was not to our good, our mortal ennemies being our Truchmen. Neverthelesse, the King of *Bungo* the place where we arriued shewed vs great friendship. For he gaue vs an house a lande where we landed our sicke men, and had all refreshing that was needfull. We had when we came to anker in *Bungo*, sicke and whole, foure and twentie men, of which number the next day three dyed. The rest for the most part recouered, sauing three which lay a long time sicke, and in the end also died. In the which time of our being here, the Emperour hearing of vs, sent presently five gallis, or friggates, to us, to bring mee to the Court, where his Highness was, which was distant from *Bungo* about an eightie English leagues. (Rundall, 1850, 23-4)

VII

THE JESUIT PRESENCE IN JAPAN

'You should not think these people are barbarians because, apart from the faith, however prudent we may believe we are, we are great barbarians compared with them. In all truth, I confess that I learn from them every day and I think that there is no other nation in the world with such and so many talents as the Japanese.'

Organtino Gnecchi-Soldi 1577
(Cooper, 1971, 137)

To appreciate how it came to pass that Jesuits were the first Europeans the *Liefde*'s survivors encountered in Japan, it is necessary to pause and look at the earliest years of Japanese-European relations.

The Portuguese had been in Japan for over half a century prior to the *Liefde*'s arrival and had known about Japan even longer. In 1515, Tomé Pires wrote in his *Suma Oriental*:

> The island of Japan (*Jampon*), according to what all the Chinese say, is larger than that of the *Lequíos*, nor (are) his subjects. He is a heathen king, a vassal of the king of China. They do not often trade in China because it is far off and they have no junks, nor are they seafaring men. (Cortesão, 1944, i, 132)

The first Portuguese to reach Japan did so in 1543. By the end of the decade, Francisco Xavier had begun missionary work in Japan. In 1543, three Portuguese who had taken passage in a Chinese junk for Liampo were driven north by a typhoon and landed on Tanegashima, a small island off the coast of Osumi, then part of the Shimadzu domains.

Liampo, although marked on early European maps of China in huge letters, was a collection of matshed huts inhabited by smugglers. Situated in all probability, on Jintang Shan, an island at the mouth of the Yong Jian, it was a precarious and temporary foothold the Portuguese then used in China. It was never

Portuguese territory, merely a convenient anchorage suitable for trade. In 1549, the newly-appointed governor of Fujian and Zhejiang, Chü Yuan, destroyed the settlement, capturing several Portuguese and killing or imprisoning many of their Chinese associates, obliterating Liampo after a mere nine years of existence. Liampo has been identified confidently with Ningpo, or *Ningbo*, but it seems likely it was some distance away from that city, which was already a considerable entrepôt in the sixteenth century. Pinto wrote that the Portuguese built over a thousand houses there, which seems an exaggeration. Even a far more modest building programme would not have been permissible within, or adjacent to a Chinese city. Chinese records relating to the era are mute on the subject of Liampo and its dramatic annihilation. The E.I.C. factory over a century later was situated on an offshore island. (Yule and Burnell, 1986, 515)

Thereafter, the Portuguese traders established another precarious foothold on Shangchuan Dao, which they called, euphonically, *São João*, or St. John's Island. It is best remembered for being the place where Francis Xavier, the 'Apostle of the Indies', died. Shangchuan Dao proved too exposed an anchorage and the Portuguese moved slightly closer to the Pearl River, to Lampakkau, then an island but now joined to the mainland by the silting action of the neighbouring estuary. From 1553 onwards, Lampakkau was the principal base for the Portuguese trading with China but in 1557, the peninsula known as Macau became their base. Permanent buildings were erected there, whereas none had been so erected at the earlier settlements. Portuguese trade with Japan thus antedates the acquisition of the foothold they established at Macau. The *Atlas of the People's Republic of China* (1989) ignores the Portuguese claim that a local Portuguese victory over pirates resulted in the Portuguese being invited to settle at Macau, saying that 'some Portuguese businessmen made a landing on the pretext of sunning their water-soaked goods.' (Yang, 1989, 21)

While attempting to alter the reduced privileges the Hirado factory had been awarded, Cocks was told that the English were afforded better treatment in Japan than were the Portuguese in China, Macau being 'a littell point or rock of no emportance'. Cocks replied that the Portuguese situation was immeasurably more advantageous since the traders at Macau paid only a 'set som for ancorage' and were not obliged to travel to court with presents, adding that the Hirado factory had 'no previleges here but faire wordes' and outspokenly wished 'the Emperour of Japon would make or previleges equall w'th the Portingales at Amacau, unto w'ch they answered little, but smiled & so past that mattr over, &c.' (Farrington, 1991, 563)

At the beginning of 1575, Gregory XIII established the Diocese of Macau, embracing both China and Japan, by issuing the bull *Super specula.* The bishop had theoretical jurisdiction over the Japanese Jesuit mission but was, in practice, restrained from exercising it; Philip II wrote to him in February 1583 to make it clear that he was prohibited from visiting Japan. This was sensible for a number of reasons; the bishop of Macau spoke no Japanese and knew little or nothing of Japanese culture, society or politics. One drawback was that missionaries in Japan, such as João Rodrigues, had to be sent from Japan to Macau to be ordained. The diocese of Funai in Bungo was established by Sixtus V in 1588; Funai was chosen in recognition of Otomo Yoshishige's unswerving assistance to the missionaries. In practice, however, the bishop resided in Nagasaki, the foremost Christian city of Japan. (Cooper, 1974, 107-9)

Although the engaging Fernão Mendes Pinto claimed to have been among the first Europeans in Japan, careful chroniclers have established that the first Europeans were António da Mota, Francisco Zeimoto and António Peixoto, sailing from Siam with a cargo of hides, deerskins and ivory. They were hospitably welcomed, and the arquebuses which they carried caused the greatest excitement. The Japanese, who had never seen firearms, at once set about copying them; and for centuries after the name for a musket in Japan was 'Tanegashima'. News of the coming of these strangers and of their weapons and other marvellous possessions soon spread to neighbouring fiefs, while the Portuguese along the China coast and in Malaya on hearing of the 'discovery' of Japan at once fitted out expeditions to trade in this new market. Within two or three years – certainly before 1549 – not only had several Portuguese ships visited harbours in Kyushu, but Portuguese traders had reached Miyako, which they described as a city of 96,000 houses – an interesting confirmation that the population of the capital, even after the Onin war which had reduced it to ruins, was over half a million, and therefore considerably greater than that of any European city of the day.

Within a few years, the traders were followed by Jesuit priests from the missions at Malacca and Goa. The traders were all Portuguese and the missionaries were all Jesuits; Portugal had at this time been confirmed by the Pope in a monopoly of both spiritual and commercial undertakings in the East and the Society of Jesus, formed in 1540, had founded in Portuguese territory its first seminaries. These two facts have important sequels in the history of Japan's relations with the West; her early contacts with European traders revealed to her international commercial rivalry in a phase of armed aggression, and her first knowledge of Christianity was gained from the most militant and uncompromising of its orders.

To the Portuguese kings, there was no contradiction in their linking of service to God and profit for themselves. In 1565, the king, Sebastián, encouraged the viceroy in Goa to promote Christianity on the island of Amboina in the East Indies, for this was 'an important means of making the country secure and would encourage the profits to be made there.' (Pearson, 1987, 10)

In September 1555, the Jesuit Balthazar Gago, writing from Hirado to his patron João III of Portugal, claimed credit for teaching Catholic converts to pray to the Portuguese monarch as their potential protector. João III was, incidentally, responsible for admitting the Society of Jesus into Portugal and its overseas possessions as well as permitting the establishment of the Inquisition and the *auto-da-fé*, despite the reluctance of the papacy. (Boxer, 1951, 167) The Inquisition was established in Goa in 1560 but its reach never extended to Macau; the Chinese authorities would never have allowed such a thing to happen.

Portugal was the only European Catholic country to have accepted all the decisions of the Council of Trent (1545-63) and to have applied them rigorously. In the early seventeenth century, Portugal possessed over 400 convents; one person in 36 was a priest or a member of a religious order.

In 1549, Francis Xavier with two other Spanish Jesuits landed at Kagoshima, where they began to preach with the full permission of the lord of Satsuma. It says a great deal for the tolerance of the Japanese that a stranger, preaching a strange doctrine, was not molested but was even encouraged by all classes, including a number of Buddhist priests who listened respectfully to such expositions of the Catholic faith as the Portuguese were able to give. Soon Xavier had baptised 150 converts, but their understanding of the new religion must have been very vague, for Japanese is a difficult language and Christianity is hard to explain. Perhaps it was because these early converts did not fully understand what their creed entailed that the Jesuits made such rapid progress in the first years of their labours.

There can be no doubt that the early missionaries in Japan were highly selective in the information they conveyed to their Japanese hearers. Catholic doctrine was represented as the one and only Christian doctrine and as late as the embassy of the four young Kyushu *samurai* to Europe, 1582-1590, the Jesuits successfully concealed the existence of the heresy of Protestantism from their charges. (Massarella, 1990, 47)

The erroneous assumption on the part of many Asians that Catholic Christianity was a singularly rigorous and demanding form of Buddhism or Hinduism was readily exploited by the Catholic missionaries, at least in the early years of evangelical endeavour:

> 'They (*the Roman Catholic priests*) assumed the character of Brahmans of a superior caste from the western world; they took Hindu names, and conformed to the heathen customs of this haughty and exclusive race, producing, in support of their pretensions, a deed forged in ancient characters, to show that the Brahmans of Rome were of a much older date than the Brahmans of India, and descended in an equally direct line from the Brahma himself,'

as a contemporary Sri Lankan historian, quoting from that Eminent Victorian Sir Emerson Tennent, has written. (Vimalanada, 1963, xxvi)

These happy days of gentle deception lasted only as long as it took for the Iberians and local converts to Catholic Christianity to obtain a firm grip on power. In Ceylon, present-day Sri Lanka, the Portuguese Catholics had no qualms about employing the same tactics the over-zealous Catholic converts in Kyushu used prematurely and with eventually disastrous results.

When the Portuguese gradually gained complete ascendancy

over the country below the Kandyan Hills, they replaced the gentler means of persuasion, inducement, temptation and blandishments by more rigorous methods. The missionaries now applied themselves with reckless ardour to the task of pulling down the structure which it had taken twenty centuries to build. 'The missionary could see in Buddhism nothing but the abhorrent creation of the devil; he did not stop to inquire what were the principles which were taught by its sages, nor what the ideals after which its lofty philosophy struggled. Buddhism was *not* Christianity, and, since by Christianity alone could souls escape damnation and hell fire, it was his duty to God to destroy Buddhism by every means in this power. He did not ask whether the people were prepared to receive his new wine or whether the destruction of the ancient beliefs might not mean the destruction of all spiritual life; his every idea was centred on the one thought that Buddhism must be wiped out of existence.' (Pieris, 1944, 80)

One providential aspect of the similarities between Buddhism and Catholic Christianity was that during the centuries of alert persecution which followed the expulsion of the bateran, Christian families and whole communities in Japan were able to disguise their 'hidden Christianity' as merely another form of Buddhism. The *Kirishitan Bunko* at Sophia University in Tokyo possesses an exquisite porcelain statue of Maria Kannon; such statues were revered in secret by Japanese Christians during the long years of persecution as images of Our Lady, the Virgin Mary. This fine example, depicted in Michael Cooper's outstanding work *The Southern Barbarians*, belonged to a Christian family at Sakitsu in the Amakusa Islands. (Cooper, 1971, 192)

In the middle of the sixteenth century, the protracted civil wars – the *Sengoku Jidai* – had eliminated all but a few powerful feudal groups from the struggle for supremacy. It was evident to all that a final contest for mastery of Japan would follow. It was at this critical point in Japanese history that the European traders and missionaries became active participants in the political evolution of Japan. The Emperor in Miyako was a powerless figurehead, his *shogun* exercised no real control over the more powerful feudal lords and a feudal chieftain of modest origin, Oda Nobunaga rose from obscurity by a judicious mixture of skilful strategy and carefully chosen alliances. Nobunaga's enemies were still strong; they included great feudal barons in North-Eastern and South-Western Japan and the great Buddhist monasteries, citadels of formidable political and military power. The *Sengoku Jidai*, the prolonged period without established central authority, was an era of virtual anarchy. Starting in the final decade of the fifteenth century, or – according to some authorities, starting with the Onin War a decade earlier – contending groups of landed barons, *daimyos*, fought ferociously amongst themselves to increase their wealth and territory. João Rodrigues, the Portuguese missionary, scholar and historian who reached Japan towards the end of this period, observed: 'Men chastised and killed each other, banished people and confiscated their property as they saw fit, in such fashion that treachery was rampant and nobody trusted his neighbour.' (Cooper, 1971, 18)

This period of instability and uncertainty was greatly advantageous to the Iberian foreigners; they could, and did, gain favour by giving limited support to one side or another, just as they had done in continental Asia and the Philippines. In Japan they could not render direct military support because of their inferior numbers but their expertise in both navigation and the manufacture and use of firearms made them useful allies. Their well-armed and all but invulnerable ships enabled them to convey cargoes safely to and from Japan, thus greatly profiting those *daimyos* whose ports they favoured with their commerce. A number of the barons in Kyushu gave special facilities to the missionaries because, having noticed the deference paid by the traders to the priests, they hoped thus to attract merchant ships to harbours in their own fiefs. Within a few years of Xavier's arrival we find one *daimyo* after another ordering his people to treat the Jesuits with respect, or even to adopt Christianity. In particular those barons who held the harbours of Kyushu – Kagoshima, Hirado, Omura, Funai – competed for the patronage of the foreign traders, sometimes to the extent of persecuting Buddhists; but more than once, when they found that no ship came, they drove the missionaries away and ordered their subjects to revert to their former faiths.

Trade was closely linked with the toleration of the religion brought by the alien *bateran* and their converts and it is revealing that the first large-scale conversions to Christianity occurred in the fiefdoms of those *daimyos* who most fervently desired foreign trade to be brought to their modest harbours. On more than one occasion a *daimyo* who found himself abruptly deprived of foreign trade took his revenge not only on the well-armed vessels and alert mariners of the *Nanbanjin*, insofar as this was within his power, but on the native Christians within his fiefdom and on his borders. Or he could prohibit missionary work without being conspicuously malevolent. For instance, Francis Xavier was foiled in catechetical work in Satsuma by Shimazu Takahisa's prohibition of baptisms; the prohibition had been ordered because of Takahisa's disappointment at the failure of the Portuguese to call at one of his ports in 1550, they had gone to Hirado instead. (Elison, 1973; 32)

The reasons for the quite remarkable successes of the Jesuits and the mendicant orders are elusive but the facts are clear. At the time Francis Xavier, Cosme de Torres and Juan Fernandez arrived in 1549, Japan had endured two centuries of civil wars and upheavals. The old social order had all but collapsed; the surviving feudal barons were engaged in a desperate struggle for power, in which treachery and shifting allegiances played no small part. There was no value system which provided the Japanese people with a sense of meaning to enable them to endure the confused period of *Sengoku Jidai* with calm understanding; the traditional religions of Japan were inadequate to the task. Quite possibly, this spiritual vacuum made the people of Kyushu, who had suffered greatly in the incessant wars, receptive to Christianity, which bore a strong resemblance to the more attractive elements of Buddhism. Additionally, the fact that the Christian missionaries were accompanied by those who offered the prospect of improved material conditions through trade made the message the more appealing. As the first Jesuits noted, the Japanese were a friendly people much given to hospitality, punctilious about manners and etiquette and extremely curious to learn new things. Since it was from China and, indirectly, from India that Japan had derived the most important elements of her cultural life, a tradition existed of willing receptiveness to foreign wisdom. The Jesuits in Japan were in the remarkable position of being participants, no less than observers, in one of the crucially important periods of Japanese history. Luís Frois and Organtino were on excellent, even familiar, terms with Oda Nobunaga. Toyotomi Hideyoshi, Nobunaga's successor, seldom admitted anyone, Japanese or foreign, to such familiarity. However, he and his eventual successor, Tokugawa Ieyasu, showed a great deal of justified confidence in their astute Jesuit interpreter, João Rodrigues. It is not an exaggeration to say that between 1570 and 1614, the Jesuits occupied a uniquely favourable position at the court of the *Bakufu*, in addition to what they could learn from their numerous influential converts in high places. The fact that the Jesuits wrote at such length about Japan and political events within the country has meant that a more accurate history can be compiled from foreign sources than could be contrived from Japanese sources alone. (Boxer, 1951, 57)

The missionaries, most especially, the Jesuits, were wholeheartedly committed to the conversion of Japan. Undaunted by the difficulties and dangers confronting them, they conscientiously attempted to adapt themselves to Japanese customs, a policy they had not condescended to adopt widely elsewhere. They also brought with them gifts for *daimyos* and other persons in important positions. Such artifacts as clocks, richly-bound books and muskets greatly impressed *daimyos* with whom they came into contact. To the extent that they succeeded in making converts among the *daimyo* class, the adherence of many, if not most, of the *daimyo*'s retainers was automatically accomplished.

The dispatch of a mission to the governor of the Philippines by Toyotomi Hideyoshi in 1592 led to the commencement of relations between Spain and Japan, conducted through the Philippines and Mexico. Spanish Franciscans came to Japan the following year, as envoys, and soon began to engage in missionary work. From the outset they were resented by the Jesuits, for a variety of reasons, not the least of which was the sensible one that Japan was too poor a country to support a mendicant order.

A minor but contributory factor in the dispute between the Jesuits and their rivals in the mendicant orders was the purely scientific or mathematical question of whether Japan lay in the Portuguese sphere or the Spanish sphere as demarcated by the Papal *diktat* of 1494. Since nobody had bothered to attempt to ascertain where the line ran in the Pacific and the East Indies until long after the Iberian powers had staked separate and often rival claims in the East, the disputants were obliged to stretch and shorten the facts on a Procrustean bed rather than to let the facts dictate which power received what. In any case, the precise circumference of the world was unknown in 1494.

F.W. Putzger's *Historischer Schulatlas* of 1960 shows that the Portuguese realm should have included the Philippines as well as Macau and the Moluccas. The Spanish, by the same reckoning, would have been entitled to all New Guinea except for the Vogelkopf Peninsula, roughly all the Eastern half of Australia and all of Japan except for Kyushu. Even had the clerical adversaries been able to agree on the cartography, it is certain that neither of them would have yielded an inch. (Putzger, 1960, 81-2)

The concordat of 1580 had confined the Japanese trade to the Portuguese, and it was in 1609 that a decree was issued by Philip III (1598-1621) permitting the citizens of Manila to trade freely with Japan and China. Equally the Papal Bull of 1585 had confined the propagation of the Christian faith in Japan to the Jesuits. That of 1600 had allowed the Begging Order to participate in the work, provided they entered the empire *via* Goa and Macao, and under the Portuguese flag. It was only 1608, after a great deal of agitation, that Pope Paul V. issued a Bull annulling the restrictions of the former two and according free access into Japan to *religieux* from any quarter. (Murdoch, 1949, 460)

Alessandro Valignano, the outstanding Jesuit *Visitor*, clearly listed the reasons 'why it is ill suited for other religious orders to move into Japan' in Chapter IX of his *Sumario* of 1583, noting particularly that the mendicant orders were too crude and brash for a sophisticated society like Japan. To Valignano, the barefoot Franciscan appeared a figure likely to undo the results of patient Jesuit endeavours over decades; it was 'extremely pernicious and baleful for Japan that any other type of religious outside of ourselves come here.' (Elison, 1973, 79) Valignano was well aware just how vulnerable the Jesuit position in Japan actually was. In his *Sumario*, he wrote '. . .we are strangers and unknown unto them and it is no small grace of Our Lord that they receive us in their lands.'

Nonetheless, the Franciscans' acts of charity among the sick and the poor, including lepers, won the grudging admiration of several Jesuits and not a few Japanese. The Dominicans and

Augustinians arrived after 1602. Dominicans encouraged Japanese Christians to form mutually supporting groups of believers, *cofradía*, which proved of great value in the years of sustained persecution after the edict of 1614.

Whether persecution could have been averted had the Jesuits retained a monopoly of missionary endeavours in Japan necessarily remains an unanswerable hypothesis.

That the Catholic Portuguese, aided by local converts to Catholicism, were not infrequently capable of hideous cruelty cannot be doubted. During the consolidation of Portuguese power in Ceylon, André Furtado, the Captain-General, 'ordered eight hundred *Badagas* and some Moors of Calicut to be beheaded, so as not to let foreigners and declared enemies remain in the realm', as Fernão de Queyroz, himself a Jesuit recorded. (de Queyroz, 1930, III, 454)

Portuguese atrocities in Asia began as soon as the first Portuguese pioneers realised that their old foe, Islam, was a force to be reckoned with in Asia as well. In 1502, da Gama set alight a crowded pilgrim ship and watched it burn. Only twenty children were allowed to escape and they were saved in order to be converted. (Pearson, 1987, 71)

The Portuguese were not alone in committing atrocities in Ceylon. During the siege of Colombo in 1655-6 which gained Ceylon for the Dutch, hundreds of non-combatants were trapped between the walls and the besiegers' lines. To make it unambiguously clear that they would not permit these unhappy people to pass through their lines, the Dutch compelled one woman to pound her child to death in a wooden mortar and display the corpse to her compatriots. (Pieris, 1944, 17-18)

In Japan, Christian converts made the appalling error of assuming that temporal power accompanied spiritual. Rather than patiently waiting for the conversion of Japan to Christianity, they strove to eradicate Buddhism in those areas where converted *daimyos* had sufficient power.

In the province of Bungo, the Jesuit persecution of Buddhism was violent and conducted upon an extensive scale. Otomo Sorin, the reigning *daimyo,* not only destroyed all the Buddhist temples in his dominion (to the number, it is said, of three thousand), but had many of the Buddhist priests put to death. For the destruction of the great temple of Hikozan, whose priests were reported to have prayed for the tyrant's death, he is said to have chosen the sixth day of the fifth month (1576), the festival of the Birthday of the Buddha.

However seductive Christianity appeared to many Japanese, there can be no doubt that Buddhist priests were slain by *daimyo* converts and their adherents and that in various times and places, it seemed that, once established, Christianity in Japan would be as ferociously imposed as it had been in Portuguese India.

It has been suggested that some '. . .leading ideas of the Catholic church have been derived from Buddhist sources, whose missionaries, while penetrating, as we know they did, to the East, and converting entire nations, may well be supposed not to have been without their influence also on the West.' (Hildreth, 1905, 59)

Outward attractions of whatever sort, or outward resemblances to Buddhism, could only assist the spread of the new religion; they could not explain the rapid progress of the propaganda.

Coercion might partly explain it, – coercion exercised by converted *daimyos* upon their subjects. Populations of provinces are known to have followed, under strong compulsion, the religion of their converted lords; and hundreds – perhaps thousands – of persons must have done the same thing through mere habit of loyalty. In these cases, it is worthwhile to consider what sort of persuasion was used upon the *daimyos*. One great help to the missionary work was found in Portuguese commerce – especially the trade in firearms and ammunition. In the disturbed state of the country prior to the imposition of Toyotomi power, the wealth and power that foreign trade offered to the *daimyos* of Kyushu was virtually irresistible. This fact has led more than one acute observer into difficulties:

> 'The *daimyo* able to use firearms would necessarily possess some advantage over a rival lord having no such weapons; and those lords able to monopolize the trade could increase their power at the expense of their neighbours. Now this trade was actually offered for the privilege of preaching; and sometimes much more than that privilege was demanded and obtained. In 1572, the Portuguese presumed to ask for the whole town of Nagasaki, as a gift to their church, – with power of jurisdiction over the same; threatening, in case of refusal, to establish themselves elsewhere. The *daimyo*, Omura, at first demurred, but

> eventually yielded; and Nagasaki then became Christian territory, directly governed by the Church.' (Hearn, 1984, 335)

There is a major flaw in this spirited account; Hearn permitted his anti-Jesuit sympathies to get the better of his good sense in the chapter of *Japan: An Interpretation* entitled *The Jesuit Peril*. There was no 'whole town' to be ceded to the Jesuits; Nagasaki was then, at best, a fishing community of little consequence. The cession of the port and town came several years later, moreover.

Father Diego Pacheco Yuuki, after having considered and compared the various accounts relating to the founding of Nagasaki, has deduced that the site of the future city was discussed in or about 1568 and that the work of building the nucleus of the new town commenced in the spring of 1571.

In his *Apologia*, written in 1598, Alessandro Valignano, the *Visitor* of the Jesuit missions in the Indies, observed:

> About thirty years ago, the port of Nagasaki, which is in the territory of don Bartolomé, Lord of Omura, was completely unknown and unpopulated. It is a naturally very good port, for a narrow promontory, which was then covered with wild thickets and brambles, juts out into the sea. As the Portuguese greatly desired to find a good port for their merchant ship and Don Bartolomé had become a Christian shortly before, a Father who was in his territories passed by the said port and saw that it was very good for the ship. There were also at that time many Christians living away from their homes, for they have been persecuted and exiled by the pagan lords because they refused to abandon the Faith and return to their sects. So this Father proposed to Don Bartolomé that it would be a good and useful thing to populate the said port and build houses on that promontory which jutted out into the sea, so that it would thus be convenient for the Portuguese to come there with their ship; he added that by dividing the promontory among the displaced Christians a start would be made towards building the town. As this was a very good plan and most profitable for Don Bartolomé and all his domain, he was greatly pleased by the idea and gave the promontory to the Father to divide among the displaced Christians. When I reached Japan for the first time, there were about four hundred houses there. (Yuuki, 1989, 31)

Luís Frois, contradicting this account slightly, wrote that Nagasaki in 1569 was an unprepossessing village (*logar inculto*) of some 1,500 souls, all of whom were baptised in the course of that year. There is a visible difference between a place with 1,500 inhabitants and one with none. (Elison, 1973, 93) By 1609, Nagasaki had about 25,000 inhabitants.

Valignano reached Japan in 1579. Nagasaki was ceded to the Jesuits in 1580, this cession being revoked by Toyotomi Hideyoshi in 1588.

Despite the reverses they, and their Japanese converts had suffered and endured since the beginning of Xavier's mission, the Jesuits still had every hope that Japan would embrace Roman Christianity. By 1600, the temporal power of the Jesuits was waning but still sufficiently strong to put the *Liefde*'s survivors in fear of their lives. Not the least remarkable aspect of Jesuit influence in Japan was that such influence was accomplished by so few; there were no more than 137 Jesuits in Japan in 1597, three years prior to the *Liefde*'s arrival.

In addition to serving as Togukawa Ieyasu's interpreter and informal advisor, João Rodrigues served as Ieyasu's commercial agent in the purchase of silk at Nagasaki. In 1602, Rodrigues' diplomatic skills did much to resolve an awkward dispute between Japanese buyers and Portuguese sellers at Nagasaki.

From the death of Henry of Aviz in 1580 until the accession of João of Brangança in 1640, Portugal was ruled by three successive Spanish monarchs of the House of Hapsburg. The domination of Portugal by Spain exacerbated existing differences rather than reconciling them. In Japan, such national antagonisms had important repercussions; the Nagasaki martyrdom of 1597 was the result of Spanish arrogance, tactlessness and stupidity, the Jesuits claimed. Contemporary Jesuits added that the antagonism between the Jesuits, on the one hand and the mendicant orders – of whom the Franciscans were the most conspicuous – the other was, *au fond*, national antagonism. The Jesuits readily conceded that difficulties would be eliminated if the Franciscans sent to Japan were all Portuguese.

If the Jesuits are to be believed, it was Don Rodrigo de Vivero y Velasco's conversations with Ieyasu that sealed the fate of Captain-Major André Pessoa and his *naó*, the *Madre de Deus*, in 1610. At the end of 1609, a great Spanish ship from the Philippines, the *San Francisco*, a ship of a thousand tons bound from the Philippines to Mexico, was forced ashore in Japan. Aboard her was Don Rodrigo Vivero y Velasco, formerly acting governor of the Philippines. He and over three hundred of the ship's passengers and crew were saved and treated well by the people of Iwawada, about thirty miles from Otaki. Soon Vivero was in Ieyasu's presence and talking expansively, one lordly aristocrat to another. Vivero pronounced himself in favour of trade relations between Japan on the one hand, the Spanish possessions of Mexico and the Philippines on the other. He also wanted *carte blanche* for Christian missionaries to spread the Christian message in Japan. Additionally, he asked Ieyasu to expel the Dutch. Ieyasu agreed to the first two requests and ignored the third. He wanted Spanish mining experts and greatly increased trade. Vivero is said to have promised to send not one but two or even three ships a year.

As well as admiring the Japanese to the point of writing that were it not for his 'loyalties as a Spaniard and a Catholic', he would prefer Japan to his own country. Don Rodrigo Vivero y Velasco wrote perceptively about the martial nature of his hosts; 'The Japanese are much braver and more warlike than the people of China, Korea, Ternate and all the other nations round the Philippines.' (Cooper, 1965, 42) Like João Rodrigues, the Portuguese historian and linguist, Don Rodrigo correctly interpreted the nature of the Tokugawa regime, writing that the *Dairi* (or O or Tenno or Mikado) was the 'legitimate Lord and King' of Japan. Rodrigues, in his *História*, had come to the same conclusion and had seen with his own eyes how decayed the Imperial house had become; the Miyako court was a miserable cluster of decayed wooden buildings 'in complete disrepair and utterly deserted', so far as could be seen. Ieyasu, who set great store on constitutional forms so long as they suited his purpose, ensured that the Imperial house and the decayed nobility, the *Kuge*, were provided with a better standard of living after his assumption of absolute power.

As Captain Major of the *Japan Voyage*, Pessoa was the Governor of Macao when a number of Japanese sailors aboard a junk of Arima Harunobu, by this time, the only Christian *daimyo* left in Japan, became embroiled in a fracas with the Macao authorities. Forty of the Japanese were killed in the armed altercation which followed and one of them was later strangled in prison on Pessoa's orders. A highly coloured version of this episode had been related to Ieyasu at approximately the same time that the Spaniards were assuring him he could dispense with the Portuguese; Ieyasu sent word to Arima that he could deal with Pessoa as he liked.

This version of events has been disputed; Vivero's offer to promote Japan – Mexico and Japan – Manila trade, together with the coincidental arrival of the Dutch, offered the prospect of releasing Ieyasu from dependence on the Portuguese trade monopoly. However, it appears that Vivero met Ieyasu in December 1609, by which time Pessoa's fate had been decided. (Cooper, 1974, 264)

Pessoa and his small crew (many of his men were on shore when Arima's intentions became obvious) struggled to reach the open sea, fighting Arima's blockading flotilla as they went.

The wind against his ship, Pessoa fought for three days before blowing up the ship, the crew, the cargo and himself rather than fall into the hands of his enemies. Relations with the Portuguese were subsequently re-established and trade continued.

Pessoa's gallant death, in the explosion which destroyed the *Madre de Deus*, led to the loss of approximately 3,000 piculs of silk, worth 600,000 cruzados, in addition to silver worth 200,000 cruzados. (Cooper, 1974, 265-6) In 1934, a Japanese diver located the wreck and searched for the silver bullion but found only cannon balls, bones and fragments. (Davies, 1985, 49) A mother-of-pearl fragment, part of a window in the doomed vessel, is in the Twenty-six Martyrs Museum in Nagasaki to which it was presented by Charles Ralph Boxer, the eminent historian. (Yuuki, 1989, 57) A cannon recovered from the seabed in 1929/30 is in the possession of Tenri University.

By the standards of any age, Pessoa was a warrior of truly heroic stature. He had distinguished himself at the siege of Malacca, during which he had been wounded fighting alongside a resolute band of Japanese mercenaries defending the city. By a curious coincidence, it was during this same campaign that Jacob Quackernaeck, formerly the captain of the *Liefde*, was killed. Pessoa's dramatic end at Nagasaki greatly impressed the Japanese. The Portuguese chronicler, António Bocarro, wrote '. . .this fidalgo behaved in such a way as to leave them astounded at his nobility of soul and how he otherwise represented the Portuguese nation.' According to several sources, the last heroic fight of his ship became part of Kyushu folklore and was recorded in several Kyushu chronicles. (Boxer, 1951; 269, 284)

This act of sanguinary revenge did not profit Arima Harunobu, Pessoa's nemesis. He was subsequently denounced to the Tokugawa shogunate for not only being a Christian, having been baptised in 1579 as John Protasius, but for plotting to seize the castle of Isahaya, (*Hizen*). He was banished to Yamura (*Kai*) and later condemned to death and executed. (Papinot, 1988, 21)

While Pessoa and his crew were fighting and dying, Vivero was a guest of Ieyasu. In fact, Vivero stayed in Japan until August 1610, having concluded an outline agreement with Ieyasu. The Spaniards completed their journey to Mexico in the *Santa Buenaventura*, the larger of the two European style ships which William Adams had built at Ieyasu's behest. With them, the Spaniards carried presents to the King of Spain and to the Viceroy of New Spain (*Mexico*).

The Spaniards' claim that they could replace the Portuguese as importers of silk and porcelain from China was absurd and empty; Chinese vessels fearfully sailed pirate-infested waters to reach Manila and thus supply the Philippine, Mexican and European markets; even the Japanese knew that the Spaniards had no foothold on the coast of China and no prospect of acquiring one. Nonetheless, embassies from Manila and Mexico arrived soon enough; both demanded the expulsion of the Dutch and Vizcaíno, the envoy from Mexico, irritated the Japanese with an ill-advised display of Castilian *hauteur.* Among his requests was the apparently reasonable one that the Spaniards should be permitted to survey the Eastern Japanese coast, taking soundings of bays and harbours. Adams told Ieyasu that in Europe such activity would be considered espionage. (Murdoch, 1949, 489)

Although Sebastián Vizcaíno caused offence unwittingly by merely bowing – 'three moderate bows. . .three times slightly more profoundly. . .three deeper bows' – rather than adopting Japanese court etiquette, he found much to admire at Hidetada's court at Edo and wrote approvingly of Hidetada's character; '. . .he does not use more than one woman; the least number of women any of his predecessors had was over forty. The prince is very upright and is exceedingly strict, especially when dealing with thieves and bad women.' (Cooper, 1965, 120)

Apart from Sebastián Vizcaíno's apparent want of diplomatic finesse, there was an unbridgeable gulf between his views and Ieyasu's on the religious issue, Ieyasu observing, mildly enough, 'The doctrine followed in your country differs entirely from ours. Therefore, I am persuaded that it would not suit us. In the Buddhist sutras it is said that it is difficult to convert those who are not disposed towards being converted. It is best, therefore, to put an end to the preaching of your doctrine on our soil. On the other hand, you can multiply the voyages of merchant ships, and thus promote mutual interests and relations. your ships can enter Japanese ports with exception. I have given strict orders to this effect.' (Boxer, 1951, 313)

VIII

ADAMS AND THE MISSIONARIES

'If the Kings and Princes of Europe do banish the Fathers out of their countries, I shall do them no injury to send them out of mine.'
Tokugawa Ieyasu to William Adams, 1613 (Boxer, 1951, 311)

Referring to the period that he daily, or hourly expected execution at the behest of the Jesuits, Adams wrote in his letter to the Britons at Bantam of October 1611: '. . .I looked everye day to dye, to be crost as the coustome of justice is in Japan as hanging is in our lande. In w'ch long time of ymprissonment the Jesuites and the Portingalles gave many evidences ageinst mee and the rest that wee were theeves and robbers of all nations, and were wee suffered to live it should be ageinst the proffitt of His Highnes and of his countrey, for noe nation should come hither w'thout robbing them; His Highnes' justice being executed, w'thout doubt the rest of our nation should feare and not come here any more; thus dayly making access to th'Emperour and procuring freindes to hasten my death.' (Farrington, 1991, 69)

It is improbable that João Rodrigues was one of these Jesuits. The records suggest that, at this period, he was busy in Kyushu. (Cooper, 1974, 193)

William Adams was credited by the Jesuits resident in Japan with having spared no effort to turn the hearts of the Japanese against the Catholic missionaries, as the Jesuit Pedro Morejón recounted in his remarkable work *A briefe Relation of the Persecution lately made against the Catholike Christians in the Kingdome of Japonia*, published in Spanish in Mexico City in 1616 and in English at St. Omer in 1619. In referring to the growing distaste the *shogun*, Tokugawa Ieyasu, felt for the Jesuits (Morejón was writing early in 1615) the Jesuit wrote 'Many noble personages in the Courtes of Yendo and Suruga did imitate the *Xoguns* proceedings in this kind but above all, the Prince of *Toxogun* did shew himselfe most cruell and rigorous moved partly by the *Xoguns* example but principally incited by the wordes of an English Pilot who spake most bitterly against religious men and Spaniardes making their persons odious unto him and all that they did suspitious.' (Morejón, 1969, 66)

There was only one man who could have qualified for this specific reference resident in Japan at this time; William Adams. The English secret service personnel, who read every line the Jesuits published in English, must have wondered who this anonymous English Pilot could have been, to be so roundly traduced by the Jesuits' printing press on the other side of the world in his own lifetime.

As Macauley, the most celebrated of English nineteenth century historians, observed:

> 'There was no region of the globe, no walk of speculative or of active life, in which Jesuits were not to be found. . .Yet, whatever might be their residence, whatever might be their employment, their spirit was the same, entire devotion to the common cause, implicit obedience to the central authority. None of them had chosen his dwelling place or his vocation for himself. Whether the Jesuit should live under the arctic circle or under the equator, whether he should pass his life in arranging gems and collating manuscripts at the Vatican or in persuading naked barbarians in the southern hemisphere not to eat each other, were matters which he left with profound submission to the decision of others. If he was wanted at Lima, he was on the Atlantic in the next fleet. If he was wanted at Bagdad, he was toiling through the desert with the next caravan. If his ministry was needed in some country where his life was more insecure than that of a wolf, where it was a crime to harbour him, where the heads and quarters of his brethren, fixed in the public places, showed him what he had to expect, he went without remonstrance or hesitation to his doom.' (Macauley, 1966, I, 542-3)

Writing of Tokugawa Ieyasu's persecutions, Morejón ascribed malign power not merely to the heretics of England and Holland but also to Satan himself, a line of reasoning which has gone out of fashion:

> 'The causes and reasons of this so rigorous sentence and proceeding of the *Xogun*, and of the execution thereof, be divers, some of old, and some of new. Of old is the hatred of the Divell, who having had peaceable possession more then a 1000. yeares of al that kingdome, and

> seing that now of late by reason of the preaching, teaching, holy life and instruction of the Fathers, many thousands of soules were daily drawne from Idolatry and superstition to the knowledge and service of the true and everliving God. . .and that very probably within smal time if they were permitted he should be altogether dispossessed of the tyrannical dominion he had so long execised upon them, did therefore al his endeavours to hinder their prosperous proceedings. . .This I say made him bestir himself, and move the *Bonzos* his Ministers to hate the Fathers bitterly, and to procure their disgrace by al means possible. . .' (Morejón, 1969, 48-50)

Morejón was certainly not alone in holding this opinion; Jesuit letters frequently stated that the Devil was busy in Japan, aiding and abetting the enemies of Christianity. Daniello Bartoli, writing in about 1650 with Jesuit materials before him, said that in Buddhism, the Devil had created a mockery of Christianity in Japan, transforming its sacraments into superstitious rites and its ceremonies into a sacrilegious cult. Xavier himself described the Buddhas Shaka (*Sakya Muni*) and Amida (*Amitabha*) as 'those two demons'. Valignano, the Visitor-General who was in Japan thirty years later, described Shaka as 'a sagacious philosopher, who, pretending to lead a holy and penitent life, commenced to preach the divine cult of Amida.' (Sansom, 1987; 121, 123)

Although Morejón was writing for a Catholic readership, it is mildly surprising that he attempted no more thoughtful analysis of the nature of Buddhism than merely to consider it the work of Satan. In 1604, the Jesuit *Annual Letter*, written by Padre João Rodrigues Girão, explained that a special course was being organised for a small number of selected converts, to train them in anti-Buddhist polemics. This course, at the Jesuit college in Nagasaki, was taught by a Japanese brother from Miyako, who had visited many of the most famous temples in Japan, not as an avowed Christian, but as a seeker after knowledge. He had heard the Buddhist texts expounded by their most qualified exponents and he had works. The students were taught to refute Buddhist doctrine, using Buddhist texts to do so, and João Rodrigues Girão was adamant that this method of propaganda was expected to prove highly effective. The *Myotei-Mondo*, one of the best-known Christian apologetics produced in Japan during those years, dates from approximately this period. (Boxer, 1951, 221)

Catholicism was assumed by many Japanese in the earliest days of the Jesuits' endeavours to be merely a more rigorous form of Buddhism and in the official grant of land at Yamaguchi to the Fathers of the Society of Jesus in 1552 the Japanese text plainly states that the grant, which appears to have included a temple called Daidoji, was made to the strangers that they might preach the Law of Buddha.

The introduction of Christianity to Japan was remarkably similar to the introduction of Buddhism a millennium earlier. In about 550 AD the first Buddhist image was sent to Japan from Korea by the king of Paikche, accompanied by a message assuring the Emperor of Japan that, while Buddhism was hard to grasp at first, it offered *the assurance of domestic tranquillity*. A few years later, an epidemic struck the court at Naniwa and the image was thrown into a canal. Some time later, one Soga no Umako, a prominent member of one of the two families contending for influence behind the throne, obtained another image, also imported from Korea, recruited the services of a Korean who had formerly been a monk and enlisted three young girls who were obliged to shave their heads and become Japan's first Buddhist nuns. Images and monks grew in number but after the outbreak of a new epidemic, Soga's enemies persuaded the Emperor to destroy the images and order nuns to be whipped publicly for insulting the native gods. After the Sui Dynasty of China (589-618 AD) gave way to the Tang (618-906 AD) the Japanese were ready to adopt Chinese culture and Buddhism wholeheartedly; by this time, there was a more powerful and impressive culture to be adopted and copied.

Buddhism was firmly established in Japan in 749 with the dedication of the Great Buddha at Nara. The difficulties inherent in reconciling the new faith with the native gods were imaginatively overcome by the monk Gyogi who stole a Buddhist relic and hid at Ise shrine. A week later, he reported that the sun goddess Amaterasu Omikami had revealed herself through the medium of Chinese poetry and announced that she and the Buddha were one and the same deity. Since the Great Buddha represented Roshanna, the *Great Shining Deity*, the Emperor could be seen both as the chief servant of Buddha and as a child of Amaterasu Omikami. Todaiji, the home temple of the image of the Great Buddha, became the chief temple of a system of temples in every province, all of which lead prayers to ensure the health, welfare and peace of the realm and Buddhism thus became an integral part of the Japanese political and cultural structure. That Christianity failed to achieve this status was certainly not due to lack of effort on the part of those propagating a religion as alien as Buddhism had once been. Rather, it was the fact that Japan already possessed a religion which met the needs of the rulers as fully as Catholicism would have done. Moreover, by the time Francis Xavier arrived in Japan, Buddhism in Japan had been transformed, over the centuries, into a specifically *Japanese* Buddhism which was entire and self-contained. While new sects, such as Shingon and Zen, might be introduced, Japanese Buddhism as a whole needed little, if anything, from abroad to sustain it. There was never any question of the necessity to acknowledge the authority of any equivalent of the Pope, for example.

Buddhism in Japan was, in the main, a tolerant religion. Various ferocious orders of sectarians existed at various times and places, but few Japanese would have felt it inappropriate for a practising Buddhist to worship at a Shinto shrine. Xavier had been cordially welcomed by the first Buddhist priests he met and, initially at least, there was no hostility on the part of the Buddhist clergy towards the European missionaries.

During the course of the Tokugawa persecutions, Buddhism was pressed into service as an arm of the persecuting mechanism of the state. It is improbable that the Buddhist clergy felt particularly pleased at being obliged to act as investigators of heresy. Unlike Catholicism or Islam, Buddhism is a somnolent, essentially tolerant and all-embracing religion, although certain sects manifest a degree of enthusiasm similar to that of the most fervent Christian zealot.

Initially, the new religion was welcomed with unfeigned interest; the first Buddhist clergy to come into contact with the missionaries thought them to be bringing a more austere and demanding version of Buddhism from India. Mutual antipathy grew; it was evident to the clergy of both faiths that mutual tolerance was impossible. The decision of the Tokugawa to press Buddhism into service merely acknowledged an existing state of affairs.

During Tokugawa Ieyasu's last years, he was treated as a living deity. Despite his atrocious treatment of such innocents as Toyotomi Hideyori's eight-year-old son, whom he had ordered beheaded after the fall of Osaka castle in 1615, it was accepted that he had constructed a lasting legacy – the *Pax Tokugawa* – and his posthumous deification under the sacred title of *Gongen Sama*, meaning an avatar of the Buddha, was assured.

One aspect of the Catholic Christianity would have impressed itself upon the minds of many observant Japanese. In Japan, no less than elsewhere in Asia, the Catholic missionaries and their converts were intolerant of all other religions. While the Jesuits and their converts were few, this intolerance was of no consequence. After Nagasaki became Christian territory, the character of the alien creed became evident; the great Buddhist temple Jinguji was burned, the conflagration implausibly ascribed to the 'wrath of God', eighty other temples around Nagasaki were burned. All religions other than Catholicism was suppressed, Buddhist priests being driven away.

The situation of the Jesuit mission in Japan was complicated by the arrival of the Franciscans in 1593, followed by the Dominicans and Augustinians. The mendicant orders were brasher and less subtle in their behaviour, the Jesuits complained. Worse, conflicting national rivalries as well as the commercial interests of Spain and Portugal tended to confuse matters greatly.

During the years of the 'Spanish captivity', the period when Portugal was ruled by the Spanish crown, Portuguese colonies and settlements, such as Goa, Cochin, Malacca and Macau, kept their autonomy and continued to fly the Portuguese flag. On the whole, there was little love between the Portuguese and the Spanish at this time, although Macau traded illegally with the Philippines.

The Spanish period in Japanese history is complicated by the rivalry between the Portuguese and the Spaniards, both subjects of the same sovereign and members of the same faith and embittered by the rivalry between the Jesuits, most of whom were Portuguese, and the friars and lay brothers of the mendicant orders, most of whom were Spanish. While it is true that the rulers of Japan desired trade with Spain, it is equally true that they were more than a little apprehensive of Spanish ambitions after 1596, the year the *San Felipe* was driven ashore at Urado in

Shikoku while *en route* between the Philippines and Mexico. Angered by seeing his fine ship deliberately wrecked by the *daimyo*'s men, the *daimyo* having decided that he wanted the cargo, the pilot of the vessel supposedly made some injudicious observations about the power and might of his master, the King of Spain. On being asked how it was that the Spanish monarch and his predecessors were lords of such vast territories, the Japanese having evidently seen a map or two of Spanish America and the Philippines, the pilot is alleged to have replied that His Majesty the King of Spain set priests and monks ahead to convert the natives to Christianity and then sent his soldiers to be guided and assisted by the new converts. Or did Francisco de Olandía really say this? Was he misunderstood? This episode and much else of the rivalry between the Jesuits and the mendicant orders has been the subject of much debate.

What is certain is that, not long after this episode, twenty-six Christians, including three Japanese converts of the *Jesuits*, who had been included more or less by mistake, were crucified at Nagasaki.

The crew and the civilian passengers were ordered to return to Manila. There were seven religious aboard; four Augustinians, one Dominican and two Franciscans. The Dominican and the Augustinians were returned to Manila. One Franciscan, the cleric Felipe de las Casa, was arrested in Miyako and included among the martyrs. The other Franciscan, the redoubtable Juan Pobre de Zamora, left Japan later and was instrumental in doing much to begin the propaganda onslaught against Jesuit 'treachery' that resulted from the affair.

Five Franciscans of the Miyako convent with some of their Christian helpers, one Franciscan of the Osaka convent and one Jesuit brother, Paul Miki, with two *dojuku* residing in Osaka were arrested. Those martyred were six Franciscans; Peter Baptist Blasquez, Francisco Blanco, Martin de Aguirre, Felipe de las Casas, Garcia Gonzalo and Francis de la Parilla. In addition there were three Japanese converts of the Jesuits; Paul Miki and the two *dojuku*, Juan de Goto and Jacobus Kisai. Both of these last two pronounced their vows before dying. Also included were fifteen lay Japanese Christians, helpers of the Miyako hospitals and similar people. All had the lobe of one ear cut off before being paraded through Miyako, Osaka and Sakai and thereafter being led overland to Nagasaki. Later, two more Christians who had followed the martyrs all the way to Nagasaki were added to the others. The whole group was crucified on the Tateyama hill at Nagasaki in February 1597, the bodies thereafter being left on the crosses for about nine months. (Jennes, 1973, 77). The martyrdom site is commemorated by life-size statues executed by Funakoshi Yasutake, erected on the site in 1962. (Cooper, 1971, 72)

The Jesuits themselves certainly believed that Francisco de Olandía had spoken unwisely, although it is quite certain that no Jesuits were present at the time. Pedro Morejón wrote:

> '. . .although he were moved thereunto principally by reason of the desire he (*Hideyoshi*) had to have taken the great Spanish galeon, called *S. Philip*, which passed by that way unto *Nova Espania*, from the *Philippines*; yet he was also not a little provoked by the foolish wordes of a certaine Pilot, who being asked how the Spaniardes had gained so many kingdomes, he answered that they went first to traffique into them, and that if therein they eyther receyved injury of any, or were not wel used, or not received by the people of the contry, that then they made warre against them, and overcomming them, tooke possession of their kingdome and estates. And being asked if they did not also for that cause send religious men before them, he answered, yes: the which although it were most false and fabulous, yet did *Taycosama* take it as a sufficient occasion to rayse a cruell persecution against al the Christians of *Iapone*.' (Morejón, 1969, 54)

The Devil, Morejón continued, attempted to do what he could to destroy Christianity in Japan. One approach open to His Satanic Majesty was to destroy the trade between Macau and Nagasaki,

> 'knowinge well how that by occasion of the traffique from the *Indies* and *Macan*, Christian religion found first entrance into *Iapone*, and how by meanes thereof it hath hitherto also beene there conserved, and that if it should cease, religion could not probably be of longe continuance there. . .' Satan also 'moved the Heretikes to go thither, to the end that by their false reportes they might bring into discredit the Catholike religion: and offer to bring them the same merchandise that the *Spaniardes* and *Portugals* have done hitherto.' (Morejón, 1969, 56-7)

The relationship between the Macau trade and the Jesuit mission was evident to all. The Jesuit Luís Frois wrote, in 1563:

> 'It was a sign of the grace of Divine Providence that the traffic and trade between the Japanese and the Chinese in their junks and *somas* had stopped. Instead, only the one yearly China Ship came with the Portuguese and their wares; and because of this very favourable opportunities, arose for our purpose, which is the conversion of souls.'

Echoing him two decades later, Alessandro Valignano wrote:

> 'Actually, I am confounded and astonished whenever I consider how great the expenses are, and I cannot persuade myself otherwise than that it was God who augmented our funds in this expenditure, doing the same as He did with the five loaves of bread and the two fishes; for in order to sustain all this machinery, we have to this day nothing but the trade of the China Ship.' (Elison, 1973; 87, 102)

The role of the Jesuits' acting as commercial brokers between buyers and sellers in Macau and Japan has been criticised severely over the centuries. Even at the time, it drew adverse comment from such observers as Jan Huyghen van Linschoten. Acting as brokers between buyers and sellers was not a role the Jesuits chose for themselves; but both buyers and sellers trusted them and the Jesuit endeavours in East Asia needed financial support from somewhere. Acting as commercial intermediaries for the Christian *daimyos*, for example, laid them under a greater obligation to the Jesuits than would have been the case otherwise. The cost of maintaining the churches, schools, training seminaries and similar activities, not to mention the eternal giving of gifts to persons in every walk of life, needed ample funds; Valignano was not overstating the case when he estimated the cost of running the Jesuits' Japan mission at between 10,000 and 12,000 cruzados annually; unlike the Buddhist establishments in Japan, the Jesuits had no income from endowments and the majority of Japanese Christians were too poor to contribute much in cash. (Boxer, 1951, 114-5)

While the Iberians and their Dutch and British rivals brought desirable trade to Japan, they were by no means indispensable. Cocks wrote of the arrival of sixty or seventy Chinese junks at Nagasaki in 1614, an estimate confirmed by a Portuguese source the same year. The Portuguese noted that the majority of the crews of these junks were Fujianese smugglers 'who settle down there (*i.e. in Japan*) and marry'. Some of these junks belonged to Chinese permanently resident in Japan, such as Cocks' friends, the Li family of Hirado. Both the Iberians and their north European rivals felt Chinese competition keenly; the Dutch felt the full force of it after the expulsion of the Portuguese and somewhat later, the establishment of the Ming dynasty in China in 1644. (Boxer, 1951, 299-300)

This junk traffic was well-established long before the first Europeans arrived in Japan in 1543; during the 1540s, around two hundred junks traded to the minor ports of Satsuma and Osumi (present-day Kagoshima prefecture) every May. The continuing civil wars prior to Oda Nobunaga's stabilisation of the country dictated the use of secluded inlets rather than the developed harbours of the Inland Sea and the northern and western coasts of Kyushu, all areas infested by pirates. (Okamoto, 1972, 12)

By the time Cocks arrived in Hirado, the country was under a strong centralised administration and the Chinese traders had no fear of using major ports where trade conditions were immeasurably better.

The *Bakufu* regarded the Macau trade as desirable but not essential; the political threat the Christian converts and the missionary influence the Jesuits and mendicant orders appeared to pose was to the stability of the country in general and the hegemony of the house of Tokugawa in particular was of greater importance.

Morejón was obliged to leave Japan in November 1614, aboard the same ship which carried the Japanese Christian hero Takayama Ukon into exile in the Philippines. He had, therefore, direct experience of the vicissitudes of fortune which afflicted the Jesuit mission in Japan. (Laures, 1942, 99)

Among the Japanese who left their native country in the years of intensifying persecution was Pedro Casui Kibe, a truly remarkable figure martyred in 1639. Kibe had left Japan for Macau in 1614, then had travelled to Rome to be ordained. It appears that he travelled by way of Goa, Ormuz, Persia and Palestine, reaching Rome in 1620, the year in which William Adams died. Ordained and admitted to the Society of Jesus in 1620, Kibe sailed from Lisbon aboard a fleet bound for Moçambique, Goa and Macau in 1623. After various adventures including leaping overboard to escape capture by the Dutch, he reached Satsuma disguised as a Japanese merchant returning from the Philippines sixteen years after his departure from Japan. For almost nine years, Kibe escaped detection, ministering in secret to the Catholic faithful. (Elison, 1973, 197)

If Christian ministry was difficult for a Japanese, it was immeasurably more difficult for a European whose appearance and imperfect language ability made deception all but impossible. Nonetheless, the Dominican Pedro Vazquez succeeded in bluffing his way into Nagasaki prison disguised as a Japanese official and hearing his coreligionists' confessions at the time of the 'Great Martyrdom' of August 1622. Equally, the Franciscan Diego de San Francisco travelled the length of Japan disguised as a *Samurai*, an astounding piece of audacity. (Boxer, 1951, 358)

Charlevoix, writing more than a century after Adams' death, echoed Morejón's observations on Adams:

> Ce Pilote disservit d'une manière cruelle les Espagnols, et tous les Chrétiens. (Charlevoix, 1754, iv, 292)

In 1605, Adams declined an offer from a Jesuit, possibly João Rodrigues Tçuzzi, of a safe conduct from Nagasaki for himself and the other *Liefde* survivors. Adams and the Jesuit engaged in an impromptu theological exchange and Adams, who the Jesuits described as an 'obstinate heretic', cited scripture to justify his case; there are suggestions that the Jesuits at one time entertained hopes of converting Adams to Catholicism, probably as a means of neutralising his influence, such as it was, with Tokugawa Ieyasu. (Laures, 1954, 149-150)

Adams rejected the offer on the grounds that Tokugawa Ieyasu had forbidden the *Liefde*'s crew to leave Japan and he probably doubted the value of such a safe-conduct. (Cooper, 1974, 206)

Adams would almost certainly have been executed had he fallen into either Spanish or Portuguese hands; no amount of recanting would have saved such a well-known and cordially detested heretic. In 1620, the E.I.C. dispatched Richard Frobisher, a ship's carpenter, to Hirado. Accompanied by his wife and their two young sons, as well as by their maidservant, a young girl called Judith, Frobisher never reached Japan. Instead, the ship on which they were travelling was wrecked on the Chinese coast. Frobisher paid a Chinese captain to convey them to Patani but their ship was intercepted by a Portuguese vessel, the captain of which evidently believed it to be a pirate ship lying in wait for Portuguese shipping, as it passed Macau.

Writing in September 1621 to Sir Thomas Smythe and the East India Company, Richard Cocks' account is clear in some respects; according to Cocks, those on the bark in which Frobisher travelled after the *Unicorn* was wrecked on the Chinese coast 'went to Amacon of their own accord'. Frobisher and his family, Cocks added, were 'sent from thence for Malacca & soe for Goa, to make use of him to build shiping.' Cocks was reliant on Chinese sources, the Hirado Chinese 'saw them arive & what else past.' (Farrington, 1991, 854)

The maid, Judith, was prevailed upon to convert to Catholicism and remain in Macau. The Frobishers were taken in two barks to Malacca, where Frobisher is believed to have been executed. In 1625, his widow was sent to the E.IC. outpost in Bantam in exchange for two Portuguese women in British hands. She said later that her two sons had died in Malacca, though some chroniclers suspect she abandoned them there. Judith, received into the Catholic Church as Julia, married a Macanese and moved with her husband to Malacca. Here Peter Mundy the English traveller and chronicler met them, observing '. . .an Englishwoman married to a Portugall Mestizo of some quality, are well to live, and have beetweene them one pretty boy.' (Coates, 1978, 50-2)

The ninety Dutch prisoners of war taken by the Manila Spaniards at Playa Honda in 1609 were executed as pirates and apostates. Even those whom Andrés de la Cámara, a Jesuit born in Ghent who spoke Dutch perfectly, converted to Catholicism were executed. Whether these converts, who included three factors, two senior pilots and two surgeons, converted from conviction or in the hope of escaping execution is unknown. It is puzzling that the Spaniards disdained to spare the lives of such useful converts. Had they been permitted to live, they would have added to the skills of one of the world's most cosmopolitan cities. Andrea Caro, writing to a friend in Rome in 1611, described the populace of Manila as

> '. . .Chinese without number, Japanese, East Indians, people of Malacca and Java, a great many Portuguese, French, Dutch, Flemings,

> immigrants from Italian, Greek and Sicilian cities; all these in addition to natives of various tongues, tribes and islands and the Spaniards both men and women. . ..'

Adams' well-founded fears for his safety at either Macau or Manila make it highly unlikely that he ventured to the latter city as an emissary of Tokugawa Ieyasu, as some writers have claimed. Adams was known to, and detested by Jesuits and the mendicant orders. His known antagonism towards the Catholic missionaries was reciprocated heartily.

The early seventeenth century was no less bigoted in religious matters than the preceding century had been. Protestant travellers who found themselves in Iberian hands might well come to a sad end, like the unfortunate carpenter Frobisher. With better luck, they might be freed, or permitted to slip away, as was Ralph Fitch after the intervention of Jan Huyghen van Lischoten and some others, such as the Dominican Thomas Stevens, during Fitch's imprisonment in Goa.

As Newberry, Fitch's companion, recorded of this incident and the providential outcome, '. . . had it not pleased God to put it into the minds of the archbishop and two Padres of Jesuits of S. Paul's Colledge to stand our friends, we might have rotted in prison.' (Yule and Burnell, 1986, 651)

Ralph Fitch, John Newberry and their companions had been arrested by the Portuguese at Ormuz, at the mouth of the Persian Gulf, and taken to Goa as suspected spies. One of the Englishmen who interceded on their behalf, Thomas Stevens, had been acquainted with Richard Hakluyt the chronicler at Oxford, an altogether remarkable coincidence. Newberry died while attempting to return overland to Europe. Fitch travelled in Asia for some years before returning to England in 1591 and subsequently having some of his writings included in the second edition of Hakluyt's *Principall Navigations* in 1599.

Less sympathy and charity might be displayed towards permanent residents. Xavier, shocked at the prevalent laxity of Goa, had recommended that the Inquisition be established speedily there. It was founded there in 1560, eight years after his death. Even before this, heresy did not go unpunished. In 1543, a 'New Christian' convert from Judaism to Catholicism, was strangled after confessing that he had relapsed.

When national and commercial rivalries were added to

unyielding religious conviction, the combination was powerful indeed. Interestingly, none of the Hirado Britons or their Dutch rivals expressed personal bigotry towards their Iberian commercial agents, for example. Both the Dutch and the British were accustomed to dealing with Catholics on a daily basis.

Religious disputes between foreigners in Tokugawa Japan were not without the occasional moment of comic relief. One such moment concerned Adams, a friar called Juan de Madrid and Melchior van Sandvoort.

Precisely what persuaded Fray Juan de Madrid that he could perform miracles will probably remain forever unknown. Having convinced himself that he could, however, he attempted to clinch a theological dispute between himself, on the one hand, and Adams and some of the *Liefde* survivors on the other by offering to perform a miracle to demonstrate the superiority of Roman Catholicism to heresy and schism. His hearers, imagining that he jested, scoffed at his claims that he could bring the sun down from the sky or cause a neighbouring hill to move, saying that the first would burn all of them and the second would adversely affect the local landowners. Juan de Madrid thereupon proposed to demonstrate the power of the One True Faith by walking upon the sea. He insisted upon doing this and was saved from drowning by the purely temporal intercession of Melchior van Sandvoort, who put off from shore in a boat and rescued him. (Boxer, 1951, 236-7)

Unabashed by his failure, the friar told all who would listen that he had every right to expect God would enable him to demonstrate the power of faith because he possessed more faith than the proverbial grain of mustard seed, according to Bishop Cerqueira.

According to Diego Carvalho, Fray Juan de Madrid was subsequently a familiar figure at Malacca and Macau, where he was known as *O Milagreiro*, the miracle-monger. That some friars could, and did, behave with a singular lack of discretion is beyond question. Fray Jerónimo de Jesús, for example, proclaimed in 1598 that he and his brethren were determined to stay in Japan in spite of 'Pope, King, prelate or governor' if need be. (Boxer, 1951, 171)

Cocks' account of the Uraga incident in his letter to Sir

Thomas Wilson in London, written in December 1614, has the deceptive immediacy of an eye-witness account although it was nothing of the sort. Bishop Luís de Cerqueira's letter of November 20 1604 to the Archbishop of Goa mentions it, as does a letter written by Fray Juan Pobre in 1605. Evidently the friar attempted to walk on water in 1604 or earlier. (Boxer, 1951, 481).

> Since I doe not well remember whether I advized yow in my former letter (because I had now tyme to take the coppie of it) of a frire that wold neds work miracles in these partes to the entent to convert on Mr W'm Adames, an Englishman, w'th certen other Duchmen (w'ch were & most of them yet are) in these partes, I say this frire promised to worke miracles to convert them to be Roman Catholicks, askinge them yf they pleased to have hym to remove a greate tree over the water from the top of one mountaine to another, or else yf they wold have hym to walke on the water as St Peter did. In fine Mr Adames tould hym he did not beleeve he could doe either the one or the other. Not that he stood in dowbt but that the power of God was abell to doe them & greater matters too, but that he fermly beleeved that all miracles ceased longe since & that those of late tyme were but fictions and nothinge to be respected. Yet this frire wold needs trie mastries and walke upon the water, and to that entent published it about the towe of Oringou, soe that thousandes of people came to behould and see the event. Soe the frire beinge well provided of a greate peece of wood made in forme of a crose, w'ch wrought from above his gerdell to his feete, a booy suffitient to have kept up any resonable swymer above the water, as this man was well knowne to be. And yet, for all his cuninge and holynesse, he had byn drowned had not a Duchman called Melchar van Sanfort gon after hym w'th a boate and saved hym, to the utter scandall of all papists and other Christians remeanyng amongst these pagonse, w'ch make a May game of it. And one the morrow after Mr Adames went to vizet this fryre to see what he wold say, and fownd hym sicke in his bed, much discomendinge Mr Adames for his unbeleefe. For (said he) had yow but beleeved that I could have donne it, I had assuredly accomplished it. But, said Mr Adames, I tould yow before that I did not beleeve yow could doe it, and now I have better occation to be of the same opineon still. Soe this frire got hym packinge out of this cuntrey for very shame and, as it is said, went to the Manillias, where the bushop of that place put hym into prison for his rash attempt. Yet others to this day canot forget soe notable a miraclemonger, & c. (Farrington, 1991, 264)

In view of the *Bakufu*'s proclaimed and demonstrated aversion to Christianity in whatever guise, it is surprising that the Hirado factory should have been so bold as to have an Anglo-Japanese child christened. Cocks recorded:

> 'Mr Henry Smith, purcer of the *Royal James*, had a child by a Japon woamon, and was christened this day per Mr Arthur Hatch, prechar, per the name of Henry; Mr Joseph Cockram and Mr Wm Eaton, godfathers, and Maria, Mr Sayers woaman, godmother'. (Thompson, 1883, II, 174)

It is perhaps curious that the Anglican clergyman should have baptised a child without first marrying the parents, a convenient combination of sacraments frequently employed in Elizabethan and Jacobean England.

Evidently the Hirado Britons assumed that Anglicanism was of no account to the *Bakufu*; nonetheless, it was fortunate that this incident, which took place several years after the 1614 decree, did not come to the notice of the Nagasaki authorities.

Although it is unlikely Adams was sent to Manila as Ieyasu's emissary, as has been claimed, he was sent as Tokugawa Ieyasu's emissary to the Spanish friars, Franciscans, at Uraga. As Cocks recorded:

> 'He, the Emperour, sent Capt Adames to Edo to the padres to know wherefore the are com in to his dominions, he having formerly banished all of their coate out of his dominions'. (Thompson, 1883, II, 81; Sadler, 1984, 263)

The episode in which Ieyasu sent Adams as emissary to the Franciscans from Mexico is indicative of the trust Ieyasu had in him. A letter written by Wickham to Cocks in October 1615 stated;

> 'The Emp'. . .hath sent Capt' Adames before to Urungava to negotiat with the 3 friers w'ch are come embasadors from Nueva Espana & are not like to have theyre dispatch untill he heare againe from Capt' Adames concerninge both theyre present & theyre busines; neyther may these prestes be suffered to come into Edoe, much lesse to appeare at the cort'.

The three Franciscans had been sent by Philip III of Spain. When Don Rodrigo Vivero y Velasco sailed for Mexico in 1610 on the second ship Adams built for Ieyasu, later named the *Santa*

Buenaventura, he carried a letter and presents from Ieyasu to the Spanish sovereign. Don Rodrigo de Vivero y Velasco, formerly the interim governor of the Philippines, was a passenger aboard a ship sailing from Manila to Acapulco, the *San Francisco*. After this ship was wrecked on the Kanto coast in July 1609, Don Rodrigo was treated kindly while in Japan and wrote admiringly about the country and its people. The Japanese seamen who accompanied Don Rodrigo to Mexico aboard the second ship Adams built were subsequently returned to Japan aboard a vessel commanded by Sebastián Vizcaíno. Vizcaíno had been in charge of two expeditions to survey the California coast before leaving Mexico in an ambassadorial role in 1611. His expedition of 1611-1612 gained Ieyasu's permission to survey the eastern coasts and harbours of Japan so that outward bound galleons sailing between the Philippines and Mexico might use Japanese anchorages in safety, equipped with charts and *roteiros*, if need arose. Vizcaíno's mission was not an outstanding diplomatic success; he insisted on observing Spanish, rather than Japanese, etiquette and threatened to return to Mexico forthwith unless he got his own way. His arrogant bearing during his audience with Hidetada, and on other occasions, caused deep resentment. When obliged to purchase another ship in which to return to Mexico he received little sympathy from the Japanese authorities and had to sell his shirts and mattresses to raise the money. He finally left Japan in October 1613 and was back in Mexico by January the following year.

His embassy to Japan is often confused with Nuño Soutomaier's Portuguese legation, which reached Japan in July 1611, a month after Vizcaíno's audience at Edo. (Cooper, 1965; 126, 412; Farrington, 1991, 74). Soutomaier was sent to Japan by the Macau senate to negotiate the restoration of Macanese trade with Japan following the *Madre de Deus* disaster. The envoy, who reached Kagoshima in July 1611, brought presents for Ieyasu and various influential officials and travelled from Miyako to Suruga with his escort mounted on forty-eight horses provided by Itakura Katsushige, the governor of the capital. Soutomaier was cordially received by Ieyasu at Suruga on August 22 and it was agreed that the *Madre de Deus* affair should be conveniently forgotten and that trade should be resumed once more. Soutomaier then visited Hidetada at Edo and Hideyori in his

Osaka citadel before embarking at Nagasaki and returning to Macau. Dom Nuño Soutomaior arrived at Satsuma uncertain of what welcome awaited him at Nagasaki. Ieyasu, by now disillusioned about the ability of the Spaniards or Dutch to replace the Macau ship, ordered that he be welcomed. Honda, known to Cocks as 'Codsquin Dono', proved affable and procured a *shuinjo* authorising trade as in the past. It is interesting to note that Honda's text commenced 'An ambassador has come from Goa to request. . .' Goa was still perceived, even at this late date, as being of more significance than Macau. (Boxer, 1951, 283). The following year Soutomaier was followed by another ambassador, Horatio Nerete, who arrived at Nagasaki aboard the heavily laden *São Felipe e Santiago* on August 17 1612, reopening trade once more. Despite the temporary debacle caused by the destruction of the *Madre de Deus*, Macau's trade with Japan continued to exist for another generation.

In June 1613, Philip III sent the three Franciscans with a letter of thanks for Don Rodrigo's reception and due acknowledgement, together with return presents. The three arrived late in 1615, and indication of how long such exchanges not infrequently took. In the drastically changed climate following Sebastián Vizcaíno's mission, Ieyasu refused to received them and Hidetada rejected their presents. The trio, sorrowful at the abject failure of their mission through no fault of their own, left Japan in September 1616, reaching Acapulco in February 1617. (Farrington, 1991, 319-320).

Ralph Coppendale, writing to the E.I.C. factors at Pattani in December 1615, wrote of the trio's efforts:

> 'Certaine Jesuites came out of Nova Espania in embassage unto the Emperor w'th a letter and a present from the King of Spaine, w'ch after a moneth or 6 weekes' attendance the Emperor rec'd, but none of the embassadors admitted to his p'sence. All the answer to theire embassage was to gett them foorth of his cuntry w'th speede, upon paine of his displeasure'. (Farrington, 1991, 343)

Coppendale mistook the religious order involved but his version of the story is otherwise substantially correct.

The three friars from Acapulco arrived in Japan aboard the vessel which had taken Sebastian Vizcaíno and Date Masamune's embassy to New Spain. Not merely was their arrival in Japan a deliberate violation of Ieyasu's edict but they apparently angered the *Bakufu* by stridently condemning the edict and condemning the destruction of Osaka castle.

Adams was hastily summoned by Ieyasu to act, in the Japanese manner, as an intermediary with the unwelcome guests. So brusque was Ieyasu's demand that Richard Cocks imagined Adams had invented the excuse because his two-year contract of employment with the Hirado factory was due to expire shortly and that a visit to Ieyasu at Suruga might well lead to Ieyasu forbidding him to leave the country, thus preventing him sailing to Siam on the E.I.C.'s business and thus, in turn, the more able to speedily resume his own business endeavours. (Massarella, 1990, 169).

The friars evidently found Adams' employment as an intermediary distasteful in the extreme; they blamed Adams for sabotaging their mission by spreading lies and misleading propaganda about Spanish ambitions in Asia. An interesting aspect of the mission was that the ship on which the friars travelled brought English cloth, which Cocks complained was sold at low rates. This cloth would have been obtained through normal commercial channels in Europe, taken by ship to Vera Cruz, by mule to Acapulco *via* Mexico City and thence by ship to Japan. A trade route as long as this would normally have been justified only by cargoes of very high value, such as those aboard the Manila galleons of the seventeenth and eighteenth centuries, which proved to be prey as desirable as the Macau *naó* had been. Captain George Anson's capture of the 1743 Manila galleon, its crew and a cargo worth £400,000 is indicative of the value of the Manila – Acapulco route.

Adams' wife was a Christian, hence the names of the couple's children, Joseph and Susanna. On at least one occasion, this led to complications; it was suspected that Adams' wife was harbouring missionaries at a time when such activity merited the death penalty. Due and discreet warning was conveyed to her. (Thompson, 1883, I, XXV). Adams must have been apprehensive, if no more, to learn that his wife was suspected of harbouring missionaries and their Japanese adherents, a suspicion which could have resulted in catastrophe for the entire family. That Adams had played an active part in encouraging the suspicions of the Japanese authorities concerning the Jesuit, and other, missionaries would have made little difference had the charges against Oyuki been pressed and proven to be true.

The suspicion that Adams' wife was harbouring priests appears to have arisen in September 1616. It seems likely, however, that these men were not priests but Spanish merchants; Oyuki apparently informed Cocks that some Spaniards were staying at Hemi. In the atmosphere of the time it seems probable that the *Bakufu* espionage apparatus assumed that *all* Iberians were priests in disguise, a reasonable assumption considering that missionaries could, and did, travel throughout the country in a variety of guises. (Rogers, 1956, 93).

Morejón, writing for a Catholic readership, most of whom felt a greater or lesser degree of loyalty towards the King of Spain and Portugal, related the salient parts of the episode concerning the *San Felipe*, and repeated the Jesuit claim that Francisco de Olandía had spoken rashly; '. . . the foolish wordes of a certaine Pilot. . .' (Morejón, 1969,54).

Having said that the hostility of the Buddhist clergy, the greed of Hideyoshi and the specific antagonism of the 'Englishmen and Hollanders, who in the time of this *Xogun* do not onely traffique but also some of them reside and dwel within Iapone' were responsible for the persecution of the missionaries and their converts, Morejón summed up the enemies of the faith as a whole but, both Spaniard and Jesuit as he was, loyally forbore to write a word concerning the antagonism between Jesuits and Friars, or between Portuguese and Spaniards.

Morejón continued the passage quoted above by referring to the European heretics' influence:

> 'This suspition was confirmed in them, yea and much increased by certeine *Englishmen*, and *Hollanders*, who in the time of this *Xogun* do not onely traffique but also some of them reside and dwel within *Iapone*: for they partly through the hate they have and beare to religious men and Catholickes, and partly for feare least the Spaniardes should be a meanes to hinder their traffique thither, have made many malicious and most vile reportes, even the very worst they could imagine or invent, both of the one and other. As for example that the religious men are dangerous persons, both wicked and rebellious: that they do not preach Christs true Religion, but onely their owne fancies & imaginations, and that for that cause they have beene ofttimes banished by Christian

princes in *Europe* out of their kingdomes and dominions; that the Spaniardes have no other end nor intention in coming thither, but onely to bereave them of their kingdom and goverment, alledging to that purpose, and as it were in proofe thereof many particuler examples to make some shew of truth'. (Morejón, 1969, 54–5)

Neither the Dutch nor the English would have needed to invent much material; the entire sanguinary history of Hispanic America was sufficient proof that Spain, for all its supposed decadence, was a first-rate military and naval power.

In retrospect, it is quite probable that the Jesuits greatly overestimated Adams' influence with the Tokugawa *shogunate*, as Massarella has claimed. (Massarella, 1990, 163). Certainly, Adams was inclined to overstate his own influence at times, such as when he claimed to have obtained peerless and unprecedented privileges for the V.O.C. factory.

In 1612 Adams was reported to have told a Spaniard from the Philippines that 'Your Honour will see that within three years there will not be a single padre in Japan', but whether he was claiming that this was likely to come about as a result of his influence remains questionable.

Valentim Carvalho recorded Adams' words to the Spanish envoy thus:

'No anno de 1612 disse o dito Adami a Domingos Francisco que foi por embaixador de Manila a corte de Daifu estas palauras Vossa Meçe verá que daqui a tres annos não ha de auer Padre nenhũ em Japão e Domingos Francisco o contou a Horatio Nerete que de Macao foi tambem por embaixador a Daifu sobre negocios daquella cidade e do comercio'. (Boxer, 1988, 83)

Adams, writing to Augustine Spalding at Bantam in January 1613, had this to say of his influence:

'The Hollandes be now settled and I hav got them that privilledg as the Spaynard and Portingalles could never geett in this 50 or 60 yeers in Jappan & c'. (Farrington, 1991, 77)

By the second decade of the seventeenth century the Tokugawa needed no persuasion to implement an anti-Christian policy of their own. While Hideyoshi's edict of 1587 commanding the expulsion of the missionaries had not been put into effect in any meaningful way, it was evident to all that times were becoming steadily harder for Christians in Japan. The presence of small numbers of Franciscans, Dominicans and Augustinians, both augmenting and complicating the labours of the Jesuits, did not make matters easier, as the events of 1586-7 demonstrated.

The Tokugawa required little prompting to consider Christianity subversive, nor were they unaware of the vague, unstated Spanish threat, even if such a threat was ludicrously hollow. It is significant, perhaps, that, around the time of the 1614 edict expelling missionaries a scandal had occurred involving Okamoto Daihachi, a Christian employed as one of Honda Masazumi's secretaries. This man was found to have forged documents which would have enlarged the domain of the Christian *daimyo* Arima Harunobu at the expense of his neighbours, the Matsuura, in whose domain both the E.I.C. and V.O.C. factories were established. Okamoto, being a Christian, declined to commit *seppuku* and was burnt at the stake instead. Many Christians regarded him as a martyr, much to Tokugawa fury. The fall of Osaka castle to the Tokugawa forces in 1615 yielded tangible proof, in the form of banners and other insignia, that many of the armed adherents of the Toyotomi had been ardent Christians. When destroying the armed opposition of Toyotomi Hideyori's adherents during the Osaka campaigns of 1614 and 1615, the Tokugawa witnessed the ranks of their enemies swelled by Christian *ronin* with 'so many crosses, Jesus and *Santiagos* on the flags, tents and other martial insignia which the Japanese use in their encampments that this must needs have made Ieyasu sick to his stomach' as the Jesuit João Rodrigues Girão recorded in Nagasaki in March 1616. (Elison, 1973,3).

Adams' letter to Sir Thomas Smyth, written early in 1617, says:

> 'Now the Emperor, heering of thees Jessuits and friers being in the castell w'th his ennemies & still from tyme to tyme against him, coumandeth all Romish Christian men to dep't out of his countri, thear churches pulled dooun & burned'. (Farrington, 1991, 569-70)

Long before the Tokugawa persecutions assumed the proportions that Jesuit, and other Catholic, chroniclers were to record in such detail, however, Adams was demonstrably lacking in the kind of influence the Jesuits claimed he possessed. In 1611 he had warned Honda Masazumi that the Spanish proposal to chart and sound Japanese ports was merely a preparation for armed invasion rather than peaceful trade. The Spanish were permitted to survey the harbours, the Tokugawa evidently declining to accept Adams' advice.

The British of the E.I.C. and the Dutch of the V.O.C. did what they could to sow mistrust of Iberian designs, such as they were. Despite this, many of the Hirado factors, of both nationalities, had Catholic servants, consorts and employees.

Ironically, the various measures taken against the Iberian missionaries and their adherents hurt the E.I.C. factory at Hirado immediately. Missionaries ignored Ieyasu's expulsion edict and disguised themselves as Iberian traders domiciled in Nagasaki. As a consequence even the Dutch and the British were obliged to confine their mercantile endeavours to Hirado and Nagasaki. Adams wrote to Specx in October 1616:

> 'All this trouble is arising from the Portuguese priests, as the emperor does not suffer foreigners to trade in the upper country for fear of the people being made Christians. All our trouble is wholly to be imputed to the Papists'. (Boxer, 1951, 328)

Cocks, writing in September 1617, observed:

> 'Capt Adames retorned from the Court with answer from the councell that the Emperour would geve our Englishe nation no larger previleges then other strangers have, only to sell our merchandiz at Firando and Langasaque. The reason he doth it is that his owne merchants of Japon shall have the profit of seling within land before strangers, as also that, under culler of buying and seling, noe pristes may lurk up and downe his cuntrey to alter religion as heretofore they have done'. (Thompson, 1883, I, 312-3)

Having done what they could to sow distrust of the Catholic missionaries, Cocks and the other Hirado Britons did not find the day-to-day reality of the growing religious intolerance and suspicion on the part of the *Bakufu* agreeable. There were, for example, suspicions of the Britons, too.

Cocks, referring to conversations with Doi Oi-no-suke Toshikatsu (*Oyendono*) and Honda Kozuke-no-suke Masazumi (*Codsquin Dono*) noted that

> '. . . all Jesuits and fryres were banished out of England before I was

> borne, the English nation not houlding with the Pope nor his doctryne, whose followers these padres (as they cald them) weare. It is strange to see how often they sent to me about this matter, and in the end gave us wayning that we did not comunecate, confesse, nor baptiz with them, for then they should hold us to be all of one sect. Unto which I replied that their Honours needed not to stand in doubt of any such matter, for that was not the custom of our nation'.

This exchange, in 1616, recalls Ieyasu's statement concerning the missionaries:

> 'If the Kings and Princes of Europe do banish the Fathers out of their countries, I shall do them no injury to send them out of mine'.

Uttered in 1613, three years after João Rodrigues had been obliged to leave Japan, this indication of what Ieyasu was thinking accurately foretold the future.

Catholic priests had not merely been expelled from England. As both Cocks and Adams were well aware, the death penalty, usually preceded by torture on the rack, was the penalty awaiting any Catholic priest apprehended in England since an Act of Parliament was enacted during the reign of Elizabeth, in 1585. Pope Pius V, a Dominican, had excommunicated Elizabeth in 1570. Significantly, this was the year following the rebellion of the Northern Earls, an ill-fated movement both feudal and religious in character. Every place occupied by the rebels saw the mass restored; in the popular mind the link between Catholicism and treason was a strong one. From 1580 onwards a tax of £240 was levied annually on each adult who refused to attend Anglican services in England; none but the very wealthiest had any choice between destitution and submission. By the time of the Gunpowder Plot of 1605, almost every Englishman of Cocks' generation saw Catholicism as a subversive, alien element in English public life.

The expulsion of João Rodrigues Tçuzzi was a serious blow to the Portuguese, and to all the Iberians. The Iberians now were obliged to rely upon Adams as their court interpreter and negotiator, on some occasions at least. Adams claimed that he recompensed evil with good, requesting and obtaining favours from Ieyasu for both Spaniards and Portuguese. During this period Adams' standing with Ieyasu was at its height; in October 1611 he wrote:

> 'I pleased him so, that what I said he would not contrarie. At which my former ennemies did wonder; and at this time must intreat me to do them a frienship, which to both Spaniards and Portingals have I doen; recompencing them good for evill. . .'

Three months later he enlarged upon this remarkable turn of events:

> 'This yeere 1612 the Spaynnards and Portingalles hav ussed me as an instrument to gett there liberty in the manner of the Hollanders, but uppon consideration of farther inconvenience I have not sought it for them. It hath pleased God to bring things to pass, so as in ye eyes of ye world (*must seem*) strange; for the Spaynnard and Portingall hath bin my bitter ennemis, to death; and now they must seek to me an unworth wretch; so the Spaynard as well as the Portingall must hav all their negosshes go through my hand. God hav ye prayse for it. . .'

It is possible that Adams was exaggerating but, if so, not by much. The period during which Adams was Ieyasu's foremost unofficial advisor as well as his shipbuilder must have been the apogee of his influence. (Boxer, 1951; 290, 488).

While Adams displayed friendship towards various Iberians, usually traders and sailors but occasionally *réligieux*, his efforts on their behalf were probably confined to minor matters. However, Adams did act as commercial agent for some Spaniards, at least, at Uraga, close to his 'lordship' at Hemi. It was here that he wished the E.I.C. to settle their factory and it was here, too, that he attempted to interest John Saris, the commander of the *Clove*, in a ship the Spanish had for sale. His general attitude was strongly anti-Catholic right up to his death. His wife Oyuki was a Christian, possibly a convert rather than a daughter of Catholics since her father, Magome Kageyu, is not known to have had a Christian baptismal name, as was common in Japan at that period. It can be assumed that both of the children born to William and Oyuki Adams were baptised, hence their names, Joseph and Susanna. Oyuki evidently chose not to use her baptismal name, which remains unknown.

To what extent, if any, William Adams had influenced Ieyasu's views remains unknown. Pedro Morejón assumed Adams possessed immense influence with Ieyasu but this was not invariably true. (Boxer, 1951, 310-311).

In the course of his conversation with Doi and Honda,

Richard Cocks did what he could to encourage suspicions of Spanish designs. Referring to two Spanish ships which had arrived at Satsuma not long before, Cocks told his hearers that he believed them to be 'full of men and treasure', having been

> 'sent of purpose by the King of Spaine haveing knowledge of the death of the ould Emperor (*Ieyasu*), thinking som papisticall *tono* might rise and rebell and so draw all the papistes to flock to them and take part, by which means they might on a sudden seaz som strong place and keep it till more succors came, they not wanting money nor men for thackomplishing such a strattagim'. (Boxer, 1951, 311)

Cocks evidently believed this to be not merely plausible but the sober truth, it appears. Cocks was wrong but such ideas had been suggested from time to time. Invariably they were speedily quashed by less reckless people; Valignano was appalled by the proposal of the Jesuit Superior, Gaspar Coelho, that Nagasaki should be fortified and the Christian *daimyo* of Kyushu supplied with arms, ammunition and a stiffening of trained Iberian troops. One of the Franciscans crucified at Nagasaki in 1597, Martín de la Ascensión, had proposed to the governor of the Philippines in 1596 that Nagasaki should be seized for the Spanish crown. By the time Cocks was living in Japan, the Iberians in east Asia had neither the inclination nor the manpower for such undertakings. (Boxer, 1951, 473-4).

The intensifying persecution appalled even so staunch a Protestant as Richard Cocks on occasion. He witnessed the martyrdom of over fifty Japanese Christians at Miyako in October 1619, by which time Hidetada had proven beyond question that he was a far more bitter persecutor than his father had been. Cocks recorded,

> '. . . all which are found are put to death. I saw fifty five martyred at Miyako, at one time when I was there, because they wold not forsake their Christian Faith, & amongst them were little Children of five or sixe yeeres old burned in their mothers armes, Crying out, Jesus recive their soules. . . There is many more in Prison in divers other places, as also heere, which looke hourely when they shall die, for very few turne Pagans'. (Cooper, 1965; 388-396).

From having been virtual pariahs in Nagasaki at their arrival, Cocks and the other Hirado Britons found circumstances greatly altered by 1620, the year of Adams' death. Referring to Dom

Luís de Cerqueira, who had died in 1614 after 15 years at the head of the Catholic Church in Japan, Cocks wrote

> 'in the time of that bishopp heare were soe many priests and Jesuits with their partakers, that one could not passe the streetes without being by them called Lutranos and *herejos*, which now are very quiet and non of them dare open his mouth to spake such a word'. (Boxer, 1951, 306)

IX

SURVIVORS

Adams states unambiguously that there were eighteen survivors after the three ashore died. Wieder's text of 1925 records the eighteen as follows:

Jacob Jansz Quaeckernaeck, of Rotterdam, captain
William Adams, pilot
Melchior van Sandvoort
Jan Joosten van Lodensteyn
Jan Cousynsen
Gisbert de Coning, of Middelburg
Jan Abelszoon, of Oudewater
Jan Gerritsz Tol
Jan Jacobsz Roos
Pieter Jansz, shipwright/carpenter
Pieter Adriaensz Blanckart, of Delft
Michiel Physz, of Leeuwarden
Thomas Cornelisz, of Dunkirk
Jacob, surname unknown
Jan Cornelisz, also known as den Dunnen
Jacob Swager
Albartus, also known as Elbert Woutersen
Willem, surname unknown

According to a Japanese source, the *Liefde* was shipwrecked, or at least very severely damaged, on the voyage from Sakai – where Ieyasu viewed the ship – to Uraga. The surviving officers of the vessel were compensated to the extent of 50,000 reals but were, along with the crew, forbidden to leave Japan.

At some stage there was what amounted to a mutiny on the part of some of the survivors; Adams' version of this is as follows:

Comming to the land of *Quanto*, and neere to the citie *Eddo*, where

> the Emperour was: being arrived, I sought all meanes by supplications, to get our ship cleare, and to seeke our best meanes to come where the Hollanders had their trade: in which suit we spent much of the mony geven us. Also, in this time, three or foure of our men rebelled against the capten, and my selfe, and made a mutinie with the rest of our men, so that we had much trouble with them. For they would not abide noe longer in the ship, but every one would be a commander: and perforce would have every one part of the money that was geven by the Emperour. It would bee too long to wryte the particulars. In the end, the money was devided according to every man's place; but this was about two yeeres that we had been in *Iapon*; and when we had a deniall that we should not have our ship, but to abyde in *Iapon*. So that the part of every one being devided, every one tooke his way where he thought best. In the end, the Emperour gave every man, to live upon, two pounds of rice a day, daily, and yeerely so much as was worth eleven or twelve ducats a yeare, yearely: my selfe, the capten, and mariners all alike. (Rundall, 1850,27)

Concerning the events Adams describes as 'a mutinie', Jan Joosten van Lodensteyn may be presumed to have been a leading spirit among the mutineers. During John Saris' brief sojourn in Japan, he observed:

> 'This Yeozen, as I am credablye informed, is a basse fellowe and was one of the Factions in the Flemish shipp long since ruinated whearof Mr Addames was pilatt'. (Satow, 1900, 99)

The version in Purchas, as quoted by Satow, quotes Saris as writing, somewhat earlier in the text:

> '. . . William Adams, an English man, who passing with a Fleming through the South-sea, by mutiny and disorder of the Marriners he remained in that Countrey and was seised vpon by the Emperour about twelve yeares before'. (Satow, 1900, 80)

This version of events is at variance with the facts. Mutiny or not, Adams and his shipmates were detained in Japan at Ieyasu's command until he, Ieyasu, consented to let Sandvoort and Quaeckernaeck leave to find their fellow-countrymen, in the hope that this would lead to the commencement of direct trade between the Dutch and Japan.

The more accurate version, quoted by Satow, concerning the ship and its crew is:

> '. . . he (Adams) came pilatt of a Fleming into this Counterye, which shipp after was hear ruinated'. (Satow, 1900, 80)

It has been suggested that the guns of the *Liefde* were employed by the Tokugawa forces at the decisive battle of Sekigahara, fought in the October of the year in which the *Liefde* arrived in Japan, but this necessarily remains surmise. (Boxer, 1931, 73; Sansom, 1990, II, 403).

The attractions such a welcome addition to his arsenal offered Ieyasu have encouraged some historians to write as though the use of the *Liefde*'s guns at Sekigahara were an established fact. (Murdoch, 1949,400). However, had the guns been so used it is probable that one or more of the *Liefde*'s survivor would have been pressed into service; there is no record of such a thing having happened. It is more plausible to assume that the muskets or arquebuses and smaller deck-guns from the *Liefde* were used by the Tokugawa forces in 1600; despite their abiding interest in the subject, the Japanese were to remain remarkably ignorant about artillery for a long time. Paradoxically, there are several records that suggest the Japanese came very close to employing artillery well both on land and, more significantly, aboard ships both large and small. In September 1578 the Italian Jesuit Organtino Gnecchi-Soldi, writing from Usuki in Bungo, referred to seven gigantic ships which Oda Nobunaga had commanded to be built in Ise Province and which he was using to blockade the belligerent Monto monks in their stronghold of Osaka. Organtino went purposely there to see them and remarked that they carried heavy artillery and were comparable in size to Portuguese carracks, suggesting that they were vessels of perhaps 450 tons. By comparison, the great *Naó do Trado,* the Macau carrack, was not infrequently a vessel of 1,200 or 1,600 tons and were the largest ships then afloat. (Boxer, 1951, 121-2). Toyotomi Hideyoshi sought to employ Portuguese shipping in his invasion of Korea but the Portuguese, accepting Jesuit advice, contrived to avoid providing any. Had the Chinese even suspected that the invasion was being aided by the Portuguese the ever-precarious existence of Macau would have come to a sudden end.

The assurance recklessly given to Hideyoshi by Vice-Provincial Gaspar Coelho that two large Portuguese carracks, together with their captains and crews, would be provided for Hideyoshi's projected invasion of Korea and China has a minor, but significant, part in the story of Iberian-Japanese relations. Hideyoshi professed himself delighted with Coelho's cooperation; Alessandro Valignano dryly commented that Hideyoshi must have thought

> 'this father-provincial is very rich and influential. One day he will make war against me as did the abbot of the Ishiyama Hongwanji against Nobunaga'.

Whether Hideyoshi thought this or not, the ships were never provided. (Boxer, 1951, 141).

João Rodrigues, while at Nagoya in Hizen, a Kyushu port conveniently adjacent to Korea, saw the fleet Hideyoshi had prepared for the Korean campaign. He noted that the most recently-constructed were protected by iron plates from the water-line upwards, the decks and gangways also being plated so that no wood was visible. By contemporary measurements, these ships were about 114 feet from bow to stern. In spite of their formidable appearance, some broke up and sank; Rodrigues omitting to explain whether this happened in port or on the high seas. According to various Japanese sources, a ship covered with iron plates had been constructed in Japan as early as 1578.

The naval operations during Hideyoshi's Korean war were undistinguished. The Koreans overcame the Japanese in sea battles repeatedly. Japanese naval operations were directed by Kato Yoshiaki and Wakizaka Yasuharu, neither professional seamen. The Korean fleet was commanded by the brilliant naval tactician Yi Sun-sin. His turtle-ships were faster and more easily manoeuvrable than the sluggish Japanese transports, no matter how well-armoured these were. The only naval engagement the Japanese won was fought at a time Yi had been temporarily replaced by the inferior commander Won Ki-un. (Cooper, 1974, 103).

The poor showing of the Japanese navy and the consequent difficulty of maintaining the supply lines between Korea and Japan did more than anything else to destroy Hideyoshi's dream of successfully invading China.

The Chinese writer Mao Yuan in his *We Pei Chih*, (*On Preparations for War*), of 1600 or thereabouts, wrote:

> The Japanese ships are not at all the same as ours. They do not nail them but only lay strips of iron along the joints. They do not caulk these with hemp and *t'ung* oil, but prevent leaks with a grass called *tanbokuso*. This is very extravagent in labour and costly for materials so that only very wealthy people can afford to build them. And those who come to raid our country are most of them poor people from the islands and the report that the *Wa* country is preparing thousands of these ships is a mere boast. . . they are wretchedly small and if they meet our big ships they cannot do them any damage but are easily sunk. (Sadler, 1937, 182)

Mao Yuan was referring to the pirates of Kyushu, who had no intention of fighting it out with naval vessels, preferring to rob the Chinese coast as and where they could as opportunity presented itself, sometimes in alliance with Chinese, Korean and Portuguese freebooters, sometimes alone.

Cannon were used with some effect by the *daimyo* of Arima at the battle of Shimabara in 1584, probably swivel-guns mounted in the prows of small boats. Otomo of Bungo is said to have used ordnance in the struggle with Satsuma in 1578 but to no avail; his forces suffered a crushing defeat. (Boxer, 1931, 70-1).

At the battle of Nagashino in eastern Japan in 1575 about 3,000 men in Nobunaga's army had matchlocks and at Hideyoshi's siege of Kanki castle in 1582 the skilful use of cannon by the besiegers played an important part in securing victory. The Japanese fascination with firearms dated from the arrival of the first Portuguese mariners at Tanegashima in 1543; Japanese sources claim that within 12 months the local *daimyo* had caused 60 adequate copies to be produced locally. Later, Portuguese-trained Japanese cast cannon at Nagasaki, just as the Dutch and their local employees cast guns at Hirado at the time of Cocks' residence there. However, in both the sixteenth and seventeenth centuries the Japanese showed a marked preference for cannon cast in Europe rather than those made in Japan, just as they delighted in possessing smaller weapons and military *impedimenta* imported from Europe; in 1588 Dom Duarte de Menezes, the Viceroy at Goa, presented a pair of pistols to Toyotomi Hideyoshi. The Portuguese cuirass, or *Namban-do*, worn by Ieyasu at Sekigahara in 1600 is still to be seen in the museum attached to his shrine at Nikko. In 1615 Jacques Specx presented two iron sakers from the *Enchuijsen* to Ieyasu and

Hidetada. In the same year the Dutch at Hirado cast a metal gun of 600 pounds, destined to be presented to Honda Kosuke-no-suke, Ieyasu's chief minister, the man to whom Cocks referred in his writing as Codskin-dono. The English *Hoseander*, which arrived in 1615, brought 5 chests of guns to sell to the Japanese.

In early 1617 Richard Cocks wrote, in a letter to the East India Company,

> 'Codyskin Dono the secretary was very ernest w'th me to write into England for 5 or 6 bras falcons or falconets, and I tould hym he might have such cast heare. But he answered me he had rather have one that was cast in England then ten of those that were cast in Japon. Soe it may please yow to send som, for he is the greatest man in the Empere next to the Emperor'. (Farrington, 1991, 567)

Whether Honda Kozuke-no-suke Masazumi was correct in his assessment of the respective merits of European and Japanese firearms or not, the view expressed to Cocks was evidently a widespread one.

However, despite the tutelage of the Portuguese and the Dutch, the Japanese remained woefully ignorant of the systematic use of artillery. When the Shimabara Christian rebellion broke out in 1637 the *Bakufu* demanded the assistance of the Dutch in quelling it. Whether they felt shame at doing so or not, the Dutch were obliged to comply. Some small 5-pounders were landed from the Dutch ship *De Ryp*, supplemented later by some additional guns, including a 12-pounder, brought round from Hirado. (Boxer, 1931, 76).

It is interesting to note that both the Portuguese and the Dutch felt grave misgivings about teaching the Japanese much about artillery, just as there were misgivings about supplying them with European-style ships. The positions of both the Portuguese and the Dutch in East Asia would have proven extremely vulnerable to determined Japanese assault backed by seagoing artillery. The Spanish in the Philippines were justifiably apprehensive at any suggestion that the Japanese were considering building European-style shipping on any substantial scale. Tokugawa Ieyasu made indirect overtures to Manila through Jerónimo de Jesús, the Franciscan missionary, seeking master shipwrights and carpenters. The request caused alarm in Manila, the authorities there believing that

> 'the Islands' greatest security . . . has always been that the Japanese have no ships and are ignorant in matters of navigation'.

This was an inaccurate observation, Japanese mariners had been issued *shuinjo* to sail to Manila in Hideyoshi's time; Japanese pirates, like those who killed John Davis, were practical navigators as skilled as any. (Massarella, 1990, 79).

The survivors of the *Liefde* met with varying degrees of success in Japan. Three were successful, the others conspicuously less so. Their careers following the mutiny have been considered in some detail by such scholars as James Murdoch, F.C. Wieder, Iwao Seiichi, C.R. Boxer, Michael Cooper and, most recently and in great detail, Derek Massarella and Michael Farrington.

Inevitably, information relating to the humbler and less successful members of the *Liefde*'s crew is sparse. In 1614 one of the two Jacobs was acting as a haulier and superintendent of overland merchandise for the Dutch at Hirado and Señor Lorenzo, their agent at Edo. (Farrington, 1991, 150). In a letter written from Shizouka by Richard Wickham in October 1615, addressed to Richard Cocks, reference is made to 'Jacob the drunkard or caulker of Edoe' relating news concerning the imprisonment of the Spanish Franciscan Fray Diego de San Francisco, a remarkable figure who was subsequently to live, and preach, secretly in Japan for twenty years or so. (Farrington, 1991, 320). Jacob was still in Japan, but hardly prospering, in 1616:

> 'Jacob the Duch man, which came into Japon with Capt Adames, came to vizet me and offerd his servis to the English. He is a cawker, a pore fello. The Duch offerd hym 3l 10s. per month the last yeare; but he refuced it, and after would have taken it, but then they would not geve it. And I put hym ofe with fayre wordes, telling hym we wanted no people, but had more than our trade did afford. I gave his wife and his (*sic*) sister each of them a single pece of chint bramport.

As Richard Cocks recorded in his diary. (Thompson, 1883, I, 171)

A Fleming, Gisbert de Coning, was employed by the English factory later. De Coning, together with Jan Abelszoon van Oudewater, had been accused by Adams of attempting to betray the survivors of the *Liefde* to the Portuguese or the *daimyo* at Bungo, or both. Richard Wickham of the East India Company's factory understood that there was little love between William Adams and de Coning, recommending de Coning for employment because the Fleming's house at Uraga had recently been destroyed by fire and because he had a wife and children to support. The Dutch were said to dislike him, a point in his favour in English eyes, and he possessed valuable experience, having worked for Señor Lorenzo, the agent for the Dutch in Edo. Gisbert de Coning's salary was to be £20 annually. Richard Cocks justified the addition to the factory's personnel on the grounds that de Coning was fluent in Japanese and that he was thought to have influence with Tokugawa Ieyasu. (Massarella, 1990, 148). He is believed to have died in 1616.

In a letter of July 1614, Richard Wickham referred to Gisbert as

> 'a Fleming whome Capt' Adams knoweth, & of his compa(ny), betweene whom there is no great frendshipp. Neverthelesse he hath shewen himself redy to doe me any service here or elsewhere. He is of late growen very poore by reason his house at Urimgava (*Uraga*), with all that ever he had, was there consumed by fire. He is desirous to seeke his living in honest fashion for that he is maried here at Uringawa, where his wife and children remayne. Yf you shall have any occasion to make use of him you shall finde him very redy to doe any service. The Dutch hee have, I meane S'r Lorenço hath, used for the exc'a' of most of his monyes & for sale as a broker for some of his goodes, & I understand he dealeth honestly, & having fawnd no other by him I can write no lesse'. (Farrington, 1991, 192)

Richard Cocks overestimated Gisbert's influence in Japan in his letter of November 1614 to the East India Company. The belief that the factory's new employee had 'entrance to speake w'th the Emperour yf need soe require' was an absurd exaggeration; it was enought to say that he was 'suffitient to doe good busynes yf occation serve to employ hym & is willing & dilligent'. (Farrington, 1991, 227).

It can reasonably be supposed that a number of the *Liefde*'s survivors continued to live and work in Japan long after 1600. The captain, Jacob Jansz Quaeckernaeck, said that twelve of the crew remained in Japan in 1605. (Boxer, 1986, I, 26). The news that there were Dutch survivors in Japan, some of whom were engaged in building ships for the 'Emperor' reached Europe remarkably soon after the *Liefde*'s landfall; Oliver van Noort encountered a Manila-bound vessel off the coast of Borneo early in 1601. The pilot, a Portuguese named Emanuel Luís, who had formerly lived and worked in Malacca and Macao, was now working for the Japanese and piloting a Japanese-owned junk. He told van Noort that a Dutch ship of around 250 tons with fourteen survivors aboard had reached Japan. An extract of van Noort's account, mentioning the men in Japan, was published in September 1601. (Massarella, 1990, 81). The suggestion that Pieter Jansz van Rotterdam, the carpenter of the *Liefde*, was among those who assisted Adams in his shipbuilding endeavours at Ieyasu's behest is not improbable. (Rogers, 1956, 32). A European shipwright would have been a welcome member of the construction crew.

Jan Cousyns, or Cousynsen, was employed by the Dutch of the Vereenigde Oost Indische Compagnie as a book-keeper at a salary of *f.* 20 per month, approximately 21s. 4d. in English money.

Quaeckernaeck, whom Wieder describes as the only one of the survivors who wished to return to Holland, never lived to see his homeland. He left Japan in 1605 in the company of Melchior van Sandvoort, having received permission to depart as well as an offer of generous trading privileges for the Dutch of the V.O.C. from Togukawa Ieyasu. A junk owned by the *daimyo* of Hirado and possessing a *shuinjo*, or vermilion seal pass, conveyed them to Malaya, where they met the Dutch. Quaeckernaeck was unable to find a vessel bound for Europe because all the ships the Dutch possessed were engaged in a desperate struggle with the Portuguese for the possession of Malacca, the strategically-sited fortress city commanding the straits between peninsular Malaya and Sumatra. Quaekernaeck therefore joined his cousin, Cornelis Matelieff de Jonge, as chief navigator of a vessel named, by an improbable irony, the *Erasmus* – the ill-fated *Liefde*'s original name. He was killed in a naval engagement with the Portuguese at Cape Rachado, close to Malacca, in 1606.

Melchior van Sandvoort returned to Japan, where he lived and traded until 1639. Unlike William Adams and Jan Joosten Lodensteyn, van Sandvoort did not become a *hatamoto* or bannerman. He was never wealthy but his endeavours as a trader who had dealings with Spaniards, Portuguese, Dutch, English, Chinese and Japanese were evidently successful enough not to oblige him to enter permanently into service with either the Dutch of the V.O.C. or the English of the E.I.C. It is known that for a period at least he lived in Sakai, the port city to which the *Liefde* was taken in 1600. Letters written by the Dutch and, even more so, by the English, give the impression that he was a diligent trader who was respected by all until the advent of *Sakoku* led to his departure from Japan. Melchior van Sandvoort, referred to frequently in Cocks' diaries as Sandford, became involved in the then flourishing trade between Japan and South-East Asia. In February 1608 the V.O.C. factor at Patani, Victor Sprinckel, gave van Sandvoort a letter to Tokugawa Ieyasu explaining that the struggle with the Portuguese had prevented Dutch vessels reaching Japan. When, in July 1609, the two Dutch ships, the *Roode Leeuw met pijlen* and the *Griffoen,* arrived in Japan – having narrowly missing capturing the doomed *Madre de Deus* en route to Nagasaki – Melchior van Sandvoort accompanied Nicholas Puik (*or Puyck*) to Ieyasu's court at Sunpu or Suruga, present-day Shizuoka, as interpreter. It is interesting, in view of the later bitter hostility between the British and the Dutch in Japan, to note that John Saris, the commander of the first British ship to reach Japan, found van Sandvoort forthcoming and agreeable, ready to share his extensive knowledge of regional trade readily, even if van Sandvoort inadvertently erred in saying that Chinese silk was readily available at Patani and at Ayuthia in Siam.

During the final struggle between the Tokugawa clan and Toyotomi Hideyori and his mother, van Sandvoort and Jan Joosten took responsibility for the stock of the V.O.C. in Osaka, which was then, as now, a thriving urban centre. These were dramatic and lawless times, Sakai was burned to the ground and van Sandvoort wrote to Hirado expressing alarm at the number of freebooters who had taken advantage of the troubles to engage in looting. (Massarella, 1990, 166). That van Sandvoort was entrusted to convey letters from the E.I.C. factory at Hirado to the Britons resident at Ayuthia is a measure of the degree to which he was trusted by the British. Considering his knowledge and experience of local conditions, van Sandvoort was not generously requited by his countrymen when, in 1609, he was employed by the V.O.C. for two months at the rate of 50 guilders per month, equivalent to £48 per annum.

Melchior van Sandvoort was married to a Japanese Christian woman and was the father of two daughters, one of whom was named Isabella. One of his daughters is known to have married a Dutchman, Willem Verstegen. After the decree of June 1639, by which an increasingly xenophobic Tokugawa *shogunate* commanded all women who had been wives or consorts of Dutchmen or Englishmen to leave Japan (the wife and children of William Adams may have been exempted from this draconian measure, hence the tomb at Hemi associated with Adams), Melchior van Sandvoort left Japan, accompanied by his wife and children. Their marriage was solemnised, somewhat late in the day, by a protestant minister in Taiwan, where the Dutch had a foothold by this time.

Jan Joosten van Lodensteyn had an interesting career in Japan. His occupation aboard the *Liefde* is unrecorded, according to Wieder. His letters, the earliest extant being dated 1614, mention more important matters than do those of van Sandvoort. Like Adams, he was treated as an unofficial advisor by Tokugawa Ieyasu and was made a *hatamoto,* being granted a small estate at Nagasaki valued at 100 *koku* of rice, one *koku* being supposedly sufficient to provide one adult's rice ration for a year and equivalent to 4.96 bushels or 180 litres. (Boxer, 1988b, 342). Like Adams, he had a house in Edo, the neighbourhood commemorating him to this day as Yayoso-gashi (now Yaesu near Tokyo station).

The elevation of Jan Joosten and Adams to the rank of *hatamoto* was not unparalleled in the East. Europeans not infrequently found favour with local rulers who utilised their talents in various fields, such as diplomacy, gunnery, fortress construction and navigation. Sir Anthony Sherley's book, *Relation of Travels into Persia,* gives an account of how that remarkable traveller was made a *Mirza* by Shah Abbas. (Sherley, 1974, 72).

Joosten declined Puik's kindly offer of a free passage home. Like Adams and van Sandvoort, he was happier to remain in Japan rather than take his chances in Europe. He seems to have thrived in Japan even though his business ventures not infrequently ran into complications and acrimonious exchanges. (Massarella, 1990, 111). The Matsuura clan at Hirado warned the English not to have dealings with him. Four years earlier they had thwarted his attempt to accompany Puik to Suruga (Makino, 1983, 81). On the other hand, at least two influential Dutchmen in the East esteemed him highly. Jan Dircksz Lam, the admiral commanding the Dutch forces in the Pacific, wrote of Joosten:

> In Japan there is a man from Delft whose name is Jan Joosten. His uncle is one of the directors of a trading company in Delft. This man helped us greatly, and is treated well by the *Shogun* and his retainers and has close and friendly connections with them. He is also of great assistance in helping us with our clerical tasks. He has been in this country for many years and has a good knowledge of its customs. (Makino, 1983, 81)

Like Adams, Jan Joosten was granted the overseas trading licenses known as *shuinjo*, literally vermilion seal documents, which permitted the holder to trade overseas. *Shuinjo*, of which 356 were issued between 1604 and 1635, were prepared by Zen monks in Miyako, present-day Kyoto. (Massarella, 1990, 133). In 1618, for example, Joosten sold wax from Cambodia to the English at Hirado, conveyed thence in two Japanese junks he owned. In 1621 Jan Joosten bought, begged or borrowed the services of a number of E.I.C. sailors who had incurred debts with brothel-keepers in Hirado. Short of men and looking for cheap labour to supplement his Chinese crew on a voyage to Batavia in Java, Jan Joosten evidently hoped to employ these wastrels usefully. (Massarella, 1990, 289). The acrimony over this unsavoury incident – certainly not the only discreditable transaction of Joosten's career – led Cocks to describe Joosten as a *foule mouthed fellow* in his Diary.

Jan Joosten, who was married to a Japanese woman, died in a shipwreck in the Paracel Islands in the South China Sea, probably in 1623. Typically, Cocks erroneously assumed that he had been murdered. (Iwao, 1958, 10-11; 20-2). In justice to Joosten, it deserves to be said that he attracted the favourable notice of the formidable Jan Pietersz Coen, who advised him to invest in Chinese silk and silk fabrics if he intended to return to Holland and who offered him a passage to Europe. (Massarella, 1990, 418).

A map carried aboard the *Liefde* has survived to the present day, as has the stern-figure of Erasmus, the *Liefde* having been called the *Erasmus* prior to the Mahu and de Cordes voyage. For decades, if not centuries, it was to be seen in the Ryukoin Temple of the Sodo sect of Zen Buddhism, in Sano, Tochigi Prefecture. Known colloquially as *Azuki-togi-Baba* (the old woman rinsing red beans), it was regarded with some awe, being popularly supposed to represent a witch. It became a National Treasure in 1930 and an Important Cultural Property in 1950. It is usually to be seen in the Tokyo National Museum but it has travelled as far afield as Rotterdam and Rome since its 'rediscovery' in the 1920s, a remarkable tale which involved Murakami Naojiro, Nagayama Tokihide, the author of *Collection of historical materials connected with the Roman Catholic religion in Japan*, and the redoubtable J.B. Snellen, a Dutch diplomat. (Snellen, 1934, 1; Makino, 1983, 125-8).

X

THE COMING OF THE DUTCH

'When as yet you did not know about our country Captain Jacob Quackernaeck was driven starving on to your shores, and though the Portuguese said that the Dutch were robbers and pirates besides other evil things, you did not listen to them but assisted our men, and for that. . . we owe you a debt of gratitude'.
Maurice of Nassau to Minamoto Ieyasu Lord of Japan, 18 February 1610 (Sadler, 1984, 234-5)

It was not long after the survivors of the *Liefde*'s appalling voyage had been helped ashore by kindly hands at Oita that the Dutch learned that a sizeable handful, if no more, of their fellow-countrymen had survived to reach Japan. Oliver van Noord of Utrecht was at anchor in a harbour in Borneo in January 1601 when he learned from the Portuguese pilot of a Japanese junk that the *Liefde* had reached Japan and that some of her crew had survived.

> 'The fourth of Januarie they set saile, and espying a Junke of Japan, learned of them that they were bound for Manilla, and forced for succour to Borneo, had spent foure moneths waiting for their voyage. The Captaine was Emanuel Powis a Portugall, then dwelling at Languasacke in Japan, the Pilot a Chinese, the company Japanders. These told them of a great Holland Ship by tempests shaken, to have put in at Japan, the company by famine and sickenesse all but fourteene dead. They came first to Bongo in thirtie foure degrees, fortie minutes, and by the Kings direction remooved to Atonza, in 36 1/2. They road there in safe harbour, with foure anchors, and had freedome of their persons and trade, and to make a new Ship to goe whether they would. They conjectured hereby that it was Verhagens his Admirall Ship of two hundred and fiftie Tunnes: being as this Captaine told them well furnished with Ordnance, Ryalls of eight, and commodities. The Generall desired this Captaine at his returne, to remember his kindest greeting to his Countrey-men, and after other kindnesses departed,

> having given him a Passe at his request, in the name of Grave Maurice'. (Wild, 1938, 5)

This account has a number of factual shortcomings. Luíz was the pilot, not the captain, of the junk. The number of survivors is erroneously reported, as is the matter of Ieyasu's permission for the crew to leave Japan. Ieyasu was unwilling to permit the *Liefde*'s survivors to leave, believing that they might prove usual to him in various ways; it was not for some years that two members of the *Liefde*'s crew were permitted to leave Japan, from the port of Hirado.

For their part, the Dutch were less than wholly forthcoming about Holland's constitution; Holland was not a monarchy but a *de facto* republic, a fact which it was considered necessary to conceal from Asians.

The Portuguese pilot, Emanuel Luís, had previously lived and worked in the Portuguese possessions of Malacca and Macau. He told Olivier van Noord that fourteen survivors from a ship of 250 tons were alive and, it seemed, well in Japan; this innocent error concerning the *Liefde*'s tonnage led the Dutch to assume that it was the *Hoop* rather than the *Liefde* which had reached Japan. An extract of the written account of Olivier van Noord's voyage was published in September 1601, mentioning the presence of the Dutchmen in Japan. The publication of the full account of the voyage was published the following year in Rotterdam with subsequent editions in other languages. It is by no means improbable that Mary Adams would have heard of this. (Massarella, 1990, 82)

While the survivors of some of the *Liefde*'s crew clearly demonstrated that Dutch voyages to Japan were possible, this was of little consolation to the backers of the expedition of which the *Liefde* had been a part, now bankrupted by the total commercial failure of the venture. (Murdoch, 1949, 465)

The expedition of Oliver van Noort had sailed from the Straits of Magellan to the Philippines, having thrown its Spanish pilot overboard *en route*. Once in Philippine waters, the admiral plundered Asian shipping and fought a brief action against the Spanish before returning to Europe *via* Borneo, Java and the Cape of Good Hope, thus completing the first Dutch circumnavigation. Although successful, the expedition pales in comparison with that of Drake, who had sacked Valparaiso, seized a treasure ship *en route* to Panama, purchased cloves in Ternate, survived a grounding in the Celebes, visited Java and returned to a hero's welcome in Plymouth in 1580.

The Dutch knew a great deal about Japan, of course. Dirck Gerritz had been there and returned safely. More importantly, Japan was perceived, somewhat erroneously, as a source of great wealth; wealth monopolised by the Portuguese, now settled in Macao and trading immensely profitably with the port of Nagasaki. These rich cargoes were there for the taking, in Dutch eyes. The Portuguese, now unwillingly subject to the Spanish crown, were enemies to be robbed as and when opportunity offered.

All that was needed was to ambush the *Great Ship from Amacon*, as Richard Cocks called the great *naó,* as she sailed between Macao and Nagasaki. All that was needed, in short, was outstanding seamanship, impeccable timing, favourable weather and an ample portion of excellent luck, a combination all too rarely enjoyed.

The Dutch, arriving in Southeast Asia in 1596, drove the Portuguese from all but a handful of strongholds over the next three decades, sharply reducing the extent, and hence the profitability, of Portuguese trade in East Asia. The key fortress of Malacca was to fall in 1641, almost the whole of Ceylon in 1659 and all the forts of Malabar by 1663. Goa itself was blockaded by the Dutch in 1638-44 and again in 1656-63. The Persians, assisted by the British, took Ormuz, at the mouth of the Persian Gulf, in 1622.

The Dutch, more numerous as well as being better-financed and better-armed, were attempting to destroy a ramshackle and dispersed empire which could be attacked as and where the attackers chose. The remarkable fact is that so much remained in Portuguese hands, for the Portuguese seaborne empire was woefully undermanned and overextended. As a contemporary noted:

> 'From the Cape of Good Hope to Japan we were unwilling to leave anything outside our control. We were anxious to lay hands on everything in that huge stretch of over 5,000 leagues from Sofala to Japan'. (Pearson, 1987, 137)

The vulnerability of Iberian power was evident to the Dutch from the first. In early 1599 the first Dutch ships, under Warwijk and Van Heemskerk, arrived at Amboina in the Moluccas. Here they made a commercial treaty with the local ruler, nominally a vassal of Ternate. Heemskerk sailed to the Banda group of islands, establishing factories on Lontar and Neira, then sailed for Bantam. Warwijk sailed to Ternate and was joyfully received by the ruler, Saïd Berkat, who desired Dutch aid against Tidore and the Portuguese. Warwijk purchased a full cargo of spices and left a handful of Dutchmen under the command of a factor when he sailed away.

In 1600 Jacob van Neck visited Ternate. To Saïd's delight, he bombarded the Portuguese fort on Tidore.

The rich cargo brought home by Van Neck's ships definitely decided the merchants of Holland to wrest control of the spice trade from the Portuguese. The better to accomplish this objective, they consolidated the various joint-stock companies which had hitherto financed expeditions to the East in one United East India Company, the Vereeinigde Oostindische Compagnie or V.O.C. Within three years of its foundation in 1602, the V.O.C. sent a total of thirty-eight ships in powerful, heavily-armed fleets to overwhelm the Portuguese establishments in Southeast Asia. In 1603 they routed a Portuguese fleet off Johore, and in 1605 wiped out Furtado da Mendoça's limited successes of 1601 by seizing the Portuguese garrisons at Amboina and Tidore and establishing a protectorate over Ternate. But the Portuguese refused to acknowledge defeat; the Spaniards in the Philippines came to their aid; and, together, they put up a surprisingly vigorous resistance. In 1606 Acuña conquered Ternate and retook Tidore, while the Dutch attack on Malacca, the key to the Indies trade route, was beaten off. In 1607 the Dutch tried to recover Ternate; they failed. Leaving a garrison to guard a bridgehead on its eastern part, they retired to strengthen their positions at Amboina and Bantam while awaiting reinforcements from Holland. Such were the opening moves in the struggle for power in the Far East which would occupy the better part of the seventeenth century.

Portuguese power in the Indian Ocean, South China Sea and Malayan Archipelago was, as Linschoten told Europe in compendious detail, far weaker than contemporaries might have supposed. Even at its height the 'Estado da India' was maritime rather than territorial. It spread along the coasts a network of factories, entrepôts protected by forts, from Sofala in Mozambique to Timor and the estuary of the Pearl River. Other empires, such as the Spanish conquests of America, constituted a political structure in a clearly-defined space; the Estado da India was more readily comparable to a trade *diaspora*, a network constituting a system of communication between various places in which the Portuguese had a foothold, whether firmly-established or tenuous in the extreme.

Until Dutch rivalry eroded the profitability of Portuguese seaborne commerce, the Portuguese trading monopolies Linschoten described at length were enormously profitable. Among the seventeen voyages 'owned' by the holder of the post of captain of Malacca was that to Macau. He could make up to 10,000 cruzados from it or could sell his rights to it for 5-6,000 cruzados. By far the best voyage was that from Goa to Japan *via* Macau, which even in the 1560s produced a clear profit of about 40,000 cruzados, and later much more. (Pearson, 1987, 37)

A Dutch source stated that 200 or more Portuguese merchants travelled to Japan from Macau aboard the annual Great Ship, an indication of how important and lucrative the Nagasaki trade was. While officered by Portuguese, these ships usually had few European crewmen; most of the crews were Eurasians, Gujeratis and black African slaves.

Every literate person in the Netherlands had either read Linschoten's writings concerning the vast value of the Macau – Nagasaki trade or had some acquaintance with the contents of Linschoten's volumes. Surely the intrepid Dutch could contrive to get their hands on some, at least of this wealth:

> 'The marchandies or ware that they carrie from Makau to Iapen, are silks, & from Iapen they return nothing but silver, whereby they doe greatly profit'. (Linschoten 1974, 42-43)

Having thus informed his fellow countrymen of the vast wealth to be found aboard the great Portuguese carracks, or *naós*, plying unceasingly between Goa and Nagasaki, Linschoten went on to describe '*The Iland of Iapen*' itself in admirable detail, He discoursed upon the location of Japan, its climate, fauna, customs, inhabitants and history among other topics. Yet it is probable that not a few of Master Linschoten's eager readers scanned the text until they found what they sought:

> 'The countrie hath some mines of silver, which from thence is by the Portingals yearely brought unto China, and there bartered for Silke, and other Chinish wares, which the Japeans have needs of. The countriemen are verie skilfull to search for Silver, and to sell their wares'. (Linschoten, 1974, 45)

Nor had precise sailing directions to this El Dorado of easy pickings been omitted. A full 140 pages of the English translation of 1598 is given over to detailed sailing directions for this was a time when no pilot in his senses would trust to a chart or map in preference to a clear rutter, or *roteiro*, composed by a fellow-pilot as a result of close observation of conditions which varied enormously by the season and which were of paramount importance in the days of sail. It is interesting to note, in this context, that Adams bequeathed his celestial globe and '*sea-cards*' to Richard Cocks, the Cape Merchant of the English factory at Hirado.

Given the wealth of information Linschoten had supplied concerning the wealth and weakness of the Portuguese maritime empire in Asian waters, disaster did not take long to strike; the Dutch were ready, willing and able to challenge the Portuguese in Asian waters.

At the end of September 1601 the citizenry of Macau were perturbed to see three unknown European vessels approaching. They hastily despatched their families and their portable valuables to the relative safety of the Jesuit College, which offered some measure of security because it was on a hill, and grasped their weapons. The Dutch, for it was indeed they who had come calling uninvited, were in two ships, the *Amsterdam* and the *Gouda*, and a pinnace. Commanded by Jacob van Neck, they had been sailing towards Canton – a city closed to foreigners – after having been blown off course while bound for Patani. The Dutch, who were masters of the underhand stratagem, sent a skiff inshore to reconnoitre the city. The Captain-Major commanding the city's defences promptly captured it. The next day, the pinnace was ill-advised enough to be caught as it approached the inner harbour. The Portuguese refused to return their twenty prisoners and all but three were executed. It is a though the gods of Olympus were angered by this atrocity, for successive disasters were to befall the Portuguese in the East thereafter. As Padre Fernão Guerreiro recorded:

> 'On the 30th July of the year sixteen hundred and three, between eleven o'clock and midday, there arrived at the City of Macau a Siamese Junk which brought news that in the previous March the carrack from China which was bound for Malacca (the richest and largest for many years) had been taken by the Dutch in the straits of Singapore. And that very same evening, when the carrack which was going from China to Japan was on the eve of departure, two ships and a pinnace of the said enemy reached this port of Macau and took the carrack where it lay without any resistance whatsoever, since there was nobody in it, everyone being ashore getting ready to embark. And forasmuch as the citizens of Macau lost virtually all of their capital in these two ships, which were each worth about a *conto* of gold, whilst they were still more deeply indebted in Japan for goods they had bought there on credit, they were all left in a condition rather to receive than to give alms'. (Boxer, 1948, 50)

The reference to the giving of alms is an acknowledgement of the open-handed generosity of the Macau Portuguese towards the Society of Jesus, the missionary efforts of which were largely supported by individual contributions and bequests, rather than by the munificence of the Iberian monarchs, as Protestant contemporaries generally assumed.

Once Malacca had been taken, Portuguese trading ventures in eastern Asia frequently realised profits of a miraculous 2,000 per cent. The importance of the possession of Macau for the Portuguese cannot be understated; Chinese silks were exchanged for Japanese silver at a rumoured overall profit of 150 per cent on bullion alone. (Scammell, 1981, 241)

Macau itself produced practically nothing. The city functioned as an entrepôt for goods purchased in Canton and, illegally but frequently, elsewhere on the Chinese coast. In 1600 the profit margin on goods purchased in Canton and sold in Nagasaki was as follows:

> Raw silk was sold at 80 taels per picul in Canton and 140 to 150 taels in Japan;
> A kind of fine quality silk was bought for 140 taels and sold in Japan at 370 taels to 400 taels;
> Gold was bought for 5.4 taels per tael and sold in Japan for 7.8 per tael;

> Cotton thread cost 7 taels per picul and was sold for 16 to 18 taels;
> Quicksilver was bought at 53 taels per picul and sold for about 90;
> Earthenware were bought at different prices and sold for two to three times as much in Japan;
> Liquorice cost 3 taels per picul in Macao and sold for 9 or 10 taels in Japan.

The supposed vulnerability of Macau and the covetousness of Portugal's foes, have impressed themselves on Portuguese chroniclers to the present day:

> 'Macau passed difficult times after the annexation of Portugal by Philip II of Spain; the Dutch and the British were intensely jealous of the position enjoyed by the Portuguese. The Dutch, English and French attacked again and again the Portuguese territories. Attempts were made by the Dutch to take Macau in 1604, 1607, 1622 and 1627, all of which were repulsed'. (Graça, 1984, 21)

Despite the best efforts of the Dutch, Macau did not fall, although the issue seemed in doubt more than once after the Dutch had established a strong presence in Eastern waters. By the time of the attack on Macau in the summer of 1622, the Dutch possessed the most formidable fleet in Asian waters, as friend and foe alike recognised.

Part of the reason for Dutch maritime success in Asia was Hendrick Brouwer's accidental and wholly felicitous discovery that south of the Cape of Good Hope strong westerlies blow throughout the year, giving a sailing vessel a clear run due east through temperate latitudes until the helmsman begins to sense the growing strength of the south-east trades and alters course for the Sunda Straits. This discovery the Dutch kept a closely-guarded secret for as long as was possible and from 1611 onwards the V.O.C. possessed a temporary monopoly of a faster, easier, more direct and far healthier and safer route to Java, the Moluccas and Japan than that so courageously established by the Portuguese a century beforehand. (Scammell, 1981, 402)

That the Dutch frequently used routes, and guides to navigation, established by the Portuguese is beyond dispute. The Dutch were maritime pioneers, too. Often, as with Hendrick Brouwer's chance discovery, this was as much by accident as by design.

It took Magellan thirty-eight days to pass through the Straits he discovered in 1520; Drake, in 1578, cleared the reefs, tidal rips and furious winds of the passage in an astonishingly short sixteen days. The element of luck, no less than competent command and seamanship, played no small part in navigating this hazardous and seemingly unavoidable waterway. Ironically, it was not until Dutch interlopers, seeking to evade the V.O.C. *diktat* that only Dutch shipping sailing with the authority of the V.O.C. could use the Straits, endeavoured to find another passage from the Atlantic to the Pacific that the Le Maire Straits and Cape Horn were discovered. Long voyages were dangerous, as every experienced sailor was aware. Magellan was slain in the Philippines. The survivors of the first circumnavigation of the world returned to Europe under the command of Juan Sebastián Elcano, a Spaniard. Even relatively short voyages, such as John Saris' journey between Bantam and Hirado, a voyage of a mere five months' duration with ample opportunities to purchase provisions *en route*, could prove fatal to several of a ship's company. Eleven Englishmen under Saris' command died on the voyage between Bantam and Japan. Richard Cocks, the Cape Merchant of the E.I.C.'s Hirado factory, died at sea while returning to England in disgrace.

The virtual impossibility of recruiting sufficient European sailors to make up the usual losses of a ship's complement led commanders to employ Asian crews. Whether Gujerati, Malay or Japanese, these proved hardy sailors and the Dutch came to rely on Japan as a recruiting-area for their wars with the Iberians in south Asia.

As Cocks was aware, the Dutch had no misgivings about recruiting Japanese mariners and mercenaries in significant numbers. He informed the E.I.C. that they could easily do the same, writing of 'desparate warlike people . . . ready to adventure for good pay'. In 1621 Hidetada forbade the employment of Japanese as sailors and mercenaries in foreign employ but this prohibition was widely flouted; nine Japanese in E.I.C. service lost their lives in the Amboina massacre of 1623.

The Dutch, who had no compelling desire to inflict their own version of European Christianity on the peoples of Asia, perceived Asia first and foremost as an immensely tempting area for trade, provided that such rivals as the Portuguese could be successfully overcome.

The Dutch in Japan missed no opportunity to calumnify the Iberians, as well they might have chosen to do. It may be presumed that Morejón, the Jesuit chronicler, had no opportunity to read the letter sent to Ieyasu by Maurice of Nassau. This missive, penned in 1610 and delivered by Specx and Brouwer in 1612, addressed Ieyasu as a 'great noble without equal in this age' and informed him that

> 'the intentions of the Spanish and Portuguese are difficult to understand because they are hidden deep in the minds of the Padres who reveal nothing, and this is a matter that you should consider very carefully. And the intention of the Padres is to convert all Japan to their faith by degrees, and as they hate other religions there is sure to be a struggle between the sects and a great disturbance in the country. And then the Padres hope to turn matters to their own advantage'.

Having done as much as could be attempted in the pages of a letter to encourage Japanese suspicions of the Catholic missionaries and their adherents, Maurice of Nassau ingratiatingly added

> 'the Dutch will do whatever you may please to require of them, and consider it a pleasure to do so. And so they will continue to do in the future'. (Sadler, 1984, 235)

It could have been in the minds of neither writer nor recipient that the Dutch would eventually abase themselves contemptibly in the eyes of European contemporaries by their acquiescence in humiliations of varying kinds during the Dejima period. It is doubtful whether Maurice of Nassau envisaged his countrymen trampling on a crucifix and pretending to be drunkards and lovelorn swains for the amusement of the Tokugawa court when he assured Ieyasu that his compatriots would do 'whatever you may please to require of them'.

In his letter to the Heeren XVII of the V.O.C. in 1614 so frequently quoted over the years, Jan Pietersz Coen, the architect of Dutch *realpolitik* in East Asia, wrote:

> You gentlemen should know well from experience that in Asia trade must be driven and maintained under the protection and favour of your own weapons, and that your weapons must be wielded from the profits gained by the trade; so trade cannot be maintained without war, nor war without trade.

Discussing the nature of Dutch mercantile efforts in Asia in greater detail, Coen noted:

> Piece goods from Gujerat we can barter for pepper and gold on the coast of Sumatra, rials and cottons from the coast (of Coromandel) for pepper in Bantam, sandalwood, pepper and rials we can barter for Chinese goods and Chinese gold; we can extract silver from Japan with Chinese goods, piece goods from the Coromandel coast in exchange for spices, other goods and gold from China, piece goods from Surat for spices, other goods and rials, rials from Arabia for spices and various other trifles – one thing leads to another. And all of it can be done without any money from the Netherlands and with ships alone. (Pearson, 1987, 92)

First, however, the Dutch had to reduce the power of their acknowledged rivals and enemies, the Portuguese and the Spaniards, and to coerce the British into accepting, willingly or otherwise, a subordinate role in East Asia.

Richard Wickham of the Hirado factory saw things in much the same light as Coen, even if the E.I.C. proved far less successful in the event. If all went well at Hirado 'the bussines of this place beeinge Carefully & honestly manniged', and the right goods purchased at Ayuthia – silk, sappan wood, deer hides and black broadcloth – the E.I.C.'s endeavours in the Far East would prosper mightily, providing Bantam

> 'wth soe great quantities of silver to stuffe all the Factories betweene this (*Hirado*) & Bantam that ther never should bee any more need to send any more money outt of England but hoally depend uppon this ffactory'. (Massarella, 1990, 191)

Coen, who was in favour of the V.O.C. adopting aggressive policies towards the Iberians and the E.I.C., had probably realised this too and was determined to prevent so successful an outcome of the E.I.C.'s efforts.

The arrival of the Dutch in Japan was not part of a detailed plan. Admiral Verhoeven, the commander of a Dutch fleet which sailed from Texel at the end of 1607, had orders to send at least one ship to Japan in order to deliver a letter from the Prince of Orange and, if opportunity permitted, to open a factory for regular trade. In fact, two of Matelief's vessels had been intended to sail to Japan in 1605, but one of them, the *Middelburgh*, was lost in the battle fought with the Portuguese at Cape Rachado in

August 1606. It was in this same battle that Quaekernaeck lost his life.

Verhoeven learned that an exceptionally richly-ladden carrack was being laden with silks and other trade goods at Macau and sent two vessels to intercept and capture this carrack, Pessoa's *Madre de Deus*. Unluckily for Pessoa, the two Dutch ships, the *Roode Leeuw met pijlen* and the *Griffoen,* failed to intercept him in the Formosa Channel. This was a disappointment for Abraham van den Broeck and his crews, for such a prize would have made them rich. However, to prepare for just such an eventuality, the ships had taken aboard some silk, cargo and lead at Pattani, it being realised that there would be no prospect of establishing a factory in Japan if neither ship carried saleable cargo. (Boxer, 1951, 288).

Having missed Pessoa's *naó* by a mere day or two, the Dutch proceeded to Hirado. Accompanied by Sandvoort, two of the merchants travelled to Suruga (Shizuoka) and were greeted by Ieyasu with unfeigned pleasure. Ieyasu granted the Dutch trading privileges and the Dutch left a modest V.O.C. outpost on the island of Hirado. Jacques Specx, a Dordrecht man, was left at Hirado as factor, aided by three assistants and a youth. One of the *Liefde*'s company, Jan Cousyns, was employed as book-keeper. Nicholas Puik, who shared command with Abraham van den Broeck, offered Adams and the other survivors of the *Liefde* passage home to Europe. Whether Adams was at liberty to leave at this time is uncertain, considering that he specifically asked Ieyasu for permission to leave Japan after the *Clove* arrived at Hirado in 1613. In any event, there is no known record of any of the *Liefde*'s survivors leaving Japan on either of the two ships.

Victor Sprinckel, the Dutch factor at Patani, wrote to Adams in February 1608 stating flatly that the reason the Dutch had been unable to send shipping to Japan prior to that time because 'our deadly enemies the Portuguese being so powerful at sea that we have enough to do to hold our own against them'. Powerful and threatening as the Dutch appeared to the Portuguese, the Dutch mariners in Asian waters did not have everything their own way until some decades had elapsed. (Farrington, 1991, 61). This letter had earlier informed Adams of Captain Jacob Quaeckernaeck's death, explaining that his cousin, Admiral Cornelius Matelief the younger, had pressed him into reluctant service against the Portuguese, being short of experienced commanders and being keen that Quackernaeck should 'gain some profit and afterwards return home with it', although Quaeckernaeck's own wish was 'rather to go home'.

The Dutch, having brought silk, pepper and 'a little lead' in 1609, were unable to return to Japan in 1610. The ships intended to sail to Japan had been involved in Admiral Wittert's crushing defeat by Governor Juan de Silva of the Philippines in April of that year. The Hirado Dutchmen felt extremely distressed at their inability to perform as they had so confidently promised and by the Iberians' claim that the Dutch were merely pirates who were unable to trade unless they had made sufficient captures at sea. In November 1610 Jacques Specx wrote to the V.O.C. observing that many of the Nagasaki Japanese were accepting the Iberian claim readily, believing that the presence of the Dutch was the main reason why no trade had come to Nagasaki from either Manila or Macau; this claim, though an undue simplification, was very close to the mark. (Boxer, 1951, 289).

A few years later Richard Cocks was saying the same to Specx;

> 'yt seemes your mastars comand yow to be comune theevs, to robbe English, Spanish, Portingalles, Chinas, Javas, and all others whatsover, without respect. . .'. (Thompson, 1883, II, 62)

The arrival of the yacht *Braeck* from Patani in 1611 restored Dutch confidence somewhat. Although the *Braeck*'s cargo was a tiny fraction of that of the Macau ship, Ieyasu seemed pleased enough and told the Dutch envoys, Specx and Segerszoon, that he was pleased to see them. Ieyasu took the opportunity of reminding the Iberians that trade was open to all, presumably to their intense disappointment. Specx noted that Adams, who acted as interpreter, was evidently in Ieyasu's favour.

João Rodrigues, whom Adams had replaced by this time, had been compelled to leave Japan in March 1610, never thereafter returning to Japan despite his repeated appeals to his superiors to be sent there again.

Adams, while considered a Dutchman by the Dutch most of the time, remained a national of a country whose interests were often at variance with those of Holland. In January 1613 he wrote to Spalding at Bantam:

> 'Had I known that our Ingllis shipes hade trade in the Indis, I had longe

a-troubled you w'th wrytting, but the Hollanders hav kept it most seeccreet from mee tell the year 1611, w'ch wast the first newes that I heerd of the trading of our shipes in the Indees'. (Farrington, 1991, 79)

Adams was not unwilling to use appropriate subterfuges when the opportunity arose. John Jourdain, aboard the *Darling* near Amboina in 1613, recorded an incident in which Adams had sent a letter and a map of Japan to Augustine Spalding, then resident at Bantam, by means of 'an English sailer'. The courier was rewarded with two reals of eight, which was hardly a vast amount considering that the Dutch would have readily punished him had they known about the concealed missive. (Farrington, 1991, 404). Loyalty to the interests of the Dutch in general and the interests of the V.O.C. in particular could be trusted to a certain point but no further, it seems.

Adams suspected the Dutch of intercepting his letters, probably justly. It would have been in Dutch interests to have suppressed commercial information of possible value to the E.I.C., as Purchas observed at the end of Adams' letter to his wife of 1605. (Farrington, 1991, 54). Letters addressed to Adams were seized, too. In his letter to Spalding in January 1613 he observed 'few coum to my hand'.

Letters took months, sometimes years, to reach Europe from Japan. An example Anthony Farrington gives is a letter Cocks wrote in December 1615. Copied in Bantam, it reached London in June 1617. A response from London could not have reached Japan before summer 1620 with the shipping available at that time. It will be recalled that Jacob Quaeckernaeck spent a year waiting for the arrival of a Dutch ship at Pattani before sailing on to Johore. Letters could be opened and deliberately withheld or censored. The Dutch would certainly have suppressed any information of commercial value in Adams' letters.

To assume that Adams felt as little hostility towards the Dutch as towards his fellow-countrymen is not necessarily to sully his reputation. Willingness to serve was more important that personal nationality, as Saris knew well, having carried a Spaniard from the Malay archipelago to Japan. Victor Sprinckel, in Pattani, wrote to Adams in February 1608 in terms which would have amply confirmed Saris' suspicions:

'The good will, love and affection which you, with some others, show

> towards the fatherland has been wonderfully pleasing for me to hear. I pray God that you and your people may continue in such sentiments, and all of us likewise, since it is God's bidding to love the fatherland'. (Farrington, 1991, 60)

It is interesting to observe that Sprinckel assumes Adams to be, in effect, Dutch in this missive.

In spite of his supposedly pro-Dutch sympathies, so distasteful to John Saris in 1613, Adams assisted two Britons to escape from Dutch custody after they had been brought to Hirado from Pattani aboard the Dutch ship *Angel* in September 1619. A third man escaped on his own, though it may have been the case that his escape was permitted by the Dutch, who did not relish being denounced to the *Bakufu* for holding Britons prisoner on Japanese soil. (Massarella, 1990, 264).

XI

THE HIRADO BRITONS

'Japan will prove by the next returne more profittable to you than it may be you expect.'
John Saris to the Court of the East India Company (Massarella, 1990, 127)

Adams had made tenuous contact, through the reluctant medium of the Dutch at Hirado, with the Englishmen of the East India Company established at Bantam in Java a considerable period prior to the arrival of John Saris aboard the *Clove*. Saris' mission in the East Indies was primarily to assist Henry Middleton in settling E.I.C. trade at Surat, in the Gulf of Cambay, close to the Portuguese fortress of Diu. Secondary objectives were Mocha, in Yemen, and, should circumstances warrant, Japan. (Satow, 1900, x-xv). Saris' commission, Ernest Satow observed, is 'carelessly drawn', much of it being copied, with slight alterations, from the commissions issued for previous voyages of East India Company fleets.

It is hard to see how this could have been avoided, given the fact that commissions were only put into writing at the last moment and necessarily full of caveats and sentences abounding in conditional tenses, reflecting the many difficulties attendant on despatching trading fleets to unknown waters. The passages in Saris' commission relating to Japan, as related by Satow, are as follows:

> Item the *Hector* and *Thomas* beinge fraighted and sent for England, then wee wishe you, Capt John Sairis, to proceede with the Cloue and, with all possible speede thatt you may, endevor your course for Japan, haueinge before att Bantam or ellswhere dilligently aduised, inquired and conferred with our Factors, or any other the best meanes you may attaine vnto the knowledge, wherby to informe your selfe for or concerninge our intended voyadge to Japan, and to procure in any of those parts (yf you may) some skilfull pilate experienced in those

Coastes and take him alonge with you, directinge your course from thence to Japan, neglectinge noe tyme, butt takeinge the benfitt and aduantage of those Wynds and Monsons as you shall most certeinlie and trulie informe your selues and learne that they blowe in their seasons.

24. Item, and being arriued att Japan, wee desier you to vse the best meanes to search out the most convenient and safest harbour to trade in, where you may sell Cloth, leade, Iron, and such other of our Natiue Comodities as by your obseruaction you shall finde most vendible there, wherein you are to be very spetially carefull, both whatt Color and sortes of Cloth and for whatt quantities will there be vented, as alsoe to giue greate chardge that your men offer noe offence to the people there, still keepinge good watch and standinge vpon your guard, and that out of the danger of any Castle, Forte, or other Gallies or friggotts, to prevent any mischeefe that may happen, and to consult and take good aduise with the rest of the Factors and espetiallie with William Adams, an English man nowe resident there and in greate favour with the kinge as wee heare, to desire his opinion whatt course should be held, both for the delivery of his Maiesties letters nowe sent, whatt presents are to [be] geuen, to whome, by whome and in whatt manner the same is to be done, with all dilligence that shall be requisitt, obserueing carefully the tymes in keepinge the Monsons in all places wheare you shall trade, for attayneinge to other portes, as occasion shall be offered. And for presennts wee haue sent with you as appeareth in the Invoice.

25. Item, and as you shall receiue incourradgment in the progresse of your affaires by the perswasion of the foresaid William Adams grounded vpon his longe experience in those partes and shall finde that ytt may be with saffetie, as beinge protected vnder the authoritie of the kinge of the Country and may proue Comodious and beneficiall for the good of the Company, Then with the Counsell of Richard Cockes and such pricipall men as are in you shipp, you may aduise, resolue and leaue such Factors as you in your discrecion shall thinke fitt with such a quantitie of goods as shall be by you thought convenient for the setlinge of a factorie and mainteyneing of a trade att Japan, together with soe many and such sufficent Marriners to attend them and guard our said goods as you shall finde to be needfull and necessarie and to prouide them a good and stronge howse for the better saffetie of such goods as shall be lefte there in chardge with them. But yf you shall finde at Japan [no] convenient meanes of ventinge our Comodities or the retourne of proffitt not to answeare the length and difficultie of the voyadge, or the dangers in prosecuteinge this trade to exceede without proporcion the advantage to be hoped, then you shall frame your course and seeke vent for such Comodities as you haue either att the Molloccoes, Philippinas

> or any other places there abouts, whether you may be incourradged by any probable hopes of peaceable and proffittable tradeinge. And yf att your departure from Japan the said William Adams shall ymportune you to transporte him into his natiue Countrie to visitt his wife and Children, Wee pray you then to accomodate him with as convenient a Cabben as you may and all other necessaries which your shipp may afford him. (Satow, 1900, xii-xiv)

At the beginning of the second decade of the seventeenth century, the directors of the East India Company were attracted by the prospect of selling England's staple export product, broadcloth, in Japan. The commission issued to the Seventh Voyage, which left England in 1611, included instructions to the factors, the senior merchants of the voyage, to explore the possibilities of commencing trade with Japan, furnishing them with a letter from James I. Peter Floris, one of the factors on the voyage, wrote a letter from Pattani in 1612 to Adams, whom the English knew to be in Japan. This letter was carried to Japan by a Dutch ship, the *Hasewint*. It was the Eighth Voyage that actually reached Japan in 1613 and established the first direct contact between the two island nations.

The three ships comprising the Eighth Voyage, the *Clove, Hector* and *Thomas,* left England in April 1611; Japan was not the main object of the voyage. (Satow, 1900, x-xvi). Primarily, the Eighth Voyage was intended to secure trade at Surat, then a flourishing port city on the Indian Gulf of Cambay. Should that prove difficult, pepper was to be obtained from Bantam in Java and spices from the Moluccas. Should these endeavours prove disappointing, the commission issued to the voyage authorised John Saris, the commander, to send a ship to Japan to explore the prospects of selling 'Clothe & leade, Iron & other of your Native Comodities as by yor obseruacon you shall finde more vendible there'. Should the market for English goods in Japan look promising, Saris was authorised to consult with the factors concerning the advisability of establishing a factory in Japan.

Surat was closed to English shipping. Saris quarrelled with Sir Henry Middleton, the commander of the Sixth Voyage, over the apportionment of spoils from seized Gujerati shipping – a conflict which almost came to blows – the *Hector* and *Thomas* procured pepper and spices in Bantam. Saris, aboard the *Clove,* proceeded to the Moluccas, where the Spaniards proved far more agreeable that the Dutch, and thence to Japan.

That the Dutch were unwilling to permit the *Clove* to trade was hardly surprising; by the time of Saris' voyage they had accepted that desperate struggles lay ahead in Asia. Even the English, who had sacrificed so much to aid Holland in the struggle against Spain, were suspect. Had the British been determined to accept the Dutch challenge in Asian waters, they could easily have done so. In the eighteen years of hostilities before James I's peace of 1604, the English captured over 1,000 Spanish and Portuguese vessels, plundered many more of other nationalities and obtained prize goods worth about 15 per cent of England's imports during the same period.

Of the treatment the Dutch in the Moluccas accorded the *Clove,* Richard Cocks wrote, in his letter to Sir Thomas Smythe of November 1613:

> '. . . they used us much worse than eather Turkes, Mores or any other heathen hath doone since our dep'ture out of England, & thretned us that yf we went about to trade w'th the Spaniard they wold take us and make prise of us'. (Farrington, 1991, 97)

Somewhat surprisingly, this period did not affect Cocks' attitudes towards the Dutch permanently. His relations with the Dutch at Hirado were, for the majority of the time, cordial and even friendly, except during the period that the Dutch were bringing British shipping into Hirado as prizes and placing, as Cocks claimed, a price on his head. Within a few years Cocks was writing the following to the East India Company concerning the hostility displayed by the Hirado Dutch:

> '. . . their generall or cheefe comander, called Adam Westarwood, sett my life at sale, promesing 50 rialles of 8 to any one would kill me, and 30 of the like for the life of each other English merchant, with many other stratagems they used against us too long to be repeated'. (Thompson, 1883, II, 317)

Normally the Dutch were content to do what they could to make the E.I.C. factory's efforts in the Japanese market unprofitable by underselling their British rivals. In December 1613 Cocks reported that the Dutch at Hirado were halving the prices being asked for their broadcloth, adding the lament that the stuff offered by the E.I.C. factory was inferior to that which the Dutch were selling, the E.I.C. factory's cloth 'being very much worme-eaten (w'ch proceeded from the ill-drying and dressing thereof. . .)' (Farrington, 1991, 117).

Writing of the difficulties he had experienced attempting to trade in the Moluccas, Saris was to write during the course of the voyage homeward to England, 'I had laden my ship w'th cloves at the Mollucoes but that the Fleminges w'th force so overcharged me both by land and sea as the naturalles could no waye com to us w'th ther spice, albeit thay wear more willinge wee should have it than thay'. (Farrington, 1991, 168).

Unusually, the Moluccas and Amboina were to be celebrated in literary form by both John Milton, in *Paradise Lost*, and in a propaganda work penned by Dryden castigating the Dutch for their cruelty.

The Dutch, being well aware of Iberian wealth no less than Iberian weakness, were determined to keep the British well away from their promising foothold in the Moluccas. The British, with the innocence of naïvité, truly and sincerely had 'probable hopes of peaceable and proffittable tradeinge' in the Philippines, conquered territory which the Spanish were determined to keep to themselves, and the fabled Spice Islands, where Drake had traded so profitably and where the Dutch and Spanish contended bitterly for mastery.

The British were not wholly ignorant about Japan, although no Briton other than Adams had been there, so far as was known. In 1577 Richard Willes, an enthusiastic advocate of the discovery of the northwest passage, published *The History of Travayle in the West and East Indies*. This, an expanded edition of Richard Eden's *Decades of the new worlde*, was, *inter alia*, the first book published in English to give an account of Japan, predating the English edition of Marco Polo's *Travels* by two years.

Willes had been a Jesuit for a time but renounced Catholicism on his return to England from studying in continental Europe. Much of the account of Japan in the *History* was culled from letters written by Xavier and other Jesuits, such as a letter written by Luís Frois from Miyako in 1565, which had been published in Naples by Giovanni Pietro Maffei in 1573. It is believed that Willes' book did much to encourage Master John Dee, Queen Elizabeth's necromancer, crystal-gazer and cosmographer, to recommend the Pet and Jackman endeavour to reach Japan by the northeast route. (Massarella, 1990, 65-7). Other works in which Japan appeared were published in English; Robert Parke's translation of Juan Gonzâlez de Mendoza's *Historie of the great and mightie kingdome of China* in 1588, which Parke hoped would encourage Thomas Cavendish to sail to Asia by the northwest passage, in order to sell English cloth, was one.

Thomas Cavendish circumnavigated the world between July 1586 and September 1588. It was aboard his ship that the first Japanese and Filipinos arrived in England. Christopher and Cosmo, two young men from Kyushu 'both of very good capacitie' were taken from a Manila galleon, the *Santa Anna*, off the coast of lower California in November 1587. Cavendish brought three Filipino boys to England at the same time, causing great interest in learned circles in England. Hakluyt, for example, wrote:

> 'Is it not as strange that the borne naturalles of Japan, and the Philippinaes are here to be seene, agreeing with our climate, speaking our language and informing us of the state of their Easterne habitations?' (Massarella, 1990, 48)

The arrival of Christopher and Cosmo in England was a sedate affair compared to the sanguinary encounter between a ship commanded by Sir Edward Michelbourne near Patani in December 1605 and a junk commandeered by Japanese pirates. John Davis, Sir Edward's pilot, was slain by the Japanese, who fought to the death rather than yield. One alone sought quarter but was hanged; while this was happening the rope broke and it is possible he swam ashore. (Wild, 1937, 77-80). Michelbourne noted that such was the reputation of Japanese mariners that no armed Japanese were permitted ashore in any Asian country, possibly an exaggeration. The emergence of a strong central government in Japan under the Tokugawa made it difficult for large *wako* bands, such as the one Michelbourne encountered, to replenish their numbers with ease. In 1600 Ieyasu commanded at least 200 *wako* from Satsuma to be crucified. These pirates had been preying on Manila-bound Chinese junks. Ieyasu desired good trading relations, if no more, between Japan and the Philippines. He also wanted direct trade with China, as Cocks noted.

Following the Spanish settlement of Manila in 1571, the same year as the founding of Nagasaki, a significant trade grew up with Chinese ports in the province of Fujian. By 1600 an average of 45 large sea-going junks (*somas*) came annually to Manila, bringing silks, porcelain and other wares which were sold for silver and gold from Mexico and Peru. It was on this trade that the Dutch preyed, much to the distress of the Chinese. By contrast, Manila's trade with Japan was insignificant; the Spaniards did not need Japanese silver and, more significantly, Hispano-Japanese relations were complicated by religious and political factors. The Manila authorities were apprehensive of Japanese designs, the Japanese authorities were all too aware that Manila was the source of the Franciscans and other mendicants who lacked the finesse of the Jesuits and, still more significantly, the *Bakufu* feared Spanish power.

The brief history of the Hirado factory of the East India Company is both an integral part of the maritime efforts of the British in the East and, quite literally, a separate world, for the armed hostility of the Dutch meant that the Hirado Britons were isolated from the world for months, even years, at a time. This state of affairs did not necessarily constitute hardship; the factors had a social life which was often agreeable, they had mistresses and interests separate from their work and they were fortunate to find themselves in one of the healthier parts of the Indies, as Asia was then known. Moreover, they were by no means the only foreigners resident in Japan. In addition to the Dutch factors of the V.O.C., there were Portuguese, Spaniards, Frenchmen, Goanese and others whose lives were centred around Hirado and Nagasaki, however briefly.

The Portuguese in Asia derived the greater part of their profit from the 'Country trade' rather than from commerce between Asia and Europe. Instead of profitable traffic in diamonds and spices carried from Asia via the Cape of Good Hope to Lisbon, the greater and most profitable trade the Portuguese drove was in more modest local commerce such as selling Arabian stallions from Qatif and Tarut to warring Indian princes, carrying cotton textiles around the Bay of Bengal, taking Timorese sandalwood to China and bartering Chinese silk for Japanese silver. This pattern was to be repeated by the Dutch and the British, both of whom found initial results disappointing. The Dutch contemplated withdrawal from Japan more than once; the British withdrew in 1623 but later attempted, too late, to re-establish themselves.

Saris' journal makes it clear that the arrival of the *Clove* at Hirado was no accident; 'I gave order to the m'r and purser to agree with 2 of the masters of the fisher boats to pilate us into Ferando', and, having anchored and shot off one piece of ordnance as a sign that the *Clove* desired to enter the port, 'soone after I was vizited by the ould king cauled Foine Same and his nephew Tone Same, at present governor of the iland. . .' (Farrington, 1991, 989). In Jacobean English, 'nephew' often meant grandson. Matsuura Shigenobu, the 'old king' of Hirado was in *inkyo*, having shaven his head and officially retired in favour of his son. Having 'retired' did not prevent him participating in Hideyoshi's Korean campaign and being accounted a formidable warrior. His assumption of formal retirement was accompanied by the formal adoption of the Buddhist name Sosei Hoin, hence the English at Hirado referred to him as King Foyne or Foyne Sama. His son had died in 1602, hence the unusual juxtaposition of grandfather and grandson as heads of the *daimyo* clan.

Hirado was not an ideal choice but it had certain undeniable advantages; it was not sufficiently Catholic as to be hostile, like Nagasaki; it enjoyed a generally mild climate and plentiful supplies; the local *daimyo* clan were welcoming, as was the 'China Captain', Li Tan, and his family. Hirado, in short, seemed to be 'the most convenient and safest harbour to trade in'.

Hirado, for all its relative remoteness, offered some surprising sights. Cocks observed cormorant fishing performed by Minami Soyemon, the steward of the *daimyo* household, a sight which he found as fascinating as had the first European chroniclers in China several centuries before. Other aspects of life on the island were less agreeable; Shosuke, the secretary to the *daimyo*, was detected engaging in commerce aboard a Dutch ship in the harbour, having 'forbad all others to doe the lyke'. He was given a choice between paying 800 taels or committing *seppuku*. He performed *seppuku*, being in no position to pay so vast a sum; 'The king demanded 800 taels from Shosuke Dono, or else to cut his belly, whoe, not having it to pay, did it'. (Cooper, 1965, 164). During Cocks' sojourn on the island two fellows, one 'a boy of 16 yeares ould' were burned to death for stealing boats.

Cocks attempted to intercede in the first instance, to no avail. He makes no mention of having tried to do the same in the second case, although he observed that the stolen boat was 'a small bark of littell or no vallue'. Cocks also noted that the punishment for permitting a house to catch fire, however briefly, was either banishment or death. Not surprisingly, the penalty for arson was death by fire. Infanticide, then widespread, distressed Cocks. He noted, with feeling, that a Hirado girl who had given birth to a child fathered by a musician aboard the *Clove* had killed her infant by treading on its throat with her foot, which seems to have been an approved *modus operandi* more humane than Spartan exposure or Chinese abandonment.

Although the E.I.C. factory at Hirado did not prosper as had been hoped in the early days, life was far from grim for the members of the first British community in Japan. Within a few months they appear to have acquired consorts, or, as a later era would style such arrangements, native mistresses of the kind Calcutta residents would describe as 'a Hindoo female friend'. While these women did not live within the English House, they lived close by and maintained their own domestic establishments with servants. Matinga, Cocks' consort, had three boys and two girls in her household.

Naturally, what many later chroniclers perceived as illicit and shameful affairs, as may be seen from the omissions in Edward Maunde Thompson's edition of Cocks' *Diaries*, was seen as perfectly normal in Japan, just as it was in most of Asia. There was doubtless affection between the women and their men; the factors gossiped about them in their letters and sent them presents; in May 1616 Richard Wickham sent Matinga the latest in Miyako fashions, for example. There were frictions from time to time, naturally. William Eaton 'sold' or transferred a girl called O-man, referred to as *Woman*, to Wickham. This upset the girl's mother greatly since she feared that Wickham would take her with him when he left Japan. The ensuing row was smoothed over and O-man and Femeja, Wickham's other consort, went up to the Kansai to stay with him in June 1616, accompanied by O-man's mother, an indication of the respectability of such liaisons. Some of the factors had children by their womenfolk. Wickham, Nealson, Sayers and Eaton all fathered children, although there is no record of Cocks having done so. Wickham's child was a daughter, who was born to O-man after Wickham had left Japan. Nealson fathered a girl called Helena. Eaton fathered three children. His daughter, Helena, was born to his consort in Sakai. His two sons were born to his consort in Hirado, Kamezo. William, the elder, travelled to England and later studied at Cambridge. The younger son was born after the closure of the factory.

Nearly sixteen years after the closure of the E.I.C. factory, the *Bakufu* decreed that all children born to foreigners were to leave Japan, together with their mothers. This decree, in 1639, was responsible for the departure to Batavia of Maria, Sayers' consort, and her daughter, Joan. Melchior van Sandvoort and his family were obliged to leave Japan, after the Dutchman had spent nearly four decades in the country. These expulsions, harsh as they were, might have been foreseen and probably were. According to one account, 287 people of mixed race and Catholic parentage were expelled to Macau. (Hearn, 1984, 329). In the nature of things there was inevitably a degree of confusion involved; some children of Catholic parentage ended their days in Batavia. One such was Jagatara Oharu, who had lived in Chikugo-machi in Nagasaki and whose parents were an Italian mariner and the daughter of a Chikugo-machi official. Oharu sent a poem on a piece of cloth cut from her sleeve to relatives, defying the prohibition against communicating with Japan. In exile she married a Dutch trader and lived to the age of 73. She has been commemorated by a monument to be seen at Kami Chikugo-machi, erected long after the Penal Laws were rescinded and the Christian era in Japanese history had become a safe subject for romantic nostalgia. (Plutschow, 1983, 39).

The merchants, or factors, who reached Hirado on June 1613, were reasonably typical of East India Company employees of their category. Their names, Richard Cocks, Tempest Peacock, Richard Wickham, William Eaton, Walter Carwarden, Edmund Sayers and William Nealson, all have a reassuringly English resonance to them.

None of the employees of the E.I.C. factory at Hirado became outstandingly proficient in Japanese, although Nealson became fluent enough to quarrel volubly in both English and Japanese. Cocks' proposal to station Richard Hudson at Miyako so that the young man might perfect his Japanese was thwarted by

Hidetada's restriction of trade to Hirado and Nagasaki. Hudson, the younger son of Henry Hudson the Arctic explorer, remained in Japan when the *Hoseander* sailed in February 1616 and remained there until the factory closed.

Cocks, whose diaries reveal him as an immensely likeable man, never prospered in Japan, was summoned home in disgrace as the scapegoat of the venture and died at sea in the Indian Ocean in March 1624. He and Adams were not infrequently at odds, but there was a great deal of mutual esteem between the two men.

Cocks' letters and diary entries are an invaluable resource for the writer of imaginative fiction no less than for the historian; he wrote as readably as Pepys. While his observations on contemporary events were often sadly amiss, they reflect the degree of ignorance that existed in Tokugawa Japan regarding state affairs, as when he shrewdly suggests that the Tokugawa were encouraging the rumour that Ieyasu had died in order to discover how the populace reacted to such news. The Tokugawa dictatorship, which Cocks called a 'terrany', could be surprisingly modern in its methods.

Cocks had hardly had time to settle in Hirado before becoming aware of some of the less appealing aspects of life in Japan; the *daimyo* of Hirado, for example, sent word to Saris and Cocks that he would not be calling on the English House as often as he had, believing 'a spie to be in Towne, sent by the Emperor to take notis what curtesyes past between us'. (Satow, 1900, 101).

For all Hirado's disadvantages, Cocks and the other Britons enjoyed life there. The Matsuura, the *daimyo* clan of the island, were minor 'outside *daimyo*', Tozama. The current *daimyo*, Matsuura Takanobu, and his grandfather, Shigenobu, made the Britons heartily welcome, well aware that the presence of more foreigners meant more trade and prosperity for their modest domain. In spite of the disagreeable necessity of having to provide presents for the Matsuura clan and their various retainers, the decade the E.I.C. Britons spent on Hirado was tolerably pleasant and harmonious, except when the rivalry between the Dutch and the Britons flared into open war. On such occasions the Matsuura acted promptly but not rashly. Guards were sent to safeguard the English house and the Dutch were sharply told to cease and desist from such behaviour. When the Dutch captured an Englishman, Richard King, and took him to the Dutch factory as a prisoner, the Matsuura promptly seized Jacques Specx and held him hostage until the Englishman's release. However, there were limits to what the Matsuura were willing to do in protecting the interests of the E.I.C. factory. Not long after King had been released, he was in a boat with Edmund Sayers and John Coaker in Hirado harbour which was fired on by the Dutch. A Japanese sailor was killed but the Matsuura proved unwilling to involve themselves and Cocks' complaint to Hidetada went unheeded.

Such dramatic events were the exceptions in a pleasant life. There was much reciprocal entertaining between the Britons, the Hirado Chinese and the Matsuura clan. Cocks also had a garden, in which he took a keen interest. This was evidently a pleasant place, with its ornamental pond for carp, *koi*, and pigeons. Apart from the remoteness of his location, Cocks might have been a tolerably prosperous Midlands squire when writing home to Hirado anxiously to insist that care be taken of his pigeons and 'fishes'.

Among the largesse the Hirado factory bestowed upon the Matsuura and their retainers were what might have been the beginnings of a new breed of pig in Japan: 'I gave 2 bore pigges and ij sow piges of thenglish race, ij to Tonomon Samme and the other ij to the Hollanders', as Cocks recorded in March 1621. The breed does not appear to have survived in Hirado. (Thompson, 1883, II, 145).

Hirado was, and remains to the present day, an island on which the Catholic variety of Christianity had established a firm foothold. Several Matsuura vassals were among the first converts in Japan and in 1580 Valignano had estimated the number of Christians on Hirado and the small islands close by as 4,000, although this may have been an exaggeration. (Massarella, 1990, 107).

Despite his dislike of Catholicism, Cocks had several Catholic friends in addition to the factory's employees and his consort. Although his diary suggests a hearty distaste for Catholic priests, Cocks displayed the compassionate side of his nature on at least three occasions. He gave some cotton cloth to a Jesuit called Tomás, a Biscayan, twice. More memorably, he gave Apolonario

Franco, a Franciscan, a meal and 15 *mas* in plate after the latter had providentially escaped from Osaka castle when it fell to Ieyasu's forces in summer 1615. (Cooper, 1982, 155; Thompson, 1883, I, 5-6).

The fall of Osaka Castle to the Tokugawa forces led Cocks to observe that it was believed that Toyotomi Hideyori had escaped; 'Nether . . . can the body of Hideyori be fownd; soe that many think he is secretly escaped'. Cocks doubted the probability of this, adding '. . . the people of these sothern parts speake as they wold have it, because they effeckt the yong man more than the ould'. (Cooper, 1965, 28).

Fray Apolonario Franco, who had escaped from the doomed fortress with 'but the clothes on his back' subsequently suffered martyrdom at the stake in Omura in 1622. Cocks was not infrequently a excellent chronicler, even if was inclined to overstate the importance of the modest E.I.C. factory in Hirado. In December 1614 he wrote to John Jourdain in Bantam, concerning the Tokugawa persecutions;

> '. . . the Emperor of Japann hath banished all Jesuitts, prists, fryers and nuns out of all his dominions of Japann and burned and pulled down all ther monestaries and churches. They laid the fault of this alteration one the arivall of our nation in thease p'tes, when it is notorious to all men that there own covitousnes and ill behaviors were occation thereof. Once howsoever I am glad thay ar gon, som of them beinge shipt for Amacau in China . . . and the rest ar gone for the Phillippinas'. (Farrington, 1991, 246)

Among those who left for Manila at this time were Takayama Ukon and Father Morejón. Morejón did, it is true, blame the Dutch and E.I.C. Britons for the persecution but it was to be many years before the Dutch brought as much trade to Japan as did the Iberians; rival theologies were of no interest to the *Bakufu*.

During his period of residence in Bayonne, in southwestern France, Cocks had been an informal intelligence agent while working as a 'factor for others', as he modestly said of himself. His experience of monitoring the movements of English Catholic exiles travelling to and from Spain probably did much to increase his suspicions of Catholic designs, whether in Europe or, later, in Japan. (Massarella, 1985, 14).

Writing from Hirado to Lord Salisbury in December 1614, Cocks displayed his knowledge of the bad feeling which existed between the Jesuits and the mendicant orders on the eve of the expulsion edict being put into effect:

> And it is worthie of notis that now at their going away being assembled alltogether at Langasaq', they fell at square amongst themselves, striveing w'ch order should be Viccar-Generall under the Pope in these p'tes over all the Christians, the Jesuistes cleamyng it by antiquetie because they came first. But all the other 4 sortes of churchmen stood out against them, viz. the Augustins, the Dominicans, the Franciscans and the seculer prists, and gave the preheminence to the Augustins. Soe that many bitter wordes passed amongst them at parting allthough for a matter of nothing, they being all quite banished the contrey & their churches pulled downe and burned, not soe much as a peece of tymber saved but cost hym his life w'ch carid it away; and amongest the rest, one saveing but a picture or painted peece of paper, & beinge fownd w'th it, had his head cut of and his body quartered. (Farrington, 1991, 257)

It is typical of Cocks that, having resided in Catholic Europe, he was able to understand the differences between the various missionary orders as well as to grasp the essence of the bitter dispute between them.

In the same letter, he refers to the apostasy of Michael Chijiwa, one of the youths who had represented Arima and Omura in the celebrated embassy of Japanese 'princes' et al to Spain and Rome. Michael Chijiwa was a vassal of Omura Yoshiaki, who had embraced Nichiren Buddhism in 1607, blaming the Jesuit João Rodrigues Tçuzzi for the transfer of Omura territory to the Nagasaki administration. In Cocks' letter, Michael Chijiwa is contemptuously described as '*a pore bare fello*'. The embassy to Europe was a matter of wonder and celebration in Catholic Europe; over seventy publications of various kinds referring to it appeared between 1585 and 1592. A portrait of Michael Chijiwa was drawn by Urbano Monte during the nobles' visit to Milan in July 1585 and is reproduced in *The Southern Barbarians*, edited by Michael Cooper. Chijiwa, fourteen at the time he left Japan, represented the *daimyos* Arima Haranobu and Omura Sumitada. Mancio Ito, twelve when he departed Japan, represented Otomo Yoshishige of Bungo. Accompanying them to Europe were Julian Nakaura, then twelve, and Martinho Hara, then thirteen. The boy ambassadors entered the Society of Jesus in July 1591. Michael Chijiwa apostatised due to pressures brought to bear on him; Julian Nakaura died a martyr's death in the pit, *ana-tsurushi*, at Nagasaki in October 1633, having been ordained in 1608. (Cooper, 1971, 70, 160).

James I of England, the 'wisest fool in Christendom', was sent one of Cocks' letters by Sir Thomas Wilson, together with such items as a Japanese almanac and an account of the *estates and revenues of the daimyo, most of them, equally or exceeding the revenues of most of ye greates Princes of Christendome*, as Wilson expressed it. Sir Thomas later had an opportunity to discuss this letter with the king, who was known to be interested in the world beyond Europe. The letter, which described Edo, the *shogun*'s magnificent retinue on the occasion of one of Hidetada's falconing expeditions, the great Buddha at Kamakura and much else, failed to impress the sceptical English monarch. James 'could not be induced to believe that the things written are true', dismissing the contents of Cocks' letter as 'loudest lyes that ever (he) heard of'. (Massarella, 1990, 329-330).

It is indicative of Richard Cocks' good sense that he usually found dealing with William Adams presented no problems. In January 1614, Cocks advised Richard Wickham to 'have a due care to geve Capt' Adams content'. Typically, Cocks added that he believed that he, Cocks, could live with Adams for seven years without a cross word, a remarkable testament to both men's characters. In fact, Cocks was unduly optimistic; while his relations with Adams seemed cordial most of the time, Cocks occasionally suspected Adams of commercial double-dealing and of having no greater regard for the English than he did of the Japanese or other European nationalities resident in Japan.

Cocks, referring to the employment of Adams by the E.I.C. factory at Hirado, wrote that the Dutch would gladly have deprived the Hirado Britons of Adams' services, even if they had no immediate use for his endeavours themselves; 'The Flemynges did what they could to have gotten hym from us, w'ch made hym to stand the more on his pointes'. (Farrington, 1991, 99). Cocks noted that Adams was 'tractable & willing to doe your Wor' the best service he may, & hath taken greate paines about the reparing our junck called the *Sea Adventure*, otherwaies she would not have byn ready to have made the Syam voyage this yeare' (1614) (Farrington, 1991, 227). Among the various services Adams provided for the Hirado factory were such mundane chores as ensuring the safety of the Company's ships. In 1615 Cocks recorded, 'And about midnight Capt Adams went out in a bark abord the *Hozeander* with many barks to tow her in, we fearing a tuffon'. (Thompson, 1883, I, 50).

The E.I.C. in London readily accepted the view that Adams was the 'onlie instram't that the Hollandes have to mediate for them w'th the Emperor', adding that Adams 'bended his affection to doe good for his countrye and contrymen, desiringe to see some English shippinge in those partes. . .' (Farrington, 1991, 191).

One aspect of Cocks' conduct as the head of the Hirado factory which has attracted unfavourable comment over the centuries was his gullibility; he permitted himself to be the victim of a prolonged confidence trick on the part of Li Tan, *alias* Andrea Dittis, the China Captain. As head of the Chinese trading community in Hirado, Li Tan was able to extract money from Cocks over a lengthy period under the pretext of employing these sums to open trade between Chinese ports and the Hirado factory. Evidently Li Tan was a confidence trickster of no mean parts for Cocks, normally an astute man, enjoyed cordial relations with Li for years without coming to the conclusion that he, and his employers, had been cheated. The E.I.C. in London, when informed of Cocks' initial discussions with Li, had snapped at the prospect with alacrity, commending Cocks for his diligence and encouraging him to do what he could to open trade with China. Cocks knew little of China and readily accepted Li Tan's assertion that the Chinese authorities were aware of the E.I.C. presence in Hirado and were greatly interested in the Company's proceedings. The reality was that the declining Ming dynasty, menaced by the inexorable growth of Manchu power, had no interest in a few foreigners operating from an insignificant island off the Kyushu coast. If the name of Hirado was known at all in Chinese official circles, which is doubtful, it would have been as a former base of the detested *wako*, the Japanese pirates who had raided China's coast for centuries.

In November 1614 Cocks recorded that the Hirado Chinese were endeavouring to open E.I.C. trade with China; in 1620 a blank royal letter brought on the *Hoseander* was, so Cocks believed, conveyed to China by the Hirado Chinese; in January 1617 delays were attributed to the Chinese Emperor's campaigns against the Tartars; in 1618 the delay was due to Dutch plundering of Chinese junks under English colours and in 1621 the delay was the result of a minor ascending the throne in Peking. (Farrington, 1991, 4).

Cocks was to rue his close dependence upon, and trust in, Li Tan before he left Hirado. Using a word derived from the Persian *na-khuda*, a skipper, the E.I.C. Council at Batavia wrote petulantly to Cocks in 1623: 'The China Nocheda hath too long deluded you through your owne simplicitie to give creditt unto him'. (Thompson, 1883, II, 341). At what point, though, *was* Cocks guilty of simplicity in accepting Li Tan's assurances? Every excuse given was plausible.

The undying hope of trading with China meant a great deal to Cocks, who was thoroughly realistic about the implications of failing to achieve this immensely desirable end. At the beginning of 1617 he wrote:

> 'And were it not for hope of trade into China, or for procuring som benefit from Syam, Pattania and Cochin China, it were noe staying in Japon. Yet it is certen here is silver enough & may be carid out at pleasure, but then we must bring them comodeties to ther lyking'. (Farrington, 1991,1)

The hopes of procuring access to the China market sustained Richard Cocks in many a bleak hour. He wrote to John Brown at Pattani that he was 'aweary of the place' and were it not for the hope of entry to the Chinese market, he 'he would rather depart from hence to-night than tarry till to-(morrow).' (Massarella, 1990, 195)

Over the years, Cocks recorded payments and loans to Li Tan and his family totalling 4,826 taels; probably more was paid over. Richard Wickham, another astute man, accepted Li's claims at face value, readily believing Li's claim to have spent his own money in the quest to open trade between the E.I.C. and China. When, eventually, the Hirado factory was abandoned, Li Tan and his clan were among the most conspicuous debtors, though whether they owed more or less than the Matsuura seems open to question. (Massarella, 1990, 181-3)

It has been claimed after careful computation that Li Tan owed the English factory 6,636 taels at the time the Hirado factory closed. (Farrington, 1991, 1554)

Even when the closure of the Hirado factory was inevitable, Cocks retained his optimism. In December 1622, he wrote; 'And our friend Andrea Dittis, the China Captain, still mentayneth that our nation may have trade into China yf they will, but not the Hollanders; which God grant may once take effect.'

Tempest Peacock died violently on the coast of Chochin-China in 1614, probably the first English-speaker to die in part of what was later to become Vietnam. The circumstances of his death remain uncertain but the likelihood is that he was killed in reprisal for an earlier Dutch attack on a local village. There is evidence to suggest he disliked Richard Cocks.

Richard Wickham travelled to Okinawa with Adams aboard the *Sea Adventure* in 1614-15 in what was intended to be a trading voyage to Siam. He left Japan in February 1617, dying in Bantam in the autumn of 1618 wealthy enough to infuriate the E.I.C. who assumed that his estate, valued at £1,400, must have been acquired dishonestly. After legal moves in England, the estate was released to his mother in 1624. In fairness to Wickham, he had shown his mettle in the service of the E.I.C. and knew from experience how precarious life could be in that service. He appears to have had a distant connection with Sir Thomas Smythe, something that was eventually to serve his mother in good stead. He had served in the Fourth Voyage, during the course of which he was captured by the Portuguese while taking in-shore soundings in Zanzibari waters. Taken to Goa, he was seen by a French traveller, François Pyrand, who described him as 'a man of proud and noble bearing, like a captain'. Taken to Lisbon along with other prisoners in August 1610, he managed to escape from the house of the Persian ambassador to the Spanish Court where he had been lodged after getting to known the ambassador *en route* to Europe. John Saris perceived Wickham as capricious and unscrupulously avaricious after a dubious incident involving possible forgery of a deceased sailor's will. One of his brothers, William, also served on the E.I.C.'s Eighth Voyage but died aboard the *Hector* in April 1612.

(Massarella, 1990, 143-4). Among the first of Wickham's activities in Japan was the establishment of an outlet for the Hirado factory's goods in Edo. Inexplicably, Adams advised him to move the bulk of these goods by sea, something the Dutch never did, and they were delayed by bad weather at Toba. In the meantime, the Dutch had taken a sufficiency of their goods to Edo overland and had saturated the market temporarily provided by the *tozama-daimyo*, or 'Outside Lords', whom Ieyasu obliged to spend their resources upon public works in Edo in addition to several other places. Although Wickham was initially inclined to doubt Adams' good faith in this instance, Richard Cocks persuaded him to set his misgivings aside. Richard Wickham certainly engaged in private trade on a fairly substantial scale considering that his salary was a modest £20 a year, considerably less than that of Peacock, whose salary was £50. Just before Saris' departure from Japan, Wickham demanded a substantial salary increase. Saris offered him an increase to £40 which Wickham scorned to accept, his wages remaining unaltered at £20. In January 1617, he claimed in a letter to Sir Thomas Smythe that his salary was barely sufficient for six months' expenses and that he would be 'ashamed to looke my ffrends in the face having spent my time to little purpose.'

On the first attempted voyage to Siam, which succeeded only in reaching Okinawa, Wickham brought ambergris back from the islands to trade on his own account, in addition to that which he brought back to trade for the E.I.C.'s account. This infuriated Cocks, although Cocks himself engaged in private trading in a modest way, largely because it was so blatant. Cocks' remonstrations had no effect on Wickham, who told Cocks to balance '. . .my gains made in Japon, or since my coming from England, with my losses and expenses, continually posting from place to place upon the Honourable Company their business by your appointment.' (Massarella, 1990, 227)

Wickham engaged in private trading; he differed from Richard Cocks primarily in being far more successful at it. Pieter Nuyts, the ill-fated Dutch Commander of Zeelandia, the Dutch fort on Taiwan, also proclaimed that he 'had not come to the Indies to eat hay' and it was generally accepted in the Dutch Indies that the accounts of remote factories were fraudulently kept and company assets used in private dealings. (Scammel,

1981, 414) So extensive were private dealings aboard Iberian vessels that commanders who captured them took great pains to search every nook and cranny for contraband being conveyed illegally to Seville or Lisbon. Individual clerics in Portuguese India engaged in private trade, as did preachers in the employ of the E.I.C. Sometimes private traders grew astoundingly rich; Augustine Spalding, the E.I.C. factor at Bantam and Adams' correspondent, was assumed by contemporaries to have made at least £28,000 from private trade in little over a decade. Remarkably, he extricated himself by voluntarily paying the E.I.C. a fine of a paltry £900, thus evading prosecution. It should not be assumed that clerical involvement in Portuguese maritime trade was necessarily for the benefit of the clerics' order. Individual clerics could and did trade in pepper in Portuguese India, defying royal decrees by so doing. In the 1630s, one of the inquisitors was among the clergy residing in India who were accused of such trade. (Pearson, 1987, 49)

Richard Wickham's letters reveal a man of sharp intelligence, keen business sense and ready wit. Writing in 1616, of Hasegawa Sahioye, the Governor of Nagasaki, he observed '. . .he hath shaved his hayre, & I doe not doubt but he will give his guttes a shaving before a yeare com about, for neyther he nor any of his kindred is in favour. . .' and, writing to Cocks about Matsudaira Tadanao, whose infatuation with a singing-girl had led him to purchase her release, he observed Matsudaira 'hath payed her master 10,000 *tayes* in oban. I would I had the money & it makes no matter who has the woman &c.' This was a truly vast sum to pay for a concubine, no matter how beguiling her charms. In February 1614, the house the E.I.C. factors had rented from Li Tan for 76 taels for one monsoon, or six months, was bought outright for 100 taels.

The 'English house at' Hirado would not have been an impressive structure. Like all but the grandest and most opulent residences, it would have required constant patching and mending. Then, as now, most Japanese residences were essentially temporary structures, easily erected and as easily demolished, or destroyed by fire.

In addition to his duties as an employee of the E.I.C., Wickham was expected to be a propagandist in the anti-Iberian cause. Writing from Hirado in October 1615, Richard Cocks instructed Wickham, who was then at Suruga or Edo, to tell his Japanese hearers of the wickedness of the Spanish monarch:

> 'Yow may lawfully say that the King of Spaine usurpeth Portingall per force & keepeth the rightfull heares out, as he doth the lyke in other parts of the world & would do the lyke in Japan yf he could, & the padres are fitt instrumentes to stur up the people to rebellion. Harp upon this stringe but be sure to take heed they secretly doe yow no mischeefe.' (Farrington, 1991, 324)

For someone as suspicious as Cocks not infrequently was, it was appropriate that he should warn Wickham against Jesuit or Franciscan revenge, which he probably thought of in terms of assassination or clandestine poison. The instructions to Wickham need to be judged in their context; the major part of the letter consists of instructions to Wickham to do his utmost to obtain the release of the Italian Damiano Marina and the Castilian Juan de Llevana from confinement aboard the Macau carrack *Nossa Senhora de Vida*, where they were confined as traitors.

William Eaton appeared in danger of execution after mortally wounding a Japanese in a dispute over the price asked for a consignment of timber in 1616 but was released without punishment at the instance of the Matsuura. He sailed to Siam twice while in Japan and left Hirado at the closure of the E.I.C. factory in 1623. His young son, William, appears to have left Japan a short while later aboard a Dutch vessel; the younger William subsequently studied at Cambridge.

Like the other E.I.C. factors, Eaton engaged in private trade. He and William Adams operated a modest lacquer-ware syndicate which by May 1617 had produced 27 taels 5 *mas* for each of the partners.

Walter Cawarden is presumed to have died at sea after fleeing from the attack in which Tempest Peacock died. Knowledgeable about gold and silver, he was greatly liked by Richard Cocks. Edmund Sayers sailed three times to south-east Asia while serving at Hirado, each time with Adams. He left Japan at the time of the factory's closure in 1623 and died either in the Indies or at sea while bound for Europe from Surat, in Gujerat. He fathered a daughter, Joan, while in Japan. Among Sayers' first endeavours in the service of the Hirado factor was an abortive effort to open trade to Korea *via* the island of Tsushima which lies between

Kyushu and Korea. Although Cocks had hopes of pursuing the prospect of trade with Korea, and possibly China as well, by means of Tsushima, this came to nothing. The Sō clan, *daimyo* of Tsushima, wanted to keep all the Korean trade in their hands. In any event, such trade as existed was carefully regulated by the Koreans; Pusan was the only port open for trade and the manner and volume of trade was strictly regulated on the Korean side. There was no room for outsiders, as the Dutch had earlier found. Cocks' view that Adams had encouraged the Dutch to trade with Korea through Tsushima was a misunderstanding on Cocks' part, as was his observation that the Dutch 'have some secret trade in Corea, or else are very likely to have'. (Satow, 1900, 170; Massarella, 1990, 152; Farrington, 1991,227)

The Sō, the *daimyo* clan of Tsushima, were fearless in the interests of their island realm. Ancestors of theirs had died defending the islands against the Mongols in 1274 and 1281, as well as against Korean and Chinese pirates. No less intrepidly, in 1606 the Sō had forged a letter from 'the king of Japan' to the King of Korea, re-establishing ruptured relations. Cocks' efforts to speak to the members of a Korean embassy to the *Bakufu* were, he noted, foiled by the 'king of Tushma', who was determined not to permit any interloper to deprive the Sō of the slightest fraction of trade with Korea.

The strategic importance of Tsushima, midway between Korea and the Japanese islands, led the Russian Imperial Navy to attempt occupation or annexation in 1861. Sir Rutherford Alcock, the British Minister to the Tokugawa court, insisted that the Russians evacuate their landing party, which they did, aware that the British had a far stronger naval presence in the Pacific than they.

A British attempt to open direct trade with Korea by the simple expedient of sailing up the coast under a flag of truce proved unavailing, disappointingly. The Koreans were resolutely determined to have no dealings with outsiders except on terms of their own choosing. Ralph Coppendale, the Commander of the *Hoseander*, attempted to go ashore in a skiff under a white flag. The inhabitants of Cheju do, or *Quelpart*, were in no mood to receive uninvited callers on that August day in 1615. Two hundred horsemen – very well mounted, Rowland Thomas the purser recorded – accompanied by footmen dissuaded the landing with gunfire. Later in the seventeenth century, the Koreans held several Dutchmen captive for long periods, treating them with kindness and some bemusement but strictly forbidding them to leave. A small *Nihonmachi* existed at Pusan, associated with the Japanese trade through Tsushima, and there were trade links with China but Korea was determined to keep foreigners strictly at a distance.

William Nealson was not a factor as such. The book-keeper and steward of the factory and the residence, the 'English House' at Hirado, he was to die at Hirado in March 1620. Cocks found him noisy, argumentative and intemperate: 'Mr. Nealson, being drunk yistarnight (as he is seldom sober), fell a quarrelling with Mr. Totton and used him out of fation.' On Cocks intervening 'he fell out with me and cald me ould drunken asse, geveing me many thretnyng speeches not sufferable'. On another occasion, 'Mr. Nealson, being drunk (as very often he is the lyke, to my greefe), fell a brawling with the chirugion, Morris Jones, and cut his head with a dagger'. In July 1618, Nealson was enraged over something or other and 'fell into this frenzy, madd, or at best drunken, humour, and in my hearing rapt out an othe, by the blood of God, that let thenglish stand clear of hyme, for, yf they used hym in such sort, he would speed som of them'. Cocks, who was all too aware that the Hirado factory was failing to prosper and that he was the obvious scapegoat in the eyes of E.I.C. and that several of the Britons in Japan thought slightingly of his leadership, wrote: 'When God is my judge I have byn taxed with all thenglish in the cuntrey for suffering Mr. Nealson to abuze all men as he daylie doth. This much I though good to note downe, whether I live or dye, that truth may be knowne.' Astonishingly, Nealson left all his property to Cocks on his death in March 1620. Still more remarkably, Cocks wrote, 'And yf God had called me to His mercy before Mr. Nealson, then had he had as much of myne.' (Cooper, 1982, 129-130)

William Nealson, like John Saris, has attracted little favourable note on the part of historians and other writers. Cocks called him *Sturton* in a letter written in March 1614 to Wickham, meaning that he was a man given to violent quarrelling. Somewhat earlier, Nealson had written to Wickham that he had slept with Cocks' mistress Matinga, the '*fayr wife*', but advising him to be 'not a blabb of your toung'. Surprisingly, perhaps, so compromising a letter has survived when so much, like Adams' maps and charts, have not. Assuming that Nealson was telling the truth about Matinga, whose true name was probably the honorific *O matsu san*, it took Cocks a long time to be sufficiently upset to break with her; it was not until March 1621 that he felt betrayed and broke with her. Her charms, no less than her wiles, must have been of a high order.

As in a Restoration comedy, Matinga's escapades with men other than Cocks were brought to his attention by her servant, Otto, or *Oto*, a bond servant whom Cocks promptly freed in recognition of her betrayal of her mistress; Cocks laconically noted that Matinga had 'abused her selfe with vj or 7 persons, as apereth under 3 witnesses.' (Thompson, 1883, II, 144-5; Farrington, 1991, 132) After Cocks had left Japan in 1623, Oto wrote a letter to him which has survived the intervening years between her age and our own. She recalls his kindness and apparently expresses the desire to leave Japan and be with him once more: 'Will you be kind enough to arrange for me to make my livelihood there?' (Farrington, 1991, 955)

John Saris, the commander, or *General*, of the *Clove*, left Japan in December 1613. Despite his brief stay in the country, his written account of his journey to Japan, his dealings with the Matsuura clan of Hirado, his meetings with Ieyasu and Hidetada and his observations of Japan and the prospects for successful British trade there, make fascinating reading to the present day. After his return *via* Bantam, Saris never sailed to the Indies again.

Saris did as much as anyone of any nationality to ensure that the E.I.C. factory at Hirado was never a commercial success; the advice he gave the E.I.C. in London resulted in grotesquely inappropriate cargoes being sent aboard the *Hoseander*, *Thomas* and *Advice*. Wickham, in 1617, wrote: 'Yf we were lerned alchemists we could not so soon turne mettles into silver as the Hon'ble Company (being deluded) are bouldly confident that we can turne these idle comodytys into mony.'

In December 1614, the East India Company considered the complaint that Saris had been 'scantinge of his people' and considered that he had acted prudently, considering that the voyage was likely to prove a long one and that it was better to impose strict rationing at the outset than to risk 'wante and scarcetie' at the end. It is noteworthy that, after a near-mutiny caused by complaints about allowances of food in the Red Sea, Saris kept daily note of the issuing of rations; *Allowance Beere and Biskett, 1 meale porke, 1 meale Rice and oyle* being typical entries. Nonetheless, there were bitter complaints in harbour at Hirado that men aboard a ship in port in a fertile country should not be obliged to subsist on the sort of fare that was all that was available in mid-ocean. (Satow, 1900, 116; Farrington, 1991, 238)

Having contrived to allay the thoroughly justified suspicions of the East India Company's Governors that he had engaged in extensive private trade in the course of the Eighth Voyage, Saris was awarded a 'gratification' of 500 marks (£333.6.8d). Saris left the Company's employ and died, relatively wealthy, in 1643. (Satow, 1900, lxxiv; Farrington, 1991, 1569) Saris had another minor difficulty concerning goods brought back from Japan, as the Court Minutes of the East India Company recorded in January 1615. 'Greate speeches haveinge bene made of certaine bookes brought home by Capt'ne Saris', there was consternation among the puritans who were then, and were to remain until the Restoration, the dominant moral influence in the City of London. Still, the Governor had 'p'cured them from Capt'ne Saris and shut them up ever since'. It being agreed and decreed that 'such wicked spectacles are not fostered and mayntayned by any of this Companie', Saris' 'lascivious bookes and pictures' were burned in front of everyone. If in scroll form, these would have been *osokusu-no-e*, otherwise *shunga* and *makura-e* would be the more familiar term for these stimulating illustrative works. While they may have been of Chinese origin and a gift from, or purchased from, the Chinese at Hirado, illustrated erotic manuscripts were known in Japan from the twelfth or thirteenth century onwards. (Farrington, 1991; 241, 276) It is an indication of changing attitudes that earlier writers about Saris have slighted his reputation on this account. Censure, if any is deserved, belongs to the Council of the East India Company; such things could have been profitably disposed of quietly. The brief saga of Saris' *shunga* recalls an incident which occurred at the time of the *Clove*'s arrival in Japan; various Christian women of Hirado were touring the *Clove* and mistakenly worshipped '*a picture of Venus. . .very lasciviously set out and in a large frame*' in Saris' cabin, believing it to be '*Our Ladie*' as Saris recorded. Was this 'very lasciviously set out' picture provided by the E.I.C., or was it Saris' own property, as seems more probable? (Boxer, 1951, 306)

Acting on Saris' claim that the Japanese were fond of lascivious paintings, the *Thomas*, which arrived at Hirado in 1616, carried a number in a mixed cargo of thoroughly inappropriate goods. One depicted Venus and Adonis, another was of '*Venus Sleeping with two saters*'. (Massarella, 1990, 194)

Posterity has not treated John Saris kindly. His journal does not reveal a likeable character, his relations with Adams were generally cool. His attitude towards Adams was dismissive and condescending, as Adams perceived clearly; '...The reason I would not go with him (*Saris*) was for dyuers injerues doun against me; the which were thinges to me veri strang and vnloked for, which thinges (*to*) write I ceass, leuing it to others to mak rellaccion thereof.' (Rundell, 1850, 68) Saris was conspicuously better-educated than Adams, as well as being approximately fifteen years younger and of a more elevated social class. Social class was of less obvious importance in Elizabethan and Jacobean England than was to be the case in later centuries but it is interesting to note the scorn with which Richard Cocks, for example, wrote that the Dutch commanders in Japan were sons of brewers and 'close-stool' makers.

Adams did not immediately endear himself to the Hirado Britons. In the first place, they seem to have assumed that he had dallied unnecessarily *en route* from Suruga. In fact the journey had taken him seventeen days. The *daimyo* of Hirado blamed contrary winds for Adams' late arrival; it may be presumed that the *daimyo* was serious when he told John Saris 'the wynds westerly was the occatyon he came not.' (Farrington, 1990, 1003) The luckless messenger who carried Saris' letter to Adams was thought to have dawdled *en route* unjustifiably and was banished from Hirado in consequence. Letters could be, and were, conveyed throughout the country by private agencies, *hikyaku-ya*, which carried private correspondence slowly and cheaply between all major population centres. However, anything of importance or urgency was carried expensively and much faster by private courier.

The obvious fact that Hirado was such a distance from major markets was a strong argument against settling the E.I.C. factory there, as Cocks was belatedly to note with some exasperation.

Relations between John Saris and William Adams were poor from the first, although a temporary improvement was discernible later; Saris stayed at Adams' 'lordship' at Hemi briefly but neglected to describe the place at any length.

Saris wrote: '...it is generally thought emongest us that (*Adams*) is a naturalised Japanner. I intreated him to make choise of anye chambers in the howse, and to aquant the Cooke what dyatt he best affected, and it should be provided. And Mr. Cocks and whoe else of the marchants should at his pleasure accompanye him in the towne. He intreated me to pardon him: he would for 3 or fowre dayes repare to his cullors, which he had put out at an ould wyndo in a poore howse, being a St. Georg made of course cloath, nether would admit of anye marchant or other to accompanye him...' This behaviour on Adams' part was disagreeable to the factors, who might have expected Adams to be overjoyed to be in the company of his fellow-countrymen after so many years. Certainly there was an element of woeful misunderstanding involved; in declining to be accompanied to his lodgings in the 'poore howse', Adams inadvertently affronted Cocks and the others, they 'thinking that he thought them not good enoffe to walke with him.' It has been surmised that the house with the cross of St. George was the house of Adams' Hirado mistress, as distinct from his Japanese wife at Hemi, near Uraga, but evidence for this claim is lacking. It seems equally probable that he felt under an obligation to stay at the house of the *bugyo* Zenzaburo, whom Saris called Zanzibar, rather than offend the man. (Satow, 1900, 109; Sadler, 1984, 260; Massarella, 1990, 112)

For whatever reason, Saris and Adams found one another's company disagreeable. Saris claimed that Adams was only fit to be sent to Ieyasu's court as interpreter when he was not commanding the Hirado factory's junk and Adams flatly refused to accompany Saris to England because of the antipathy between the two men. Adams also observed that he desired to become wealthier before returning to his native country. Adams was, however, all but indispensable to Saris and Cocks, however much the former might suspect Adams' servant of theft and complicity in aiding the *Clove*'s fugitives to seek refuge with the Iberians in Nagasaki. (Satow, 1900, 163)

These seven deserters, five Englishmen and two Dutchmen,

had taken the *Clove*'s skiff and deserted to the sanctuary provided by the Spaniards and Portuguese at Nagasaki early in October; 'The occasion they said was for that they which had command over them used them more like dogges than men'; adding further, that if 'but twentie resolute Spaniards would take the matter in hand, with a small boat or two they might easily take our shippe'. (Satow, 1900, 163)

It proved possible to recover the skiff but the men slipped away to Manila or Macau, as Saris reported. (Satow, 1900, 176) Deserters forfeited their wages, naturally. When the father of Christopher Evans, one of the deserters, petitioned the East India company for his son's wages in 1615 he was refused, according to due precedent, but was awarded a paltry forty shillings from the poor-box as he 'seemed to bee in necessitie'. (Satow, 1900, lxix) Evans and another of the deserters, John Bowles the quarter-master, had been Spanish galley-slaves together and had distinguished themselves as notorious troublemakers during the *Clove*'s voyage. (Farrington, 1991, 102)

Paradoxically, one of the Dutch in the Moluccas had attempted to defect to the *Clove* on its voyage to Japan, offering to persuade all the other Dutch on the island of Bachan, 'the Captain and preacher excepted', to come with him. For some ill-explained reason, Saris did not take the man, probably fearing serious trouble with the Dutch had he done so, but he took the opportunity to learn a great deal about the local trade. This man, Leuen Martson, felt himself ill-requited by his employers, who paid him only 'in victualls' and who 'inforsed' his local wife from time to time, they having obliged him to marry her in the first place. (Satow, 1900, 24-5; Massarella, 1990, 106)

Some while before the encounter with the disgruntled Martson, Saris had offered room aboard the *Clove* to one Richard Welden, who had been in the Moluccas since leaving the *Expedition* there, the *Expedition* having left England in the Fifth Voyage in 1609. Welden was by now in the employ of the ruler of Boeton. Saris 'resolved to have taken him along with me' but Welden made an 'exceeding lamentatyon' at this prospect, protesting that he was 'in the waye of doing himselfe good heare' so Saris gave him some European clothes and bade him farewell. In Cocks' letter of November 1613 to Sir Thomas Smythe,

Welden was described as one in the service of the ruler of Boeton, or *Butung* or *Buton*, 'for whome, it is said, he hath doone very desperate service & is in great creddit w'th hym.' (Farrington, 1991, 96) Welden, who had a native consort, subsequently returned to England and was appointed chief factor at Banda. (Satow, 1900, 15-16; Massarella, 1990, 105; Farrington, 1991, 96-102) The role of deserters and prisoners-of-war in the east is a fascinating one; the defection of a few gunners to a local sovereign could alter the balance of power quite suddenly, as the Portuguese found to their cost in India.

The transfer of technology between Europe and Asia was really accomplished in such areas of expertise as their ship-building and gun-founding. European renegades taught both skills to the subjects of local rulers willingly; Gujerati ship-builders emulated European techniques of construction and Asians enthusiastically recovered guns from wrecked European ships, Diu in India alone possessing over 100 such guns by 1503. (Scammel, 1981, 265)

The matter of the deserters apart, Adams and Saris had other differences. Adams was keen that the E.I.C. factory should be established at Uraga; Saris assumed that this was for Adams personal convenience, knowing of Uraga's proximity to Hemi, where Adams possessed the 'lordship' Ieyasu had bestowed upon him. There was the matter of Adams seeming to favour the Japanese and Dutch – and even, on occasion – the Spaniards and Portuguese over his own countrymen. There was the matter of Adams trying to sell a ship at Uraga to Saris for more than the latter was willing to pay. There was the matter of Adams' salary, a squalid piece of petty haggling which should never have happened. There was also the question of court etiquette, which Adams understood and Saris did not.

Ieyasu's 'privileges' of October 1613 specified that the E.I.C. factors were at liberty to use any port in Japan and stated that the E.I.C. factors were at liberty to choose a place in Edo to erect houses and warehouses, implying that this land would be given to them by the *Bakufu*. (Farrington, 1991, 88) As a proposition, this was a far better deal than Hirado turned out to be. Apart from paying rent to Li Tan, alias Andrea Dittis, the *China Captain*, and enduring the ceaseless importunities of Matsuura and their numerous retainers, the E.I.C. at Hirado necessarily incurred substantial costs travelling to and from Edo, where they were expected to offer gifts of the same kind they would have been required to give had they settled in Edo, or a port close to it such as Uraga or Hemi. Ieyasu favoured the factory being established close to Edo or at Suruga.

The importance of foreign trade to the Matsuura *daimyo* of Hirado is illustrated by the fact that although an earlier *daimyo*, Takanobu, who died in 1598, had been described by the Jesuits as 'an astute abhorrer of the Christian faith, a gentile to the bones', he had unhesitatingly offered permission to the Augustinians to build a convent on the island provided that this resulted in trade from Manila being brought to the domain. (Massarella, 1990, 108)

It is a delicious irony that Adams was writing from Hirado rather than from Edo, Hemi or Uraga, when he wrote to Augustine Spalding at Bantam in January 1613:

> '. . .yf a ship do coum, let heer not coum wheer the Hollanders (are), for it is not good, but a very bade place for sall of goodes. But yf a ship do oum leet her coum for the esterly p't of Japan. . lying in latitude 35*d* 10*m*, whear the King and the Emperour court is; for coum our ships to Ferando, whear the Hollanders bee, it is farr to the courte, about 2301 a werysoum way and fare. The citti of Edo lyeth in 36, and about this esterlly p't of the land thear be the best harbors and a cost soo clear as theayr be no sholdes nor rokes ½ a myll from the maynland. It is good allso for sall of marchandis. . .for ships and security; for w'ch mysellf I hav been alongs the cost in the shipping that I have made for the Emperour, that I have experienc all (*along the?*) cost (*from?*) Ozakis (*and?*) Sakay to Edo to, w'ch lieth in 36*d* &c.' (Farrington, 1991, 78)

Assuring his reader in distant Bantam of the welcome the E.I.C. ships would receive, Adams added: 'Yf it be that there coum a ship neer unto the estermost p't, let them inquir for me. I am called in the Japann tonge Angin Sama. By that nam am I knowen all the see cost allonge, and feear not to coum neer the mayn for you shall have barkes w'th pillots that shall carry you wheer you will. . .' (Farrington, 1991, 79)

Saris considered Uraga an excellent port, noting that ships might ride as safely there as in the Thames at London and that the approaches were safe. The only shortcoming of Oring Gave, or *Oringgaw* as he termed Uraga, was that Uraga was 'not so well replenished with victuall and fleshmeat as Firando is'. The strongest point of all in favour of Uraga was that it was 'but fourteene or fifteen leagues' from Edo. (Farrington, 1991, 1019) It is the more remarkable that Saris did not order the factors to move from Hirado forthwith; only his antipathy towards Adams can explain the decision. Adams, acting as a commercial agent for the Spaniards on occasion, attempted to interest Saris in 'the hull of a shippe w'ch was the Spannyards', asking 100 pounds sterling for it. He would 'abate nothing thereof' and Saris declined to purchase it. It may well have been that Adams *was* asking too much but there was no chance that he was trying to sell Saris and the E.I.C. an unseaworthy craft, since he would be sailing in it.

Concerning his salary as an employee of the E.I.C. factory at Hirado, Adams was offered 80 pounds sterling a year, rather than the 12 pounds per month he had asked when requested to name an appropriate monthly salary. There was some undignified haggling about the figure. As Adams recorded, Saris 'w'th much adoo agreed w'th me for a 100*li* the year.' (Farrington, 1991, 114)

The remembrance which Saris wrote and left with Cocks suggests a deep dislike of Adams;

> 'And pro Mr. Adames he is onlye fitting to be m'r of the junke & to be used as a linguist at corte when you have no imployment pro him at sea. It is nessesarye that you stirr him, his condition being well knowne unto you as to myself, otherwayes you shall have little service of him, the counterye affording great libertie, whereunto he is much affected. The forsed agreement I have made with him, as you knowe, could not be eschudd, the Flemings and Spanyards making false p'fers of great intertainment, and himselfe more affected to them then hes owne natyon, we holye (*destitute*) of language.' (Farrington, 1991, 120)

Later, in the same letter, Saris counselled Cocks against trusting Adams with E.I.C. money without constant supervision and instructing Cocks not to heed any request Adams might make visit Suruga to obtain specific permission from Tokugawa Ieyasu to leave Japan temporarily aboard the Company's junk, '. . .for his wish is but to have the Companye beare his charges to his wife.' At the same time, Saris was realistic enough to understand, and to impress on Cocks, that losing Adams' services would prove a major impediment, dryly noting that were Adams to insist that he needed to travel to Edo, close to where his wife and family resided at Hemi, Cocks should 'make a vertue of a nessecitye and let him goe.'

Adams' dislike of Saris was not the only reason he chose not to return to England aboard the *Clove*. In the contract of employment he signed with Cocks, Tempest Peacock and Richard Wickham at Hirado in November 1613, Adams is quoted as saying that '. . .his desyre is to goe home for his native contrey of England, but not in this shipp; only his stayinge is for a certen tyme to get somethinge, havinge hetherto spent his tyme soe many yeares in vayne & wold not now goe home w'th an emptie purse. . .' (Farrington, 1991, 94) In Cocks' letter to Sir Thomas Smythe and the East India Company in London, written from Hirado in the same month, Cocks says of Adams that he '. . .aleadged he was a pore man and that he had spent 14 yeares allready to now purpose & now wold be loth to retorne for his contrey a beggar. . .'

In his letter to Thomas Best in Bantam, written in December 1613, Adams wrote of 'soum discourtissies' offered to him by Saris, adding that he had obtained Ieyasu's permission to leave Japan; Ieyasu '. . .gave me leav in all frindship to tarri or to goo.' (Farrington, 1991, 113)

Saris found the etiquette demanded at Japanese formal occasions trying in the extreme, although he had Adams on hand to advise him. Saris tried his best to insist that James' letter should be handed directly to Ieyasu. On being told this was impermissible, Saris threatened to return forthwith to his lodgings, which earned Adams a rebuke for having failed to instruct Saris adequately in the accepted procedure for such matters. In the end, the letter was handed to Honda Masazumi, Ieyasu's secretary, who then passed it to Ieyasu. Ieyasu touched it to his forehead, thanked Saris and bade him withdraw. (Massarella, 1990, 114) Subsequently, Adams translated James I's letter from English to Japanese written in the *kana* syllabary; it was then re-written in *kanji*, Chinese characters with an admixture of *kana*. (Farrington, 1991, 63)

The episode concerning the amended, and inferior, privileges awarded to the Hirado factory after Ieyasu's death, which were only translated and fully grasped sometime after Cocks had received them from Hidetada, makes it probable that Adams' knowledge of the complexities of written Japanese in official documents was rudimentary. It is possible, however, that Adams had assumed, as had Cocks and Eaton, that the privileges were unaltered and had not bothered to examine the *Bakufu*'s document with adequate care. (Massarella, 1990, 198)

Soon after the arrival of the *Clove* at Hirado, Richard Cocks arranged to rent a house from Li Tan, the 'China Captain' or leader of the Chinese trading community resident on the island. This building was later purchased outright. Additions and repairs were made to it, neighbouring houses were bought and demolished and considerable numbers of men from the locality were employed to complete the building programme; by June 1616 over 3,897 taels had been spent on the work. This local expenditure and the various gifts the family received was of more importance to the Matsuura than any considerations of prestige that the presence of the Dutch and the British factories bestowed on an otherwise insignificant place. The expenditure on the Hirado factory, together with the goodwill the E.I.C.'s expenditure had created, naturally had the effect of committing the Britons to staying at Hirado, in spite of the island's obvious shortcomings. Unlike expatriate Britons of a later generation, the Hirado factors appear to have possessed no sentiments of racial superiority towards the Japanese. Apart from their sexual liaisons, in which emotional ties necessarily created close bonds, they worked with and depended upon, Japanese and other non-Europeans on a daily basis. The standard of living and life expectancy in Japan did not differ markedly from that which they would have known in Britain; the concept of Europe as the most civilised of places did not exist and probably never entered their heads. In all likelihood, everyday dealings between the Hirado Britons and their Hirado hosts were warm and friendly; they liked some Japanese, disliked others, loved still others and, inevitably, distrusted and hated some, too. The distance between expatriate males and the local populace in the East began to widen when European women began to cross the oceans in large numbers, a phenomenon still far in the future.

Richard Cocks called the Tokugawa regime a '*terrany*' with some justice. However, Ieyasu's government and that of his successors, differed from centralised, authoritarian, European governments primarily in its efficiency. Adams, whom John Saris considered to be virtually a naturalised Japanese, had observed in a letter written in 1611, '. . .their justice is severely executed without any partialitie upon transgressors of the law. They are governed in great civilitie. I meane, not a land better governed in the world by civill policie.' (Cooper, 1965, 6) It is probable that his fellow-countrymen shared his sentiments to a greater or lesser extent. Cocks, who was a man with a genuinely kind nature and who interceded for the lives of thieves condemned to execution more than once, wrote 'Yf it were not for this strict justice, it were no liveing amongst them, they are so villanouse desperate,' a somewhat pessimistic view of the Japanese character. (Cooper, 1965, 159) Adams noted that murderers were readily denounced by the offer of a cash reward for information leading to their discovery; '. . .for the lukar of so moch monny it coumes to light,' adding that Japanese cities were so safe that one might walk through them at night without fear. This could not have been said of Elizabethan or Jacobean London, as any contemporary would have known. Street riots in Elizabethan and Jacobean England were violent and bloody, if infrequent. During at least one apprentices' riot in Elizabeth's reign apprehended rioters were hung on the spot by the sheriff's men. The Europeans in Japan in Cocks' time were not unduly hesitant about inflicting severe penalties. In 1615, Cocks recorded that the Dutch had 'cut a slave of theirs a-pieces for theft, per order of justice'. (Thompson, 1883, I, 19)

Adams was not the only seventeenth-century Englishman to compare Asian standards favourably with those prevailing at home. Peter Mundy, the chief factor on John Weddel's 1637 voyage to China, wrote of the Chinese Empire; '*This country may be said to excel in these particulars: antiquity, largeness, richness, healthiness, plentifulness. For arts and manners of government, I think no kingdom in the world comparable to it, considered altogether.*' (Coates, 1989, 54)

When the *Clove* sailed from Hirado in December 1613, the main goods left to form the greater part of the new factory's stock – the rest being comprised of money – were 50 pieces and remnants of broadcloth, 6057 pieces of Indian cloth, 124 elephant tusks, 315.14 peculs of pepper, 46 barrels of gunpowder, 238 hundredweight of lead, 6 cannon with shot, 20 taels' weight of gold, 2 pipes of Zant oil and 1188 pounds of tin. (Farrington, 1991, 5)

Unfortunately, this sort of stock offered few attractions to Japanese purchasers; being 'not veri vendibel', as Adams tactfully expressed it. The Dutch and Iberians had flooded the market with broadcloth and ivory, tin offered no profit, Japan was self-sufficient in cotton cloth and the demand for pepper and spices was modest. Adams' advice was disregarded; future British ships, such as the *Hoseander*, the *Thomas* and the *Advice* brought more of the same. It was not until the short-lived Anglo-Dutch alliance, the period of the Fleet of Defence, that the E.I.C. Hirado factory did well and that was a temporary phenomenon brought about by the blockade of Manila and the plundering of Chinese junk traffic. The English half-share of the total plunder was nearly £40,000, ten times the amount Cocks was alleged to have wasted during the decade of the factory's existence. (Farrington, 1991, 12) When the E.I.C. factory closed, it was owed 12,000 taels.

Aboard the *Clove* when it left Japan were fifteen Japanese sailors provided, or recommended, by the Matsuura. Saris originally wanted twelve seamen but he evidently had second thoughts and decided a larger number would be justified. The *Clove* left Japan with a crew of sixty-nine, including George Peterson, a man returning home after nearly a quarter-century in Spanish service. (Massarella, 1990, 122)

Only eleven of the Japanese who had left Hirado aboard the *Clove* returned with the fleet commanded by Keeling. These eleven reached Hirado on the *Advice* in August 1617. On the 18th August, they got into a dispute with Adams about wages owed to them, one of them seizing Adams by the throat. (Farrington, 1991, 278)

Adams' dealings with his countrymen, so long-awaited, were usually more friendly than acrimonious except on those occasions when he was assumed to favour the interests of other Europeans or Japanese before the interests of the E.I.C. factory. Having signed a contract of employment with the Hirado factory, Adams considered himself bound by it so far as was commercially realistic; unlike Cocks and Wickham, he knew the country well and he was well aware of what was possible and what was totally unrealistic. Having obtained Ieyasu's express permission to leave Japan and return to England, Adams would seem to have concluded that no hero's welcome, knighthood or vast fortune awaited him there. Probably he decided to leave the decision until a later occasion, at least until the Hirado factory had started trading profitably.

Whatever the Hirado Britons occasionally thought and wrote about Adams' loyalty, for example Cocks' intemperate outburst to the effect that Adams esteemed the Dutch 'much better then us that are of his owne nation', Adams probably felt no inner conflict at all. He served the Hirado factory for the two years stipulated in his 1613 contract of employment and worked for Cocks and the other factors sporadically thereafter. It may be presumed that his later services were duly and adequately requited but the records are mute. Adams maintained cordial relations with the Dutch while in E.I.C. employment, but surviving letters do not suggest that commercial confidences were breached.

A junk, the *Sea Adventure,* was purchased, Saris having disdained to buy the Spanish ship at Uraga in which Adams had attempted to interest him. The *Sea Adventure* turned out to be a poor choice. Whether the ship Adams attempted to sell Saris would have been a better deal is an unanswerable question.

XII

CONFLICT AT HIRADO

During the *Clove*'s voyage to Hirado in 1613, relations with the Dutch in the Moluccas had been strained but relations between the Dutch and the E.I.C. factory at Hirado were cordial, even hospitable, if guarded from time to time. From the first, commercial rivalry marked the relationship; Saris' suggestion that the two factories at Hirado should sell cloth at the same price was briskly rejected by the Dutch, who promptly reduced their own prices to maintain market share. The Dutch were contented to watch the Britons attempt to open trade with Korea *via* Tsushima, an effort which proved as unavailing as the earlier Dutch attempt to do so.

Peace prevailed, however. Dutch ships carried letters written by Cocks and the other Englishmen, even if they opened some, as Cocks claimed. The Britons reciprocated. Presents were exchanged when ships arrived, a cargo of Dutch-owned ebony was shipped aboard the *Hoseander* at Hirado and carried to Bantam, freightage being charged for space and weight which would have otherwise have been wasted on ballast. (Massarella, 1990, 257) This straightforward commercial transaction earned Cocks the wrath of John Jourdain, the chief factor at Bantam. George Ball, who served as President in Bantam from March 1617 to November 1618, called the transaction, 'a haynos offence' and severe criticism of this nature probably did much to make Cocks wary of entering into commercial cooperation with the Dutch subsequently.

Friction arose over such issues as which of the two factories possessed the equivalent of diplomatic precedence when the *daimyo* of Satsuma visited Hirado. (Massarella, 1990, 258) This reflected thinking among men of Cocks' generation and background in England, who knew well just how much Holland owed the English in winning her independence;

Cocks tartly contrasting 'the mighty and powerfull governm't of the king of England' with that of Holland, a 'small state govend by a couty (*committee*)'. Like the rival Iberians before them, the Dutch and the British had taken their rivalry to the shores of Japan. In the waters of East Asia, the British were neither mighty nor powerful, as the Japanese were well able to judge.

Relations between the two factories deteriorated sharply. Whereas in March 1618, Jacques Specx, the chief of the V.O.C. factory at Hirado, could write to Jan Pieterszoon Coen stating that the Dutch and British in Hirado were 'good friends', in August of the same year the captured British ship *Attendance* was brought into Hirado harbour 'in a bravado & shot affe many guns out of her', as Cocks noted. Specx, who may have been surprised to see a captured British vessel brought into Hirado, offered the ship and its contents to Cocks, who rejected the offer with contempt, remarking that the commanders of the Dutch were evidently commanding men like Specx to be 'comune theevs'. Specx retorted that he valued Cocks' friendship and would endeavour to maintain good relations until he received orders to the contrary, when the Dutch would do 'as they thought good'; the period of open, if undeclared hostilities between the V.O.C. and the E.I.C. isolated the E.I.C. factory at Hirado for two years between 1618 and 1620.

Cocks and Nealson departed for Edo to protest to the *Bakufu*, efforts to persuade the Hirado Chinese to lodge a joint protest having proven unavailing. Adams, who had travelled to Edo with a Dutch party before the *Attendance*'s arrival, was contacted and asked to support his fellow-countrymen of the E.I.C. Although unwilling to do so, Adams complied unavailingly, just as he, or the Chinese or the Iberians, could have predicted. Cocks felt that Adams' sympathies were in doubt and called him 'altogether Holandized' prior to his efforts on the E.I.C. factory's behalf. The *Bakufu* referred the business to the Matsuura clan to adjudicate as best they could, Cocks having played a minor role in demonstrating Tokugawa legitimacy by delivering a present to Iemitsu, Hidetada's son. (Massarella, 1990, 260)

Early in 1619, another British ship, the *Swan*, was brought into Hirado as a prize. Accompanying the captured ship was a fleet of Dutch ships, six in all, the crews of which augmented the European population of the quiet town dramatically. Cocks and the Hirado factors were taunted with jibes, threats and catcalls. Three Englishmen aboard one of the Dutch ships escaped to the English house, prompting a Dutch demand to the *daimyo* for their return, a demand the *daimyo* rejected with the scornful suggestion that the Dutch take their complaint to the *Bakufu* if displeased. The Dutch, if Cocks' account is to be believed, 'ment to have entred our English howse & cut all our throates, w'ch they wanted but littell to have effected, geving 3 assalts against us in one day, they being 100 of them to 1 Englishman. Yet God preserved us from them, the Japoneses, our neighb'rs, taking our partes.' This account was written in March 1620 to the Clothworkers' Company of London. (Farrington, 1991, 776) This and the letters to Sir Thomas Wilson and Sir Thomas Smythe necessarily compressed events which took place over a period of two years and the dramatic attempted storming of the English house was, in all likelihood, a case of men hardened by over-indulgence in alcohol losing control, as Derek Massarella has suggested. (Massarella, 1990, 262) Still, even allowing for a degree of exaggeration on Cocks' part, the events were serious enough; Gourden, Payne and Williams were held captive aboard the *Angel*, the escape of the first two being facilitated by William Adams, as Cocks reported in his letter to Sir Thomas Smythe. (Farrington, 1991, 785) John Coaker, an Englishman, was wounded in an assault; 'a company of them entred our howse armed w'th piks, swordes and cattans, where they wounded John Coaker and another, thinking they hadd kild one of them, at least as they made their braggs after.'

Cocks and Specx were obliged to 'geve a writing in Japones before witnesses' that neither nation would abuse the other 'nether in word or deed' but soon afterwards, a Japanese was killed by a Dutch musket-shot while in a boat with Edmund Sayers, Coaker and Richard King not long after King had been seized by the Dutch and held a captive in their factory until the Matsuura seized Specx and imprisoned him until King's release.

The Matsuura were less distressed by Anglo-Dutch conflict than might have been imagined. The *daimyo* clan needed the trade and employment that the V.O.C. and E.I.C. factories brought and were willing to endure occasional rowdiness, commotion and even bloodshed if that was what the presence of the two factories entailed. Far from wishing the foreigners would take their business elsewhere, the Matsuura went to great lengths to ensure that both factories stayed in Hirado. Apart from commercial factors, there was the consideration of 'face'; so long as the Dutch and British were established at Hirado, Hirado was a place of some consequence. When, as eventually happened, first the British then the Dutch left the island, Hirado returned to being an quiet backwater of no great significance.

It was in the interests of the Matsuura to attempt to calm things down; the loss of either factory would have been a bitter loss to them. Cocks had already considered the merits of moving the E.I.C. factory to Nagasaki but was aware that the factory's loans to the Matsuura effectively checked a precipitate move to the more prosperous place.

Cocks made as much fuss as possible but was ignored; 'Yet from that tyme till now, there is nothing donne although I have divers tymes very instantly desired it of the kinge, whose best answer I eaver could gett was that the Hollanders hadd kild no Englishman but a Japonar, his owne vassale, w'ch yf he were content to pardon, what hadd I to do therw'th.' (Farrington, 1991, 786) Cocks alleged that the commander of the Dutch fleet, Adam Westerwood, had offered a reward of 50 reals to the man, or men, who assassinated Cocks, with an accompanying reward of 30 reals 'for the life of each other English m'rchant,' adding that some of the Dutch 'enformed me of the noble parentadg of their Lord Comander Westarwood, telling that his father is a close-stoole maker at Amstardam or thereaboutes, & the best of their other capt(ains) either sumakars', carpentars' or bearbrewards' sonnes. God blesse such an honorable wor'll generation, I meane God blesse me from them.' (Farrington, 1991, 778)

Snobbery apart, Cocks was justified in his apprehension about the Dutch. From the Dutch point of view, matters were more complex; the E.I.C. was attempting to establish a trading foothold in the Spice Islands and seizing market share in a region the Dutch had penetrated at great risk to themselves. The British could counter that Drake had traded in the Spice Islands long before the Dutch and that the seas were open to all. Paradoxically, the mutual suspicion and occasional hostility in the Far East was paralleled by proposals to unite the E.I.C. and the V.O.C.; negotiations were attempted in 1610, 1613 and 1615. Jan Dirckszoon Lam, the Dutch admiral, assured Cocks that if all that needed to be settled between the E.I.C. and the V.O.C. were purely financial questions, they 'could not chuse but sowne be decyded,' as Cocks recorded. Jan Pietersz Coen held that the English rather than the Iberians were the real threat to the V.O.C.'s interests in the Indies, however, and by early 1617, open hostilities had broken out over the E.I.C. presence on the island of Run in the Spice Islands; events in Hirado merely mirrored the outbreak of conflict further south.

Evidently, the Dutch assaults against the E.I.C. factory were sporadic in nature. William Eaton, writing to Cocks from Hirado in August 1619, remarked 'Wee are all in good health & the Duch quiett innowe etc.' (Farrington, 1991, 759)

In the period of undeclared war, the Dutch had the upper hand from the first; their mariners captured eleven British ships, including one laden with silver, while the E.I.C. fleet succeeded in capturing a single Dutch vessel.

During the period of hostilities at Hirado, the E.I.C. factory was effectively paralysed. The Dutch, however, were successfully combining trade and piracy; their business was doing well enough in spite of the problems which might have been caused by Chinese, Iberian and British complaints to the *Bakufu*. Even Coen expressed misgivings on this point in a letter of January 1619. Adams' role during this period was necessarily ambiguous. The Dutch regarded him as a Dutchman while the English of the Hirado factory were inclined to question his sympathies. The probability is that Adams attempted to distance himself from the contending parties except when there was no choice; he handled a formal complaint about the Dutch seizure of British shipping, for instance. By the time the *James Royal* brought formal notice of the signed peace accord to Hirado, in July 1620, Adams had died. It was aboard this ship that the first instalment of Adams' legacy to Deliverance, his daughter in England, was sent home.

The Dutch penchant for robbery with violence on the high seas had a simple purpose: to oblige the Chinese to open their ports to Dutch trade. In this, it proved a failure until the Dutch seized the Pescadores, or *Penghu Liedao*, in 1622 following the disastrously unsuccessful attack on Macau. The occupation of the Pescadores and the subsequent Dutch settlement of Zeelandia on Taiwan, near present-day Tainan, in 1624 after the negotiated evacuation of the Pescadores, transformed the Dutch from being a marginal, disruptive force in East Asian trade profiting from the plunder of Chinese and Iberian vessels to full participants in the trade.

The period of open hostility between the Dutch and the British which so perturbed Richard Cocks was brought to an end by a short-lived alliance which was, in turn, rudely broken when word of the Amboina massacre of 1623 reached the ears of the E.I.C.

Eaton, writing from Hirado in December 1620, hoped that the peace between the two companies would lead to a joint Anglo-Dutch monopoly of trade; '. . .nowe I hoope by the helpe of God that in a smale tyme all the trade of the Easte Indies will be in yours & in the Hollanders' hands'. (Farrington, 1991, 817) Cocks, typically, wrote 'God be pr'sed for it', adding the hope that the Dutch would 'fermly follow the orders prescribed, as I make no dowbt the English will doe, and then their will noe occation of discontent be offered hereafter.'

XIII

ADAMS IN JAPAN

The years William Adams spent in Japan between the landfall of the stricken *Liefde* in 1600 and the arrival of Adams' long-awaited fellow-countrymen aboard the *Clove* in 1613 are poorly documented, so far as the day-to-day details of Adams' life are concerned. Precise dates are lacking; no record exists which states exactly when Adams was granted *hatamoto* status, married his Japanese wife or became prosperous. There was no secular chronicler who was the equivalent of the meticulous Jesuits, other than, after 1613, Richard Cocks, whose Diaries are incomplete as well as capricious.

After the crew of the *Liefde*, following what Adams described as a mutiny, went their separate ways, Adams was forbidden to leave Japan, as were other members of the *Liefde*'s crew. Whether this prohibition was rigorously enforced is unknown; some members of the crew are recorded as having cast guns at Hirado, others were active in commerce with widely varying degrees of success.

> In the ende of fiue yeeres, I made supplication to the king to goe out of this land, desiring to see my poore wife and children according to conscience and nature. With the which request, the emperour was not well pleased, and would not let me goe anymore for my countrey, but to byde in his land. Yet in processe of time, being in great fauour with the Emperour, I made supplication agein, by reason we had newes that the Hollanders were in *Shian* and *Patania*; which reioyced vs much, with hope that God should bring us to our countrey againe, by one meanes or other. So I made supplication agein, and boldly spake my selfe with him, at which he gaue me no aunswer. I told him, if he would permit me to depart, I would bee a meanes, that both the English and Hollanders should come and traffick there. But by no means he would let mee goe. I asked him leave for the capten, the which he presently granted mee. So by that meanes my capten got leave; and in a *Iapon* iunk sailed to *Pattan*; and in a yeares space cam no *Hollanders*. In

> the end, he went from *Patane* to *Ior*, where he found a fleet of nine saile: of which fleet *Matleef* was General, and in this fleet, he was made Master againe, which fleet sailed to *Malacca*, and fought with an armado of Portingalls: in which battel he was shot, and presently died: so that as yet, I think, no certain newes is knownen, whether I be liuing or dead. (Rundall, 1850, 23)

Adams almost certainly erred in assuming that no news of him had been communicated to the British, through the medium of the Dutch. Quackernaeck would have told the Dutch in Matteliefs fleet of events in Japan and Adams would have mentioned more than once. Whether news of Adams' survival had reached England is doubtful, however.

Adams found favour with Ieyasu, who evidently esteemed him highly. This did not necessarily mean that Ieyasu felt himself bound to accept Adams' advice even when it was solicited; Adams' observation that a detailed Spanish survey of the eastern coast of Japan would be considered espionage and preparation for a possible invasion were it conducted in Europe was ignored. Nor was Adams the only advisor on matters beyond the shores of Japan; João Rodrigues, the learned and bilingual Jesuit, was an advisor and interpreter for many years, as was Jan Joosten van Lodensteijn, one of the ringleaders of the mutiny among the *Liefde*'s survivors.

In 1605, Adams obtained permission for Jacob Quaeckernaeck, the *Liefde*'s captain, and Melchior van Santvoort, the factor, to leave Japan and establish contact with the Dutch known by this time to be resident and trading in Java. Quaeckernaeck and Santvoort left Japan aboard a junk provided by the *daimyo* of Hirado, arriving at Pattani on 2 December 1605. Quaeckernaeck was killed in Dutch service but Sandvoort returned to Japan, living to trade for many years and leaving Japan with his family in 1639. It is probable that he outlived everyone else aboard the *Liefde*.

Adams' attainment of *hatamoto* status, achieved also by Jan Joosten but not by Sandvoort, made him a direct retainer of the *Bakufu* rather than a samurai whose primary allegiance would have been to a *daimyo* clan. Apart from the guaranteed income which possession of *hatamoto* status provided, it was visibly indicative of a measure of official favour in a feudal society like Tokugawa Japan.

During the period of Ieyasu's rule, *hatamoto* were numerous and were considered the mainstay of the Bakufu armies. If called to active service, each had to provide 13 men for the first 500 *koku* of their revenue and a similar number for each additional *koku*. Only *hatamoto* of the highest rank had a revenue of 300 *koku* or more. Under Hidetada's successor, Iemitsu, *hatamoto* were forbidden to engage in trade and many of those with modest holdings were deprived of their petty feifs and given fixed stipends instead. This had the wholly unintended effect of turning a formerly productive class into swaggering idlers disturbing the peace of castle towns and commercial cities.

Adams was, understandably, proud of the esteem in which he was held and his letter of October 1611 to the Bantam E.I.C. factors, referred to his 'lordshipp' thus:

> 'Now for my servis that I have done and doe daily, being employed in th'Emperor's servis, th'Emperor hath geven me a living, as in England a lordshipp, w'th 80 or 90 husbandmen that be my slaves or servaunts, w'ch, or the like, were here never before geven to a straunger. Thus hath God provided for mee after my great misery. . .' (Farrington, 1991, 72)

Under the Tokugawa, *hatamoto* could be unmade as swiftly as they had been created, of course.

The size of Adams' 'lordship' has been variously described as 150 or 250 *koku* of rice, a *koku* being about 5 bushels or 182 litres. As was the case with similar *hatamoto* holdings, the estate was a modest one and Adams' eighty or ninety husbandmen would have lived no better than most Japanese peasantry of the period. Cocks, who was given to exaggeration on occasion, visited Adams' 'lordship' in September 1616 and recorded that it included over one hundred farms and households and that Adams 'hath the power of life & death over them, they being his slaves & he absolute authorities over them as any *tono* (lord) in Japaon hath over his vassals'. (Massarella, 1990, 80) Both John Saris and Richard Cocks stayed at Hemi at different times. Cocks, visiting Adams' estate at Hemi in September 1616, noted that Adams' tenants brought him 'oringes, figgs, peares, chisnutts and grapes, whereof there is abundance in that place'. Jan Joosten's *hatamoto* estate at Nagasaki was smaller, valued at approximately 100 *koku*.

During Adams' residence in Japan the peasantry constituted at least ninety percent of the population. Their standard of living was extremely low and their amusements few. Honda Masanobu, Ieyasu's trusted advisor, wrote that the peasant was the foundation of the state and needed to be governed with care, allowed neither too much nor too little. The *Bakufu* later devised detailed rules and regulations to govern peasant life; peasants were to rise early and cut grass for fuel before beginning field work. Tea and *sake*, rice, cotton and silk were forbidden to them. Peasant households were obliged to spend their evenings making straw rope or straw bags. These draconian orders, formulated in 1642 and issued in detailed form in 1649, are indicative of what village life was like in Tokugawa Japan. In 1640, Tairo Doi Toshikatsu, a *Bakufu* official, visiting his estate after an absence of a decade, exclaimed on seeing comfortable houses rather than wretched hovels; 'These people are too comfortable. They must be more heavily taxed!'

As well as being a minor landlord, Adams was a coastal trader known all along the coast, as he claimed. Adams' activities as a trader led to him being known as Miura Anjin, joining the term for pilot with the place-name Miura, his 'lordship' being at Hemi in the Miura district southwest of Edo, close to Uraga. His trading ventures led him to acquire a house in the Nihonbashi district of Edo, a place later named to commemorate his residence there; Anjincho. The arrival of the Dutch obliged Adams to adopt an entirely new role. The Dutch arrived in two ships in 1609, settling in Hirado. Adams acted on their behalf, claiming that he obtained peerless privileges for them. This claim has been disputed on the grounds that Adams would have found it impossible to obtain more than the Tokugawa were willing to grant.

The dramatic end of Pessoa's ship, the *Nossa Senhora da Graça*, also known as the *Madre de Deus*, in January 1610, together with a convoluted legal dispute in Nagasaki, led to the expulsion from Japan of João Rodrigues in March 1610, after a virtually unbroken sojourn of thirty-three years in Japan. He was unofficially succeeded in his capacity as court interpreter and trade negotiator by Adams. It was to this aspect of his activities that Adams was referring when he described the Iberians being obliged to have their negotiations conducted 'through his hands.'

Shortly after the arrival of the E.I.C. ship, the *Clove*, at Hirado, Adams accompanied Saris to Ieyasu's court at Sumpu, or Suruga, assisting the E.I.C. to establish themselves in Japan. As has been said, he obtained Ieyasu's permission to leave Japan if he so wished but evidently decided for various personal and financial reasons, to delay the decision. The mutual dislike between Adams and John Saris appears to have played a significant part in this decision.

Early in 1614 Adams assisted Richard Wickham to establish agencies of the Hirado factory at Edo and elsewhere in Japan. Relations between the two were not always harmonious, for various reasons. Richard Wickham certainly distrusted Adams' brother-in-law. Writing to William Eaton in June he said, '. . .once more I advise you to have a specialer care to Andres & your *jurabaso*, that they join not in one to deceave you.' (Farrington, 1991, 296)

Thereafter, Adams was instrumental in purchasing a junk for the Hirado factory's use. This vessel, the *Sea Adventure,* left Hirado in December 1614 with Adams, Wickham and Sayers aboard. The voyage, intended for Siam, proved abortive; the *Sea Adventure* was unable to proceed beyond the Ryukyus. The junk returned to Hirado in June 1615.

Following the factory's unfortunate first attempts at trading beyond Japanese shores, Adams found himself acting as a negotiator once again after the *Hoseander* reached Japan late in 1615. This ship, the second British vessel to reach Japan, was commanded by Ralph Coppendale, a shrewd man whose letters are as readable as those of Cocks, if less amusing and interesting. Unlike Cocks, he perceived that the Hirado factory was in no position to wait patiently until trade with China could be peacefully achieved. Writing to the Pattani factors in December 1615 he observed. 'Either, I say, we must p'cure a peaceable trade in China or elles, as the Hollanders doe, to trade w'th them per force.' It is probable that Adams assisted Coppendale and the other Britons at their audience with Ieyasu in October 1615.

In December 1615, Adams left Japan for a second time, again aboard the *Sea Adventure*. He was accompanied by Edmund Sayers and a Japanese crew and the voyage was successful, reaching Siam and trading profitably. They returned to Hirado in June 1616, by which time, Ieyasu had died and been succeeded by Hidetada. The E.I.C. ship *Advice* had arrived at Hirado some days before the return of the *Sea Adventure* and it was considered desirable to ensure cordial relations between the Hirado E.I.C. factor and the new ruler. Cocks, Adams and their party were received by Hidetada at Edo in September 1616, receiving what they fondly assumed was a reissuing of the E.I.C's trading privileges. On closer examination, it proved that the new dispensation confined the Company's trading to Hirado, a change of fortune which distressed Cocks greatly.

The curtailment of the privileges accorded to the Dutch and the British came as a severe blow to both the V.O.C. and E.I.C. Following Ieyasu's death in 1616 the Matsuura informed Cocks that the trading concessions awarded by Ieyasu would have to be renewed by his son and *de facto* successor Hidetata, who had been de jure *shogun* for some years prior to Ieyasu's death but visibly in his father's shadow. The arrival of two British ships, the *Thomas* and the *Advice*, in June and July 1616 was a further incentive to visit the *Bakufu*'s court; the arrival of shipping was duly noted in Edo and presents were expected. Adams had returned from Siam providentially in time to accompany the party to Hidetada's court.

Prior to the Britons' departure for Edo, the *daimyo* of Hirado had told Cocks to refrain from selling any of the goods which had arrived aboard the *Thomas* and the *Advice* without obtaining permission from Hidetada to do so, a departure from normal practice which might have served as a warning.

Hidetada received the Britons' presents with genteel affability, considering how modest they were – they included English broadcloth and three dozen rabbit skins – and Cocks duly received a new *shuinjo* for the *Sea Adventure*'s forthcoming voyage and what he assumed was a confirmation of the Hirado factory's existing privileges. It turned out to be no such thing; the Britons were restricted to trading in Hirado rather than being free to buy and sell wherever they wished. Prior to the realisation that conditions had suddenly altered for the worse, Cocks had been subjected to repeated questioning concerning the religion of the British crown; a *Bakufu* official questioned why James I was styled 'Defender of the Faith' and warned Cocks and the other Hirado Britons to ensure that they did not receive mass or any similar sacrament with the Catholics. Cocks assured his hearer that the Catholics were enemies of 'the state of England', referred to the attempted assassination of James and the English parliament in the Gunpowder Plot of 1605 and imaginatively suggested a Japanese conquest of the Philippines, assisted by the British and the Dutch. (Massarella, 1990, 197-8) In spite of Cocks' despairing observation that Hirado was a poor fisher town of no sales and that the 'Emperour' might as well have banished the factory out of Japan altogether as confined them to Hirado, it seemed that there was at least a faint possibility of the decision being reversed at a future date.

Returning to Edo, Cocks, Adams and Eaton were unable to secure a reversal of this decree; all they succeeded in obtaining was the minor concession that Japanese agents might sell any goods then stored outside Hirado but it was made clear that in the future, the E.I.C. factory's sales were to be confined to Hirado.

At the end of 1616, Adams received his outstanding wages from the E.I.C. and became a free agent once more. Characteristically, he continued to assist his fellow-countrymen from time to time, although documentary evidence concerning how much he was paid on these occasions appears to be lacking.

Between March and August 1617, Adams made a voyage to Cochin China aboard a junk he had bought from Cocks, named the *Gift of God*. Shortly after his return to Japan he set out for Edo, joining Cocks there early in September. Attempts to obtain the earlier privileges proved fruitless; all Hidetada was prepared to grant were two *shuinjo,* or *goshuin,* for Siam and Cochin China. However, Hidetada confirmed the *hatamoto* status bestowed upon Adams by Ieyasu; from time to time Adams sold goods on Cocks' behalf as though they were his own, a practice evidently ignored if done discreetly.

In March 1618, Adams sailed again for Cochin China as pilot of a junk owned by a Chinese merchant of Nagasaki. As was the case with the *Sea Adventure*'s first voyage, the junk got no further than the Ryukyu Islands and Adams soon returned to Japan, having missed the monsoon. In July 1618, Adams travelled to Edo as interpreter and negotiator for a Dutch commercial embassy to the *Bakufu*. Shortly thereafter, a captured British ship was brought into Hirado by the triumphant Dutch, a state of *de facto* hostilities having begun in Asian waters.

The seizure of the *Attendance* and her arrival at Hirado not merely distressed Cocks, the incident and events stemming from it led him to question Adams' good faith. Adams was peremptorily ordered to cease aiding the Dutch and do what he could to protest to the *Bakufu*. Adams replied, not unreasonably, that he was not a servant of the E.I.C. and that protest would be unavailing. Cocks, having been told this both in writing and in person by Adams, felt angered enough to write, 'Pray God protect us from our hidden enemy who has the face of a friend.' (Makino, 1983, 73) The most surprising element of this disagreeable tale is that Adams set his misgivings aside and duly protested, even though he knew well that the protest would be unavailing. Over the years, bitter complaints had been made to the *Bakufu* by Iberians and Chinese about Dutch predation on their shipping. To each complaint, the answer was that piracy in waters far from the Japanese coast were of no interest to the *Bakufu*.

The British case against the Dutch stood no chance of being acknowledged by the *Bakufu*, as Adams was well aware. It is illustrative of Adams' determination to serve the interests of his countrymen as best he could that Adams found himself engaged in so fruitless a task as to demand redress from a government which paid little or no heed to such pleas.

Concerning the seizure of Chinese vessels by the Dutch, Cocks had an interesting and revealing conversation with Tonomon Samme, the brother of the *daimyo* of Hirado, on this subject. On being asked why the English refrained from seizing Chinese ships, Cocks replied that 'we could not take any that were frendes to the King of England, as the *Chinas* weare and all others till wars were procleamed.' In the course of this conversation, Cocks' interlocutor sagaciously observed 'that the Hollanders and we were frendes but from tooth outward and not cordially, as neighbours and frendes ought to be.' This exchange, in 1617, is revealing; the Japanese authorities in Hirado evidently guessed that trouble was brewing long before it erupted in open conflict. (Thompson, 1883, I, 270)

Adams, considered by the Dutch to be a Dutchman and by the Hirado Britons to be an Englishman, was in an unenviable position at this time. Unfortunately, no letter of his dating from this period has survived. It can be surmised that Adams was fully aware of the delicacy and ambiguity of his position as an emissary for both the Dutch and the British at a time when the two nations were in a state of undeclared war in East Asian waters.

The war between the Dutch and the Iberians was an ideological conflict with economic implications. Philip of Spain, who had become concurrently the king of Portugal in 1580, closed the port of Lisbon to the traffic of his rebellious Dutch subjects in 1594, the year in which that portion of the Netherlands known as the United Provinces became entirely free from Spanish occupation. The closure of Lisbon spurred Dutch ventures to attack the Iberians at the places where their trade was most vulnerable, with the clear intention of bringing as much booty to Holland as was possible. The struggle between the Dutch and the Iberians was both economic and ideological; the later struggles between the Dutch and the British were purely predatory and mercenary. The Dutch, although well aware that the English had done much to realise Dutch independence, resented the presence of the E.I.C. in the East Asian waters where they were contending for mastery with the Iberians.

Acting on behalf of the Hirado factory, William Adams attended Hidetada's court daily for two months in the hope of receiving a satisfactory response to the British complaint. The delay can only be considered a calculated snub on Hidetada's part, indicative of the changed circumstances in which Adams, and indeed all foreigners, found themselves after Ieyasu's death. Eventually, the reply was given that captures which took place in waters distant from the Japan were of no concern to the Japanese authorities. Ironically, this was not dissimilar to the reply Ieyasu had made to the urging of the Portuguese that the *Liefde*'s crew deserved to be executed as pirates after their arrival in 1600.

Adams' efforts on behalf of his aggrieved fellow-countrymen in pressing their complaints against the Dutch probably struck many members of the *Bakufu* as ironic; in 1615 the Dutch had seized a Portuguese junk called the *São António* and brought her to Hirado. Ieyasu permitted the Dutch to keep her as 'good prize', on Adams' representation. The junk was carrying a cargo of ebony and tin, together with some gold and 'much conserves'. (Boxer, 1988, 87) A Portuguese captured aboard the *São António* visited Cocks, who drily noted that this was the fifth time the man had been 'taken. . .at sea' by the Dutch. (Thompson, 1883, I, 35, 59)

By the time Adams received Hidetada's belated answer to the E.I.C. complaint, Cocks and Nealson had left Edo. The unavailing protest had been time-consuming; Cocks and Nealson had embarked to lay a formal protest before Hidetada in late August. It was not until early December that Adams rejoined them at Osaka.

Adams' last voyage, as the pilot of a Japanese-owned junk, was to Tonkin. He left Hirado in March 1619 and returned to Hirado in August.

In September 1619, Adams was evidently too ill to travel from Edo to Hirado, although requested to do so by Richard Cocks. Eaton report of Adams 'I knowe not when Capt' Adames will goe up, in that hee is sickly & minded to take vissick'. Adams was sufficiently well by February 1620 to assist Cocks with the sale of lead to Hasegawa Gonroku, the *bugyo* of Nagasaki, however. Hasegawa was a reluctant persecutor of Christians, despite strict orders from the *Bakufu* to be unrelenting. At his request, he was relieved of his duties in 1626. (Farrington, 1991, 761)

Adams' death, in the house of his Hirado host Yasimon Dono, was on 16 May 1620. His will, written and witnessed earlier the same day, is a splendid example of unsophisticated Elizabethan – Jacobean English:

> In the name of God amen. This 16th of May 1620 I, William Adams, mariner, that have binn resident in Japon the space of some xviii or xx years, beinge sick of boddey but of perfect remembrance, laude and prayse be unto Almighty God, mak and ordeine this my present testament, contayning herein my last will in manner and forme followinge that is to saye:
>
> Imprimis, I commend my soule unto Allmightie god my Maker & Redemer, trusting through the merritt of His deerely beloved Sonne to inherit eternall lyfe. Next I bequeth my bodey to be buryed in the earth from whence it came.
>
> Item, I will that all such debts & dueties as I owe of right or of conscience to any person or persons be well and trully contented & payed by mine overseers hereafter named, or elce ordeine soe for to be payed without any delay or contradice. And after my debts payed & my funerall expences performed, I will that my monney, goods and debts shalbe devided into ij equall parts, whereof I will & bequeth unto my lovinge wyfe & children in

England the one halfe part thereof which I have heare in Japon or in any other of these Eastern parts. The other halfe parte of my aforesaied monney and goods I will and bequeth unto my ij loveinge childerene Joseph and Susana, liveinge in Japon.

Item, I will and bequeth unto my lovinge & good frend Mr. Richard Cocke, Cape M'chant of the English in Japon, for a rememberance of my good wille, i selestiall globe in a case and all my seacards & plates & my best cattane. The others of my cattans and wagadashes I will and bequeth unto my aforesaied sonne Joseph.

Item, I will & bequeth unto my loving frend William Eaton, one of the English factors resident in Japon, for a remembrance of my good will, all my bookes and sea instruments that I have.

Item, I will and bequeth unto my servant Anthony v tayes in money, w'thall his liberty.

Item, I give and bequeth unto my maied-servante called Jugasa i chody, ij new cattaberas that came last from Miaco, & 2 bars of silver qt eight tayes six mas.

Item, I give and bequeth unto John Phebe 1 bar of silver qt foure tayes three mas, w'th all else that he is indebted unto me.

Item, I give and bequeth unto my host Yeasom Dono & unto his wyfe sixtey tayes, of w'ch he hath in his hands fiftey tayes allredey, and the rest to be given hime by my overseers.

Item, I give and bequeth unto Mychaell, a Coriane, ten tayes w'ch the sayde Mychaell oweth unto me.

Item, I give unto John Osterwick, Richard Kinge, Abram Smart & Richard Hudson, each of them, one kerymon of the best I have.

Item, I will and ordaine for overseers of this my will & testament and for the execution of the same, my lovinge frends Mr. Richard Cocke and William Eaton. I utterly revoke and adnull all & every other former testaments, willes, legasies & executors and overseers by mee in any wise before this tyme named, willed and bequeathed. And soe hearunto I have sett my hand, these whose names are hearunder written beinge wittnesses. Per me, W'm Addames.

Ric'Cocks W'm Addames
William Eaton
Jo' Osterwick
Richard King
Abram Smart his mark
Tho' Bacup

Probate clause in Latin: Administration issued to Mary Adams by

Edmund Pope, LL.D., Surrogate of Nicholas Langford, M.A., Commissary General, 8 October 1621, because no executors named [in England]
Endorsed: 1620. The true coppie of Capt'W'm Addames his testament, written the 16th of Maye, in which day at 5 a clocke in the afternowne he dep'ted out of this miserable world in the house of Yasomon Dono his host at Firando in Japon.

On 8 October 1621, Mary Adams was made executrix of Adams' will, his estate in England being valued at £165 9s 10d, a not inconsiderable sum. (Massarella, 1990, 265)

Rundall (p. 88) quotes an inventory which is no longer extant, as follows:

'In the name of God, Amen, 1620, May the 22nd day.
The inventory of the estate of the deceased, Capt. Wm. Adames, taken at Firando, in Japan, after his death, pr. me Richd. Cock, and Mr. Wm. Eaton, factors in the English Factory at Firando, in Japan, left by testament his overseers, viz., of all the monies, debts, merchandiz, and moveabls, being as hereafter followeth.'

The succeeding extract shews that William Adams had accumulated about £.stg. 500 at the period of his death, viz.

'The totall is:	ta.	m.	co.
In ready money	0365	0	9
In bills of debt	0890	0	0
In merchandiz, rated at	0638	7	0
In moveables, sould for	0078	4	5
	1972	2	4
	ta.	ma.	co.
	1972	2	4'

(Farrington, 1991, 795-6)

The swords Adams bequeathed to his son Joseph were handed over by Richard Cocks late in 1621, in what was evidently an emotional moment for both.

Adams refers to 'children' in England. Was he, perhaps thinking of a child who had died in infancy, as so many children did in Elizabethan England? Cocks, writing in December 1620, referred clearly enough to 'his wife and childe in England' and to 'Mrs. Adames & her doughter'.

Adams' letter of October 1611 to the Britons at Bantam referred to 'my poor wife and 2 children', adding that 'in a manner my wife is a widdow and children fatherles. . .' (Farrington, 1991, 71)

The commission issued to John Saris by the East India Company referred to Adams' 'wife and children' in his 'native countrie', so it is possible that another child, other than Deliverance, was alive in 1611. By the time Deliverance, now married and surnamed Goodchild, petitioned the East India Company for the release of Adams' estate, in August 1624, Mary Adams had died, bequeathing her share of Adams' estate to her daughter. (Farrington, 1991, 961)

According to Cocks, Adams was determined that the 'English' half of his legacy should be divided between Mary Adams and Deliverance; '. . .for yt was not his mind his wife should have all in regard she might marry another husband & carry all from his childe, but rather that it should be equally p'ted betwixt them. . .' (Farrington, 1991, 822)

The question concerning Adams' third Japanese child is somewhat vexing. There are two references in Cocks' diary, both of 1621: February 20. . . 'Captain Adames childe in Firando was brought to me per the mother, unto whom I gave ii tais in small plate, and offerd her to pay for the bringing of it up to schoole, yf she would deliver it to thenglish nations protection.' April 16: 'And I paid ii tais I *mas* for 2 peces Japon taffety to lyne Capt. Adams and Coa Jnos. childrens coates.'

Obviously, these references did not apply to either of Adams' two children by his Japanese wife, O-yuki, the daughter of Magome Kageyu. Magome Kageyu was, at the time Adams met him, the superintendent of the packhorse exchange at Demma-cho in Edo; certainly not, as has been claimed, a member of the *samurai* class.

Neither the gender of the Hirado child nor the mother's name is known, but a guess can be made. In his will he left various minor bequests, including the following:

> Item, I give and bequeth unto my maied-servante called Jugasa i chody, ii new cattaberas that came last from Miaco, & 2 bars of silver qt eight tayes six *mas*.' (Farrington, 1991, 795)

It is not impossible that Jugasa was expecting Captain Adams' child *without being aware of the fact* at the time of his death. Whatever may have been his relations with European missionaries, Adams was not known to be vindictive in his personal relationships; it is improbable that he would have left no provision for the Hirado child *had he known of the child's existence.*

Anthony Farrington has suggested that the reference to the Hirado child's schooling suggests that the child was probably a boy. Literacy was far more widespread among the humbler classes of society in seventeenth-century Japan than was the case in Elizabethan and Jacobean England, however. Even such people as Oto, Matinga's maidservant, could write, if only in the relatively simple *kana* script, as opposed to the mighty host of Chinese characters a truly learned person would have been expected to know.

Following Adams' death, Richard Cocks, whose relationship with Adams had not always been satisfactory, wrote:

> '. . .I canot but be sorofull for the losse of such a man as Capt' W'm Adames was, he having byn in such favour w'th two Emperours of Japon as never was any Christian in these p'tes of the worlde, & might freely have entred & had speech w'th th'Emperours when many Japon kings stood w'thout & could not be p'mitted. And this Emperour hath confermed the lordshipp to his sonne w'ch th'other Emperour gave to the father.' (Farrington, 1991, 824)

It was a generous obituary considering the annoyance Cocks had frequently felt towards Adams, as Dr. Massarella has observed. Earlier in the same letter, Cocks referred to 'our good frend Capt' W'm Adames, whoe was so longe before us in Japon.'

Cocks erroneously overstated Adams' influence with Hidetada, who had little interest in the company or discourse of foreigners. After Ieyasu's death in 1616, Adams' influence, such as it was, had waned markedly. However, it is noteworthy that Hidetada confirmed Joseph in possession of Adams' modest 'lordship' at Hemi.

Joseph Adams was still trading from Japan in 1633, the year in which his was one of the seven households permitted to engage in the *shuinsen* trade overseas. (Massarella, 1990, 343) A mere two years later, an edict forbade any Japanese to sail overseas, thus ending the *shuinsen* trade completely.

Adams never sailed northwards while in Japan, nor did any of the Britons or Dutchmen resident in Japan during the period of Adams' life there record that he had sailed northwards while in

Dutch service prior to leaving Europe in 1598. The prospect of northern discoveries from Japan interested him greatly, as both he and his contemporaries record.

In December 1613, Adams wrote, in his letter to the East India Company:

> '. . .I hav byllt 2 shipes in this country for the Emperor. The on of them sold to the Spaynnards uppon occacion, and the other I sayld in myselff uppon dyvers vyages uppon this cost. Now the one of them that was sold to the Spaynnards wass uppon this occassion; that a great ship of 1000 tounes w'ch cam from the *Manilia* w'ch was cast away uppon this cost, whearin was the Governor of *Manilia*, to whoum the Emperor lent hir to carry him to *Akapulca*, a plac in *Nova Spaynia*; w'ch shipp theay found so good ass theay never retturned agayn, butt sent so much monny ass shee was wourth, and afterwards wass imployed in the vyages from *Nova Spaynia* to the *Phillipines*, &c. Soo that nevertheles by my profession I am no shippwrit, yet I hop to mak such shipping as shalbe necessary for any such discovery.' (Farrington, 1991, 108)

The discovery to which Adams referred in this letter was the short, northern route thought to exist between Europe and the Far East. No such voyage was made; the Hirado factors found other uses for Adams' abilities, the Hirado Britons and Dutch never attempted to sail north.

The prospect of finding a miraculous short cut to Japan continued to fascinate both the English and the Dutch in Japan. It fascinated the Spaniards less; their interest lay in the discovery of fabled isles of silver and gold, somewhere in the northern seas close to Japan. The Japanese, more practically, knew only that furs and salmon were to be had in abundance in the large island of Yedzo, or Yezo, to the north of Honshu. The only Japanese settlement on Yezo, as *Hokkaido* was then known, was Matsumae, the centre of an important fur trade. The *daimyo* there was Matsumae Yoshihiro (1550-1618), whose authority had been confirmed by Ieyasu in 1604. (Farrington, 1991, 82)

The population of Yezo increased dramatically after the discovery of commercially feasible gold deposits early in the seventeenth century. According to Jesuit sources, a gold rush of dramatic proportions ensued. Two Jesuits, Jerónimo de Angelis, in 1618, and Diego Carvalho, in 1620, visited Yezo to say mass in the miners' settlements. Both of these courageous men were later martyred, in 1623 and 1624 respectively.

Father de Angelis was the first European to write an account of the Ainu people of Yezo. He noted, as have so many since, that they were hairier than the Japanese and that, like Celts and other primitive peoples, they had a weakness for strong drink. Jerónimo de Angelis innocently did much to mislead later geographers and cartographers by stating that Yezo was not an island 'as it is depicted in our old maps' but connected to Tartary and very close to the American continent, being separated from that great land-mass by the narrow 'strait of Anian'. (Boxer, 1951, 336)

Remarkably, no effort was made by Europeans to exploit the export potential of a trade in furs obtained in Yezo, Sakhalin or the Kuriles, all known to Japanese mariners. When Captain James Cook took sea otter skins from the Pacific Coast of North America to Macau nearly two centuries later, the merchants of Canton clamoured to buy even the shabbiest at premium prices. (Reader, 1990, 122-3)

In the days of the Russian American Company, vast numbers of furs were shipped from the Alaskan island of Kodiak to the Chinese market between 1747 and 1791, earning the Russians millions in silver.

At the time of Saris' audience with Ieyasu, Ieyasu expressed interest in the Westerners' desire to sail northwards, offering to direct Matsumae Yoshihiro to give any British expedition all possible assistance. (Farrington, 1991, 105) Adams was enthusiastic about such a venture in 1613, telling the East India Company how best to equip a ship to venture northwards, detailing such requirements as *poldavy*, a kind of coarse canvas used in sailmaking, together with tar, pitch and compasses. Cocks was of the opinion that the Dutch would have already sent an expedition northwards from Japan in search of either the north-east or north-west passage, or both, from Japan, had they not been busy with contending for mastery in the Moluccas with the Spaniards.

At the end of 1614, Cocks was writing that Adams 'hath a great desire to find out the norther passage for England from hence and thinketh it an easie matter to be donne in respect the Emperour of this place offreth his assistance. . .' Cocks added that he would willingly go himself. (Farrington, 1991, 227) John Saris, on his return from Japan wrote from his cabin aboard the *Clove* at Plymouth to the East India Company,

> 'I p'posed to have bought a junke and to have sent him (Adams) upone discovery of the iland called Yedzo in this draught of Japan w'ch I send yow hearw'th, and is said to yeald great store of gould, silver and rich furrs. The Emperor, understandinge of my determination, liked it so well as he interested that a man or 2 of his might goe alonge w'th us, who should carry his order to his subjectes to ayd and assist us in the busines. But the tyme of the year would not p'mitt mee. Itt is to be thought that ther is great hope of findinge the norwest passadg that way, and is this year putt in practice by the Fleminges yf ther Mullocco busines have not hindred it.' (Farrington, 1991, 213)

It is mildly surprising to find Cocks so eager to sail to the northern seas, but Cocks was neither a coward nor a fool, as his behaviour in a potentially hazardous situation in the Red Sea on the outward voyage had amply proved. In a letter to Lord Salisbury, written in December 1614, Cocks insisted, 'And I for my p'te will adventure myselfe in p'son in the action as willingly as any man it hath pleased them to imploy into these p'tes of the world', after briefly discussing the 'greate hope there is to find the northerne passages from this place for England by meanes of th'assistance of this Emperour of Japan, whoe offereth us all the furtherance he maye' and referring to Adams' capacity and willingness to 'take the matter in hand.' (Farrington, 1991, 259) The Court Minutes of the East India Company, March-April 1615, suggest that the E.I.C. was as enthusiastic about the business as Cocks, Adams, Saris and Ieyasu thought:

> And they entringe into some consideration of the conveniencye of makinge trialle for the discov'y of the North-West Passage from thence, held him (*i.e. Adams*) a very fitt instrument to bee employed therein yf yt shall bee held convenient by the factors there to bee enterprized. And therefore, wisht to have yt enlargde in the l're unto them to p'cure the furtheraunce & assistance of the Emperor soe much as hee shall be willinge to contribute and to have a paier of globes and some mappes sent unto them to give some light in the discov'y yf it shall be thought a fitt accion to bee undertaken. (Farrington, 1991, 290)

The E.I.C. are hardly to be blamed for their studiously guarded enthusiasm; like the Dutch, they had seen ships, men and money lost in various attempts to find the northern routes to the riches of Asia. There were more pressing matters to be addressed, just as more pressing matters in Japan led to the northern voyage's indefinite postponement.

Referring to the possibility of finding possible northern passages to Europe from Japan, at the end of November 1613, Cocks wrote to Sir Thomas Smythe and the East India Company;

> 'Mr. Adams hath drawn out the plot of Japan, w'th p'te of that iland (*Yezo: Hokkaido*) & Corea & other bordering places, & sendeth it to your Worships per this conveance. Ytis certen that the Hollanders had taken this discovery in hand before now but that they have soe many irons in the fyre allready w'th their wars in the Molucos against the Spaniardes.' (Farrington, 1991, 99)

Sadly, this map is not extant; it would throw a great deal of light on the way a practical navigator perceived the waters around Japan and the neighbouring countries.

Adams, in a letter to Thomas Best in Bantam written in December 1613, recounted his interview with Ieyasu in some detail:

> 'So w'th divers speeches of our countri he asked me yf our countrimen could not find the norwest passedg. I told him our countri had made manny discoveris, and still douth, but as yeat had not found it. So he asked me yf we knew of a land not above 10 leagues from his land, upon the north p't, in w'ch land his peopell had 30 days' journes in his countri frindship. The countri is called Yedzoo. By all liklihood it is a kind of Tartores, w'ch, ass he told mee, is a greatt land; by my judgement is a promentary that striketh w'th a great bytt or elbo from the cost of Corea and so trenteth againe to the north-estward to Cattay or the land of the Great Cam.' (Farrington, 1991, 111-2)

As a practical mariner, Adams added that Ieyasu's pass would greatly facilitate matters; '. . .the King's pass of frindship into thoos p'ts so far as His Majesti hath frindship w'th, w'ch is a great matter. . .' Another point made in the letter to Best was that interpreters who could speak Korean and other appropriate languages were readily available in Japan. Obviously, such tongues as Portuguese, by this time the *lingua franca* of seaborne commerce in East Asia and Malay – a language which factors like John Saris, for example, spoke – would be of little use in an expedition to northern waters. Portuguese and Malay were often the appropriate languages for communication between traders of differing nationalities in East Asia but necessity and chance in the Pacific often dictated some surprising choices of language; when Nikolai Rezanov of the Russian American Company met Commandante Luís Arguello at San Francisco in April 1806 their exchanges were in *Latin*. The British belief that a discoverable route to the wealth of East Asia lay through Arctic waters was to last until the nineteenth century. Before, during and after Adams' lifetime, many futile efforts were made. In 1497, the Venetian John Cabot left Bristol, with some royal financial backing, to make a westwards passage to Asia. It is uncertain whether he reached Labrador, Newfoundland or Maine but he unhesitatingly claimed to have reached '*the country of the Grand Khan*'. His son, Sebastian, in 1508-9, examined the eastern shores of North America and may have reached Hudson Bay. No Chinese were encountered in this or subsequent voyages, but the English refused to be deterred by successive disappointments; Henry VIII sent an expedition in 1527-8, another in 1536 followed. Sebastian Cabot, who had left England in 1512, returned after thirty-five years in Spanish service, convinced that the northeast route offered the fairest prospect of a northern passage to Asia. In 1553, a joint-stock company was formed under Cabot's governorship and a fleet commanded by Hugh Willoughby and Richard Chancellor departed optimistically for Cathay, *via* Norway. Willoughby died in Novaya Zemlya, Chancellor traded with the Russians in Archangel. Stephen Borough reached the Kara Sea in a small boat in 1556; Henry Hudson reached Spitzbergen in 1607 and explored part of Novaya Zemlya in the following year.

In spite of disappointments and losses, interest in the northwest passage never faltered for long; in 1576, Martin Frobisher, a former pirate and slaver, reached Baffin Island and returned with an abducted Eskimo (*Inuit*) and his kayak, together with samples of what were believed to be gold ore.

In 1578, Frobisher, having earlier identified the body of water now known as Frobisher Strait as the route to Asia, sailed to Hudson Strait, claiming it to offer still better prospects. The ore turned out to be worthless 'fool's gold' and the Cathay Company sank into bankruptcy. In 1585, John Davis sailed up the coast of Greenland, accompanied by Walter Ralegh and Humphrey Gilbert. In 1610, Henry Hudson entered the immense bay which bears his name and survived the winter there in great misery, to be set adrift with his son by his mutinous crew. Further heroic efforts were made by Thomas Button and William Baffin in 1612 and 1616, adding little to the store of knowledge and nothing to the wealth of the realm. It is remarkable that so much effort, so much wealth and so many lives were so recklessly ventured in retrospect but is significant that seemingly limitless resources could be drawn upon to aid an undertaking which offered so dazzling a prospect of gain. After Thomas James' expedition in 1631-2, the English lost interest in northern navigation for some decades, having resigned themselves to using the route *via* the Cape and the Indian Ocean to reach East Asia. Eventually interest was to revive; in 1776 Captain James Cook made his third voyage to the Pacific with instructions to search for the passage leading from that ocean to Hudson's Bay. Unable to find a way through the ice north of the Bering Straits, Cook was an unsuccessful as his predecessors but had the surprising fortune to begin the trade in sea otter furs between the Pacific coast of North America and Macau, a brief but enormously profitable business.

The dream of a northwest passage from Europe to the riches of Asia fascinated Europeans for centuries. Many mariners left their names behind; Baffin, Hudson, Davis, Foxe, Parry, Bylot and Sverdrup. Many gave their lives. Sir John Franklin's expedition of 1845-8 met disaster, losing two ships and 129 men, inspiring several subsequent expeditions to find and rescue him. Finally, in 1903, the Norwegian Roald Amundsen sailed through the passage from east to west in a motorised sailboat. Unlike the northeast passage, now used by the Russians every year during the brief Arctic summer, the northwest passage is not a commercial waterway.

The Dutch, emulating the English, endeavoured to search for the elusive but enticing routes to East Asia through the icy northern waters. Efforts were made in the 1590s to push eastwards of the White Sea fishing grounds, already well-known to Dutch fishing fleets, and in 1596, Willem Barentsz reached Spitzbergen. Trapped by ice blocking their homeward route, his crew wintered in Novaya Zemlya, the survivors reaching the Russian mainland in an open boat in the spring. The Dutch, in spite of a reputation for dogged persistence, never evinced the same degree of unshakeable belief in the existence of either northern route as did the British. However, Arnoldus Montanus' *Atlas Japannensis* of 1670 recorded how a group of ten sailors from a ship that set sail from Batavia in Java 'to discover by the East of Japan the Northern Coasts of Tartary' landed for provisions in an inlet or an estuary of the northern Japanese coast far from Nagasaki, by this time the only permitted port for foreign shipping, exclusively Dutch and Chinese. Captured, they were assumed to be instrumental in landing missionaries on the coast. Taken before Inoue Chikugo, the chief inquisitor, they were interrogated at length and eventually, before their conveyance to Nagasaki and subsequent departure, compelled to witness the torture of one or more of the Jesuit missionaries of the Second Rubino Group. (Elison, 1973, 200) This was in late 1643; it is surprising that the Dutch authorities in Batavia should have permitted a Dutch vessel to approach the Japanese coast at all, knowing that suspicious conduct of this kind might well endanger the V.O.C. outpost on the islet of Dejima in Nagasaki harbour.

In spite of romantic Victorian claims that Adams was the 'founder of the Japanese navy', whispers of which persist into the twentieth century, Adams built a mere two ships in Japan, the combined tonnage of which amounted to a fraction of that of one of the Macau-Nagasaki *naós* in the golden age of Luso-Japanese commerce.

Writing in December 1613 to Thomas Best at Bantam, Adams said of his shipbuilding experience:

> '. . .I myseelf hav bylt 2 shipes in Jappan, the on by occassion sold to the Spaynards went for Nova Spaynia, w'ch ship on viage uppon this cost I made w'th heer, being of burden 170 tounes, the w'ch now being in the Spaynnards' hands saylles from or betwenn the Philipiness and Accpullca. And the other ship I saylled uppon this cost about 2 yeers, so that for making of shiping and vittalling of shipping and saylling w'th shipping by Japanes I hav experenc theerof' (Farrington, 1991, 112)

In an earlier letter, that to his *unknown friends and countrymen* at Bantam in Java, dated October 1611, Adams set his shipbuilding endeavours squarely in their context:

> So in processe of four or fiue yeeres the Emperour called me, as diuers times he had done before. So one time aboue the rest he would haue

> me to make him a small ship. I aunswered that I was no carpenter, and had no knowledge thereof. Well, doe your endeavour, saith he: if it be not good, it is no matter. Wherefore at his commaund I buylt him a ship of the burthen of eightie tunnes, or there about: which ship being made in all respects as our manner is, he comming aboord to see it, liked it very well; by which meanes I came in more fauour with him, so that I came often in his presence, who from time to time gaue me presents, and at length a yearely stypend to liue vpon, much about seuentie ducats by the yeare, with two pounds of rice a day, daily. Now beeing in such grace and fauour, by reason I learned him some points of *jeometry*, and vnderstanding of the art of *mathematickes*, with other things I pleased him so, that what I said he would not contrarie. (Rundall, 1850, 28)

Concerning matters of mathematics, astronomy and navigation, Adams was by no means the only European to give instructions to prominent Japanese. Carlo Spinola, yet another future martyr, who arrived in Miyako in 1605, is said to have met Tokugawa Hidetada and various *daimyo*, and to have refuted Buddhist monks in discussions on astronomy. The Jesuit church in Miyako, the *Nambanji*, possessed a terrestrial globe and various astronomical instruments and it is recorded that the Emperor, Go-Yozei, secretly sent a court messenger to the mission residence asking for a demonstration and explanation of the instruments. Spinola established a regrettably short-lived academy of mathematics and science at the Miyako Jesuit residence, transferred to Nagasaki in 1611. In conjunction with the Jesuit Giulio Aleni at Macau in February 1612, Spinola made the first truly scientific observation of a lunar eclipse in Japan and was thereby able to calculate the latitude of Nagasaki within a margin of error of less than three minutes, a remarkable accomplishment for the period (Cooper, 1971, 141)

According to Japanese sources, Adams built both ships at Ito, a small town on the Izu Peninsula, hence the commemoration of Adams' shipbuilding efforts by the Ito Tourist Association; the Anjin Festival. Ito was chosen because of its proximity to Edo, the availability of skilled shipwrights locally and the abundant supplies of excellent timber on Mt. Amagi, a mountain close by. Assisted by Mukai Shogen Tadakatsu, Ieyasu's admiral, and by Yojuro, a shipwright, and Shikanosuke and Koshinosuke, pilots, Adams assembled a team of local shipwrights and constructed the first vessel, satisfying himself that it sailed adequately in open water, though details are lacking. (Makino, 1983, 39) At Ieyasu's command, a second was constructed. Japanese records, the *Annals of the Keicho Period*, state that Adams constructed the first of the two vessels built at Ieyasu's behest by a method well-known to local shipwrights; logs were laid down on the beach and the ribs and keel built up from them. When the ship was all but finished, sand and shingle was dug from beneath the logs, causing the ship to sink into a trench. This was then filled with water from a minor river called the Tojingawa. A larger river, the Matsugawa, was then dammed. When there was sufficient water behind the dam, the dam was breached thus bearing the ship to the sea. (Purvis, 1926, 73; Makino, 1983, 39) Interestingly, the same source refers to carpenters and shipwrights trained by Adams either building a European-style ship, or possibly repairing an older semi-derelict one, at Sendai in 1613. This carried Date Masamune's mission to Spain and Rome *via* Mexico.

Mukai Shogen Tadakatsu, to whom Richard Cocks referred as the '*Amerall of the Sea*', supervised the building of the ship which carried the Date Masamune embassy to Mexico in 1613 and was keen that Adams become 'pilot of a voyage they pretended to the northward to make conquest of certain ilands, as he said, rich in gould' as Cocks recorded in January 1617. Adams demurred, telling Mukai Shogen that he was currently in the service of the E.I.C. factory at Hirado. (Farrington, 1991, 556)

A generation later, in 1636, the third Togukawa *Shogun*, Iemitsu, decreed that all vessels of European build and all large vessels of native design were to be destroyed. This, the fourth *Sakoku* Edict, was a decree which ensured that only small junks suitable for coasting purposes could be built thenceforth. However, there were a few official exceptions; the *Nippon Maru* which had been built by Kuki Yoshitaka to Hideyoshi's orders in 1591, remained at anchor at Toba, to which port it had been brought after the Korean campaign ended. Refitted, repaired and renamed *Tairyu Maru,* it remained at Toba until 1856, when it was broken up. A contemporary sketch depicts a ship easily capable of sailing to Java or the Philippines. (Sadler, 1937, 183)

Of the activities of Adams as Ieyasu's shipwright, there are grounds for believing that Adams and the surviving members of the *Liefde*'s crew who may have assisted him were not the first European shipbuilders in Japan. An allegedly defrauded Spanish-Peruvian merchant, who charged certain of the Nagasaki Portuguese with fraud in August 1592, busied himself with construction of a vessel large enough to trade with China and Peru. A shadowy figure, de Solis and *another* Spaniard, a merchant from the Philippines, sought to intimidate the Jesuits by threatening to tell the Japanese authorities what they could of the Jesuits illegally resident in Japan. (Hildreth, 1905, 113; Boxer, 1951, 178)

If anything came of Jean (or *Juan*) de Solis' shipbuilding venture, no record remains. However, the Spanish authorities in the Philippines were well aware of the vulnerability of their position at Manila were the Japanese to construct an armed seagoing fleet.

Innocently, Adams noted:

> You shall vnderstand that the first ship that I did make, I did make a voyage or two in, and then the King commaunded me to make an other, the which I did, being of the burthen of an hundred and twentie tunnes. In this ship I have made a voyage from *Meaco* to *Eddo*, being as far as from *London* to the *Lizarde* or the *Lands end of England*: which in the yeere of our Lord 1609 was cast away a great ship called the *S. Francisco,* beeing about a thousand tunnes, vpon the coast of *Iapon*, in the lattetude of thirty fiue degrees and fiftie minutes. By distress of weather she cut ouer-boord her maine mast and bore vp for *Iapon*, and in the night vnawares, the ship ranne vpon the shore and was cast away: in the which thirtie and sixe men were drowned, and three hundred fortie, or three hundred fiftie saued: in which ship the Gouernour of *Manilla* as a passenger, was to returne to *Noua Spania*. But this gouernour was sent in the bigger ship which I made in *ann*. 1610, to *Acapulca*. And in *ann*. 1611, this Gouernour returned another ship in her roome, with a great present, and with an Embassadour to the Emperour, giuing him thankes for his great friendship: and also sent the worth of the Emperours ship in goods and money: which shippe the Spaniards haue now in the *Philippinas*. (Rundall, 1850, 30)

In one letter, Adams gave the tonnage of the second ship as 120 tons, in another as 170 tons. Ieyasu, according to one report, provided 4,000 ducats to equip her. Manned by a Japanese crew *en route* to California, she subsequently remained in Spanish service for many years. The crew returned to Japan aboard the ship which carried Sebastián Vizcaíno to Japan. (Murdoch, 1949, 480)

Don Rodrigo, who died at the age of eighty-one in 1636, was the interim Governor of the Philippine between June 1608 and April 1609. His accounts of Japan remain fascinating reading to the present day. He found much to admire in Japan, observing that the Japanese were braver and more warlike than the Chinese or the Koreans but his Castilian pride obliged him to declare that the Spanish monarch was the greatest and most powerful in the world. Possibly to undermine his confidence in the veracity of this assertion, Ieyasu staged a minor sideshow during his audience with the latter at Sumpu in 1609; 'one of the greatest nobles of Japan' entered silently with tribute in the form of gold, silver and silk robes of a value Don Rodrigo estimated at more than 20,000 ducats, prostrated himself without a word and withdrew, Ieyasu not condescending to notice his presence. (Cooper, 1965, 118)

Adams' second ship, named the *Santa Buenaventura* in Spanish service, made landfall at Mantanchel in California at the end of October 1610, hence the occasional participation of American naval bands in ceremonies commemorating Adams.

The most surprising aspect of Adams' activities as Ieyasu's shipwright was that Adams was required to do so little. Since the second ship could, and did, sail across the Pacific it would have made excellent commercial sense for Ieyasu to have commissioned another twenty such vessels. To have copied a really large ship, such as the Macau carrack, would not have proved unduly difficult after a permanent workforce of shipwrights had acquired some experience. The Spanish friar, Luís Sotelo, was involved in the preparations for Data Masamune's expedition to Mexico, thus incurring the distaste and suspicion of his fellow-countrymen at Manila: Los Rios Coronel stated that he should not be permitted to return to Japan, fearing that the Japanese would learn shipbuilding through his efforts. When Richard Cocks was attempting to interest the Tokugawa admiral, Mukai Shogen Tadakatsu, in the prospects of a Japanese invasion of the Philippines in 1616, Shogen showed much interest 'and in the end said that they wanted such ships as ours were.' An earlier governor of the Philippines, Don Pedro Bravo de Acuña, writing to Spain in 1605, expressed apprehension that the Japanese might learn gunnery, shipbuilding and navigation from the Dutch. The Japanese lack of expertise in these sciences was the only reason they had not attempted an invasion of the Philippines already, he added. The only Dutchmen in Japan at this period, apart from stray Flemings in Iberian service, were the handful of survivors of the *Liefde*. (Boxer, 1951, 267-8)

None of the various maps drawn by Adams and sent to Europe are known to have survived. The only tangible evidence concerning Adams' activities as a cartographer is conjectural at best. A map of Japan, still in excellent condition and safely kept in the National Museum in Tokyo, has been confidently identified as a Portulan chart by the hand of Cornelis Doedtsz of Edam, the cartographer commissioned to furnish maps for the ill-fated expedition of Mahu and De Cordes. A *palimpsest*, or careful amendment, altered the coastline of Honshu on the map. It may be presumed, knowing what we do of the friendly relations between Tokugawa Ieyasu and William Adams, that this alteration was performed at the behest of the former and executed by the latter. C.R. Boxer considered this possibility at length in *The Transactions and Proceedings of the Japan Society of London XXXIII, London 1936*. More recently, a Portuguese translation, by C/Alm. José Manuel Teles Pereira Germano, has appeared in Macau. (Boxer, 1989, 52) This map and the stern-figure of Erasmus are the only known surviving artifacts of the *Liefde*.

It has been suggested that Adams was employed, albeit probably informally, as a cartographer by the *Bakufu*. A Jesuit letter tells of a terrestrial globe in Adams' possession, presumably either part of the *Liefde*'s contents recovered from the peasantry of Bungo or made in Japan subsequent to Adams' first audience with Tokugawa Ieyasu. According to Diogo do Couto, Adams made this terrestrial globe while in Japan and a Portuguese copy of this was later taken to Macau. (Boxer, 1936, 23) At the time of Adams' death in Hirado in 1620, he possessed 'i selestiall globe in a case', which he bequeathed to Richard Cocks. (Farrington, 1991, 795) Charts, globes and rutters (*roteiros*) possessed a value and a mystique it is hard for contemporary readers to envisage. There was an active black market in Europe in stolen and copied charts. (Scammell, 1981, 394)

Carvalho, the Jesuit provincial, called Adams 'a great engineer and mathematician', which, coming from a Jesuit, was high praise indeed. (Murdoch, 1949, 486)

The 'vearey Large Letter' written by Adams and despatched to the East India Company aboard the *Clove* requested that the Company send 'coumpasses, rounning glasses, a payr of gllobes for demonstracion, and soum cardes or mapes contayning the wholl world' to Japan. (Marakami and Murakawa, 1900, 40) The reference to hour glasses – *rounning glasses* – is interesting; mechanical timepieces were too expensive and fragile to be part of the timekeeping and navigational equipment of ships for many years after Adams' era.

In the letter Cocks sent to England aboard the same ship, he said:

> 'Mr. Adams is of the opynion that, yf eaver the northeast or northwest passages be fowned out, it must be from these partes, and offreth his best services therein, the Emperour promisinge his best fortherance with men or letters of recommendacions to all prinses, and hath entrance allready into an iland called Yedzo, which is thought to be rather som parte of the continent of Tartaria. Mr. Adams hath drawne out the plot of Japan, with parte of that iland and Corea and other bordering places, and sendeth it to your Worships. . .' (Thompson, 1883, II, 258)

So far as is known, Adams' '*plot of Japan*' has not survived. *Yedzo*, now known as Hokkaido, was thought to be part of the Asian mainland by many at the time Cocks was writing. The Japanese contented themselves with trading to Matsumae and other modest settlements on its south coast rather than circumnavigating it and settling the issue. Paradoxically, Korea was long thought to be an island.

Nomenclature, no less than geographical knowledge, has changed greatly since Adams' era; Morejón's translator, William Wright, informed English readers that Mexico was in the *West Indies*. William Eaton the younger, the half-Japanese son of William Eaton the Hirado factor, wrote that he had been '*borne in Japaon one of the remotest parts of the east Indyes*' in a petition to Charles I in 1640 or 1641. (Massarella, 1990, 322)

Several Portuguese-Japanese portulan charts dating from the early seventeenth century have survived. Painted on vellum and often liberally decorated with the *Cruz de Christo* as well as windroses, compass lines and scales in maritime leagues, they are obviously of Japanese manufacture. Nomenclature is in *kana*, with few European letters used. The coasts of Japan and neighbouring countries are shown with far greater accuracy than on contemporary European maps; as in many other areas of learning, the Japanese had learned much from European mentors. During the period of artistic and cultural cross-fertilization in the late sixteenth and early seventeenth centuries, a distinct variety of *namban-byobu*, Southern Barbarian picture-screens, came into existence. These depicted world maps in the style of the *Theatrum Orbis Terrarum* of Abraham Ortelius and their depiction of Japan, China and Korea is considerably more accurate than the delineation to be found on European maps of that period, probable evidence of detailed correction from local sources. Some of these depicted the mysterious gold and silver islands, *Kinjima* or *Rica de Oro* and *Ginjima* or *Rico de Plata*, which fascinated seamen and navigators of all nationalities at that time. (Boxer, 1951, 201)

It is surprising, but true, that originally *shuinsen* vessels were obliged, by Japanese regulations, to carry Portuguese pilots. This regulation was seldom enforced, however. All the same, there were plentiful Portuguese in Japanese service at a relatively late date, such as Emanuel Luís, the pilot of the Japanese junk encountered by Oliver van Noort off the Borneo coast in January 1601. Luís, typically, had lived and worked in Malacca and Macau. By the time he met the Dutchmen he was a resident of Nagasaki. (Boxer, 1951, 265; Massarella, 1990, 81)

XIV

VOYAGES

In his earliest years in Japan, Adams was prohibited from leaving the country by the personal edict of Tokugawa Ieyasu. That he almost certainly could have made good his escape, had he so desired, is immaterial; by the time Adams became a man 'called in the Japann tonge ANJIN SAMMA (and) by that nam I am knowen all the sea cost allong', as he stated in his letter of January 1613 to Augustus Spalding at Bantam in Java (Rundall, 1850, 44), he was comfortably situated in Japan, a trusted, respected and tolerably wealthy member of society. His situation in Togukawa Japan was wholly unlike that of many Europeans, mainly mariners but also including some gunners, who were unable to leave the Asian societies in which they found themselves, being closely guarded to prevent any attempt at escape. After Saris' visit to Ieyasu, Adams was at liberty to leave Japan. The reasons he gave for not doing so were threefold; he had not yet made sufficient money to enable him to return home in appropriate affluence, he had grown to dislike the company of John Saris, the *Clove*'s commander and, lastly, he desired to serve the East India Company, especially were they to pursue the *chimaera* of the northwest passage. Adams was also esteemed and successful in Japan. (Massarella, 1990, 223)

Vermilion-seal documents, *shuinjo,* made clear the distinction between legitimate merchants, like Adams and Jan Joosten on the one hand and pirates like those who slew John Davis in 1605. Also referred to as *goshuin*, and – by Cocks, *inter alia* – as *goshon*, they invoked the Bakufu's protection, as André Pessoa found to his cost. In this they were like the pass issued to the Portuguese pilot Luís by the Dutch whom he encountered on the Borneo coast and the Portuguese *cartaze*. (Massarella, 1990, 132) In spite of possession of *shuinjo,* a number of the *shuinsen* vessels had no hesitation in behaving like pirate ships. Some would attack any ship or coastal settlement for booty and were duly feared throughout southeast Asia in consequence.

Among those who received *shuinjo* during the early seventeenth century were William Adams, Jan Joosten and several Iberians resident in Nagasaki. A number of Chinese residents of Nagasaki and Hirado received *shuinjo* as did various *daimyo*. The Arima junk whose crew caused disturbances in Macau which, eventually, resulted in the destruction of Pessoa and the *Nossa Senhora da Graça* (or *Madre de Deus*) was in possession of a *shuinjo*. Possibly this was one of the factors which impelled Ieyasu to permit the *daimyo* of Arima to settle matters with Pessoa, the honour of the *Bakufu* having been insulted. Also listed as awarded *shuinjo* was Thomas Araki, Kirishtan *Bateran* Tomasu, one of the very few Japanese priests to have been ordained in Rome. He was expelled from the ranks of the Jesuits for unchastity, subsequently apostatising and becoming a bitter foe of the foreign missionaries and those around them. (Boxer, 1951, 263)

It was this, Adams' first voyage southwards from Hirado, that Saris was anticipating in the written instructions, or '*remembrance*' he left with the Hirado factors. The factory's junk was to sail to Ayuthia and Pattani to meet Chinese traders who were expected to be actively trading there. The outward cargo was to be English broadcloth, Cambay cloth from Gujerat in India, ivory and coinage in the form of reals, worth approximately 3s 6d to 4s 6d in English money. Goods to be procured for sale in Japan were silk, deerskins and sappan wood as well as merchants travelling with their goods, a common practice of the era.

As a *shuinsen* merchant, Adams made a number of voyages. It can be reasonably surmised that many records relating to these still survive intact, awaiting discovery, like the contemporary Christian letter which turned up in the lining of a Japanese screen in Evora in Portugal, or the important document 'lost' for centuries and located by chance in Oxford or the stern-figure of the *Liefde* itself, revered as a Buddhist deity for decades. (Elison, 1973, 18-19; Massarella and Tytler, 1990, 189; Snellen, 1934, 1)

The records of *shuinjo,* vermilion seal documents authorising the possessor to make an overseas voyage, were kept by Zen monks in Miyako. (Massarella, 1990, 132-3) It is not improbable that more accidental discoveries await researchers.

Among the surviving records relating to Adams the mariner are those relating to his association with the East India Company factory at Hirado, painstakingly researched by Derek Massarella and considered in some detail in *A World Elsewhere: Europe's Encounter with Japan in the Sixteenth and Seventeenth Centuries*. (See Bibliography) Anthony Farrington's outstanding work, *The English Factory in Japan,* reproduces the complete original texts.

Prior to his arrival in Japan, Adams had sailed in European waters and, probably, to North Africa. The journey to Japan had taken him to the coast of Africa and thence to the Magellan Straits, the Chilean coast and the trans-Pacific crossing *via* either the Hawaiian Islands or, possibly, the Marshalls or the Marianas if the reference to 16°N latitude in his letter of 1605 was accurate. While associated with the factors of the E.I.C. factory at Hirado, Adams made five voyages from Japan. Three were successful, the other two failed. The first two voyages had Siam as their intended destination and were performed in 1614 and 1615, of these, the first reached Okinawa before being forced to return to Japan. The third and fourth voyages had Cochin-China as their intended destination and were performed in 1617 and 1618; the second of these was unsuccessful, reaching Okinawa before circumstances forced the vessel's return. The fifth and last voyage was performed in 1619 and successfully reached Tongking.

Indo-China had close trade relations with Japan up to the time of the *Sakoku* decrees. There were several *nihonmachi*, Japanese trading communities. Faifo, or *Hoi An*, and Tourane, or *Da Nang*, had Japanese residents in significant numbers, as did Ayuthia in Siam and Phnom Penh in Cambodia. During the period 1604 – 1634 over 300 Japanese voyages were made to Southeast Asia, approximately a quarter of these trading to what is now Vietnam.

THE SIAM VOYAGE OF 1614

The Siam voyage of 1614 was the second overseas venture of the East India Company's factory at Hirado. The first had ended in disaster and loss; Walter Carwarden and Tempest Peacock, employees of the factory, failed to return; Peacock having been killed in Annam and Carwarden having drowned (according to one account). This loss, which entailed the loss of a sizeable portion of the Hirado factory's stock, was as yet unknown to Richard Cocks of the Hirado factory at the time preparations were being made for the first voyage to Ayuthia, then the capital of Siam.

The E.I.C. factory employed its own junk, the *Sea Adventure,* bought for 2,000 taels and refitted at an additional cost exceeding a further 2,000. As Japanese official regulations required, it carried a *shuinjo,* or vermilion-seal document, which Adams had obtained at Suruga.

The cargo consisted of 5,000 taels in silver and just under 130 taels in ready money, with which it was intended to purchase sappan wood, deer hides, silk and other goods which would be suitable for the Japanese market. An assortment of Cambay cloth, Japanese weapons and Japanese armour for presents and for sale was included with the rest of the cargo, the total value of which was over 5,800 taels, over 25 per cent of the Hirado factory's stock. Additionally, the junk took letters for the E.I.C. factors at Ayuthia and Patani as well as letters to be forwarded to England *via* Bantam in Java.

Adams was designated master of the junk, being accompanied by Richard Wickham of the Hirado factory, acting as Cape Merchant, and Edmund Sayers.

Wickham was specifically instructed by Richard Cocks to avoid conflict with Adams, to keep his eyes open for other saleable goods, such as the shark skins the Japanese liked to use to decorate scabbards, and to avoid putting into Cochinchina if Ayuthia could not be reached. In any case, Wickham was told, the junk was to return with the monsoon even if not fully laden. In accordance with Japanese practice, the Japanese crew were permitted to load merchandise for private trade. Additionally, a number of Japanese traders and their cargoes sailed with the vessel.

The *Sea Adventure* left Hirado for Kochi, or *Kawachi,* late in November. Junks outward bound from Hirado usually anchored in the roadstead at Kochi, or *Kawachi,* prior to their departure. This was a league from Hirado, but because it was essential for ships to catch the tide at the precise moment, time and tide waiting for none, Wickham, for example, took lodgings there prior to the *Sea Adventure*'s departure at the end of 1614. (Farrington, 1991, 270)

The sailing southwards, in mid-December, was attended by misfortune; after encountering bad weather to the south of the Goto Islands, the junk sprang a leak and rather than return ignominiously to Hirado, Adams, Wickham and Sayers decided to steer for the Ryukyus in order to make appropriate repairs. What was intended to be a short delay turned into an enforced stay of nearly five months; the *Sea Adventure* lost the monsoon and was forced to return to Hirado. The voyage, which failed to reach Siam, turned into an expensive fiasco for the English factory at Hirado although the writings that have survived the ravages of time throw an interesting light on the Ryukyus, or Okinawa.

Among those who sailed aboard the *Sea Adventure*'s first voyage between December 1614 and May 1615 were the Italian Damiano Marina and the Castilian Juan de Llevana. Employed as commercial agents for the English in Nagasaki, they were seized by the Portuguese in Nagasaki after returning to Japan. Accused of treason to the Iberian monarch and, one presumes, the Catholic faith, they were imprisoned aboard the Macau carrack *Nossa Senhora da Vida*, which had arrived at Nagasaki in August 1615. In October of the same year, Adams obtained the Bakufu's order for their release. Both men left Japan aboard the *Hoseander* in February 1616. Although Catholic and Iberian power was waning in Japan, European Catholics who were too close to the Dutch and the British were justifiably apprehensive about being punished for their associations, especially in such places as Macau and Manila, where the Iberians had absolute power. Cocks described Juan de Llevana as a poor man in a letter to Wickham written in December 1614, adding that had 'not byn forgetfull to geve him somthing out of my povertie' and suggesting that Wickham do the same. (Farrington, 1991, 244)

Okinawa lay in the sea lanes used by Western ships which approached Japan. According to Pinto, an engaging if occasionally misleading chronicler, there was an interesting proposal concerning the Ryukyus in 1556:

> '. . .a Portugal arrived at *Malaca*, named *Pedro Gomez d'Almeyda*, servant to the Grand Master of *Santiago*, with a rich Present, and letters from the *Nautaquim*, Prince of the Island of *Tanizumaa*, directed to King *John* the third. . .to have five hundred *Portugals* granted to him, to the end that with them, and his own Forces, he might conquer the Island of *Lequio*,

> for which he would remain tributary to him at 5000 Kintals of Copper and 1000 of Lattin, yearly.' (Yule and Burnell, 1986, 514)

This proposal, if indeed it was made, illustrates clearly that some *daimyo* during the *Sengoku Jidai* were willing to consider alliance with European monarchs and ready enough to employ European mercenaries in the same way that they were employed in Burma and Siam.

The Spanish came from Mexico and the Philippines about 1580; the Dutch established themselves at Hirado in 1609. Japan's rulers had ample reason to dislike and mistrust the Spanish and Portuguese missionaries, but Tokugawa Ieyasu was eager to encourage trade. He granted a liberal commercial charter to the British and opened all ports to British ships disabled by storm. By extension through Satsuma, Naha came under these general provisions and was used as a port of refuge and as a way station on the run between Japan, the Philippines and Siam.

The Ryukyu Islands, nominally subject to China, were invaded on the orders of Shimazu Iehisa (Tadatsune), *daimyo* of Satsuma, in 1609. An annual tribute was levied in the islands. The circumstances in which this came to pass are less than wholly creditable to Japanese pretensions of overlordship stretching into the mists of antiquity. In 1608, Shimazu Iehisa, who had recently attracted Ieyasu's favourable attention, wrote to the 'king' of Luchu, demanding to know why the latter had failed to send any tribute for a long time, despite being a vassal of the house of Shimazu and demanding that tribute be paid forthwith. Accompanying this missive were two Buddhist priests and a layman; these confronted Sho Nei, the 'king', and his three generals. This demand was refused and the envoys, having paused to map the islands and steal a religious image greatly esteemed by the islanders, left. In the second month of the next year, Shimazu despatched a force of 1,500 men, 734 of them armed with firearms. Despite inflicting 300 casualties on the invaders, the islanders were obliged to submit and Ieyasu granted the territory to Shimazu. Attempts to subdue the ferocious and determined aborigines of Taiwan, or *Formosa*, were signally less successful. Arima Haronobu sent an expedition there at about the same time as the Shimazu conquest of Rykyu but met with stout resistance. In 1616, the *daikan* of Nagasaki, the ill-fated

Murayama Toan, despatched an expedition which met with shipwreck and disaster. (Sadler, 1984, 248)

Toan's abortive Formosa venture was if anything, counter-productive. After one of the thirteen junks involved had been ambushed in a creek on the island, the crew committing *seppuku* rather than be taken alive by the Taiwanese headhunters, the remainder embarked on a piratical expedition against the Chinese coast, 'boot-haling', as Cocks expressed it. There they were said 'to have killed above 1,200 Chinas, and taken all the barkes or junks they met withal, throwing the people overboard'. (Boxer, 1951, 298)

This expedition was an attempt on Toan's part to save himself from the *Bakufu*'s growing anger at him for having exhibited himself conspicuously as a penitent Christian in the flagellant penitential procession held in Nagasaki under Dominican auspices in May 1614. Additionally, Toan had acquired powerful enemies determined to accomplish his downfall. The intended invasion of Taiwan was, Richard Cocks recorded, 'to look for Fidaia *Samme*,' the young Hideyori. Earlier Toan had sent assistance to Hideyori in Osaka Castle. Toan's own son, the priest Francisco, perished when the castle fell to the Bakufu armies in 1615. (Elison, 1973, 161) The fall of Murayama Toan and his clan was as thorough, swift and appalling as any invention on the part of a Greek dramatist; his position undermined by Suetsugu Heizo João from early in 1618, he was banished to an island close to Edo. In November 1619, his eldest son, André Tokuan, was executed in Nagasaki for concealing missionaries – the same offence as that of which Adams' wife had been suspected. Toan was beheaded in Edo in December 1619 as was his son Juan Shuan, the Formosan adventurer. Two other sons, Pedro and Paulo, were executed in Miyako.

In a letter dated December 23, 1614, Richard Wickham reported to his chief at Hirado, Richard Cocks:

> 'The people [of 'Liquea'] much resemble the Chinese, yet speak the Japan tongue, although with difficulty to be understood of the Japans, they wear [their] hair long bound up like the Chinese, with a bodkin thrust through, but it is made up [on the] right side of their heads; they are a very gentle and courteous people.'

While this letter was being written, Adams was limping towards

Naha port in the damaged junk *Sea Adventure*. With a crew of Japanese sailors, he had set out from Japan on November 28 for a voyage to Siam. The ship proved unseaworthy. On December 22 a gale forced the leading craft inshore at Amami Oshima. Finding no suitable anchorage, Adams took the *Sea Adventure* on down to Naha, putting in on December 27 for repairs.

Naha was the capital of this Lilliputian insular 'kingdom', which still maintained a fragile semi-independence at the time of Adams' arrival. The seat of government was in Shuri castle, later to be smashed to rubble during the Allied assault in 1945. Restored painstakingly over a period of more than three years prior to 1992, the castle has been rebuilt to what was intended to be its original state, using old picture scrolls and similar records as visual guides.

The presence of the *Sea Adventure* was disturbing to the Ryukyu officials. Although owned by Europeans, it was obviously a Japanese ship. Trade with China continued despite the Satsuma invasion of 1609 and the presence of the *Sea Adventure* was a violation of a 1611 agreement between Ryukyu and Satsuma that all foreign trade and ships entering or leaving Ryukyuan waters should have Satsuma authorization. Curiously, this stipulation did not upset an official from Satsuma who was in Naha at the time; he genially offered his assistance to the ship. (Massarella, 1990, 158)

There were approximately 125 passengers and seamen aboard. Shuri gave them permission to land their stores and to begin repair work. 'We found marvellous great friendship', worte Adams, but after thirty days the Okinawan officials began to urge the strangers to hasten their departure. Junks were expected to come in from Ch'uang-chou, said the anxious Okinawans and the Chinese would be angry if they found rival traders at Naha; trade relations with China might be broken off. Chinese junks were officially forbidden to call at Naha. It is probable that the Okinawans were ordered to conceal the presence of Satsuma's agents aboard the Okinawan vessels returning from the China coast. There were other reasons too; the idle crew and passengers were bickering among themselves, making demands upon Adams and creating disturbances in the port. A mutinous quarrel broke out between a score of armed men, led by a Japanese named Shobei, and about forty other boisterous seamen.

Shuri's chief magistrate was called down to mediate and by March 15, restored order.

The people of Naha and Shuri treated these uninvited guests with courtesy. Adams was received most cordially; his close friendship with Tokugawa Ieyasu was well known to Satsuma's agents at Naha and to the king's officials, and he himself made a great effort to establish good personal relations; for instance, his diary notes polite words and phrases which he had transcribed for guidance. This was certainly the first time anyone had put together a short phrase-list of English and the Okinawan dialect. Adams recorded such useful phrases as:

> *yaabero* I will not, or no no
> *shaberan* I know not
> *wiasabero* I drink to ye
> *obocooii kattakina* I thank you, but clouwnish spech

(Farrington, 1991, 1071)

At Naha, Adams dickered for a cargo of grain and ambergris and directed repairs on the *Sea Adventure*. It was slow work; the voyage to Siam was given up as an unseasonable venture; and on May 22 Adams sailed for Kawachi in Japan, carrying sweet-potato plants for Cocks' garden at Hirado and such cargo as he had been able to buy at Naha. On June 10, the *Sea Adventure* made port safely.

The record of British expenditures at Naha demonstrates the cheapness of goods and the low value placed upon Okinawan currency. Wheat, 'Liquea wyne', a 'great Liquea cocke', and 'Liquea trenchers' (possibly lacquerware) were among the articles brought in from Naha by the foreign merchants. Cock's *Diary* notes that on June 2, 1615, Wickham took a gift of two pieces of Okinawan cloth and a 'dish of pottatos' to the feudal Lord of Bungo. On June 26 he recorded: 'Bongo Dono sent to me to have had a jar of Liquea wyne (or *rack*) for that the Emperor hath sent to him to come to Miaco, and therefore, he sought for such matters to give in present to greate men for a novelitie.'

Some traffic in spices took place by way of Fukien. Adams noted on June 14, 1615, that 'the new botswayn of the junck brought me 2 Liquea brushes and a box of synamon of same place, the best that ever I saw in my life and Jno. Japan our *jurebasso*, brought me a present of Liquea cloth one peece.'

The Ryukyus had an unusual export, remarked upon by all travellers who recorded their impressions; 'Leque Grande yeeldeth greate store of amber greece of the best sorte', as Ralph Coppindale observed. (Thompson, 1883, II, 272)

Sometimes Adams suspected that his agents at Naha sequestered valuable items which should have been delivered to the English trading depot. He records a quarrel with Damiano Marina, who had bought up the local Okinawan supply of ambergris, kept in a 'chist' which Adams wanted to inspect. Wickham, too, reports on supplies of this valuable commodity which could be obtained in the Ryukyus. In other entries for 1615 and 1616, Cocks records the desertion of a Japanese employee in Okinawa and a sum set aside for investment in ambergris at Naha. He also notes that 'thirteen barkes laden with souldiers' had left port, ostensibly for Formosa, but he was of the opinion that they were searching throughout the Ryukyu Islands for refugees scattered after the fall of Osaka Castle, where Hideyoshi's heirs and their adherents had been destroyed.

Under date of July 28, 1618, Cocks notes that he had received letters 'from Antony the Negro' and two others then stationed at Naha, and in that year, Adams made his second visit to Okinawa en route to Indo-China.

The English company had no illusions concerning the source of basic authority in the Ryukyus, for Cocks at Hirado was on most friendly terms with 'the King of Xaxma [*Satsuma*] whose vassall the King of Liqueas is. . .' William Eaton at Naha, reported to Cocks that he received cordial assistance from the Okinawans because the Lord of Satsuma had ordered them to be helpful to the British. Edmund Sayers, who was often at Kagoshima, noted that 'Soyemon Dono told me that the King of Shasma did much esteem our English nation and would suffer us to trade into the Liqueas or any other parts of his dominion.' (Kerr, 1984, 173) Adams' logbook of this ill-fated voyage consists of 79 folios of two different kinds of Japanese paper. It was bequeathed to the Bodleian Library by Sir Henry Savile but its earlier travels are unknown.

A minor part of the mythology which was grown up around William Adams is the folk belief that he introduced sweet potatoes from the Ryukyus to the main islands of Japan. Cocks recorded, in July 1618, that the 500 small potato roots he planted in his garden at Hirado were sent by William Eaton from the 'Liques' (Thompson, 1883, II, 59)

Adams' account of the journey and the frustrations of attempting to repair the junk adequately in Okinawa make the affair sound nightmarish. The Italian Damiano Marina and Richard Wickham found one another's company irksome; 'Mr. Wik' & Damian did fight together' being followed in the log a month later with 'This day wass Mr. Wikcam & Damian mad frinds.' The accounts contain 'Item p'd for men hired w'ch wached w'th me when our men forsook the ship'.

THE SIAM VOYAGE OF 1615

Readied once more for service in the open sea, the *Sea Adventure* left Japan in December 1615 with Adams as master and Sayers as Cape Merchant. Over 1,690 taels had been spent to make the vessel seaworthy, Cocks suspecting that the Japanese purser of the vessel had contrived to pocket over 50 taels of this, with Adams' complicity.

The cargo this time was valued at just under 3,000 taels, of which 2,400 taels was in reals and silver plate, the remainder of the cargo laden by the factory being similar to that sent on the abortive first voyage to Siam.

The *Sea Adventure* skirted the Fukien coast, forbidden to Japanese shipping. Just after a month after the departure from Japan, the junk reached the mouth of the Chao Phraya, Sayers proceeding upriver in a smaller vessel provided by the local governor and arriving in the capital on the 14th of January 1616. Two days later, authorised by a pass which Sayers had obtained, the *Sea Adventure* docked at Ayuthia and Sayers set briskly about his task of bestowing presents of Japanese swords and armour upon the king and court officials, before purchasing goods from resident Portuguese, Japanese and Chinese merchants. By early June, all seemed ready until it emerged that there were disputes over the amount of cargo space for the Japanese crew, accustomed to the *shuinsen* practice of lading a vessel aboard which they served with their own goods. In the case of sappan wood, space was at a premium and Adams, who also loaded his own cargo, strongly supported the crew, 'alleging that they were all true men and might lade what they pleased.'

Benjamin Farie, the E.I.C. cape-merchant in Siam, concluded

that the E.I.C's interests 'ar exseedingly abused herin by his (*Adams*') lardg prevyledges granted to his purser & rest wherby I thenk the Jonk to be 2/3 laden by himself & marners'. Farie was evidently unaware that this was standard practice among Japanese mariners; as in Europe, one strong argument in favour of permitting sailors to carry individual cargoes for their own intended profit was that their financial commitment would encourage them not to desert the vessel in the event of shipwreck or other catastrophe.

Two additional junks, one owned by a Japanese, the other by a Chinese, were duly chartered and loaded but even then 30 peculs of sappan wood – a considerable quantity, considering that a pecul was slightly more than 133 lbs *avoirdupois* – had to be left behind.

Sappan-wood was a valuable commodity used in dyeing. Bocarro the Portuguese chronicler, writing about the trade of Ayuthia in 1616, refers to Sappan-wood (*sapão*), deer-skins and silk from Cochin-china and Chincheo, the port in the Chinese province of Fujian. (Yule and Burnell, 1986, 794)

The *Sea Adventure* reached Hirado in late July 1616. The junk owned by the Chinese merchant Giquan was only saved from shipwreck by the strenuous efforts of Sayers, reaching Satsuma in September, her owner and most of her crew having perished. The junk owned by the Japanese, one Shoby-dono, did not reach Nagasaki until the following June, adverse weather conditions having forced the vessel to winter in Champa, now the southernmost part of Vietnam. After all the saleable goods had been sold and the Satsuma *daimyo* given presents to induce him to release the junk on which Sayers returned to Japan, the voyage had not been an outstandingly profitable affair. Nonetheless, Cocks and his subordinates felt encouraged, believing that trade between Ayuthia and Hirado would blossom in the future. (Massarella, 1990, 178)

Giquan's junk ended up in the hands of the Hirado factory after various bills had been settled as satisfactorily as was possible in the light of Giquan's death. Adams purchased this from the Company for 750 taels with the intention of refitting it for a voyage to Cochin-China the following year.

The quarrels concerning cargo owned by crewmen caused a temporary breach between William Adams and Richard Cocks.

Adams supported the crew, knowing Japanese practice intimately. Cocks' bitter complaints to the Matsuura resulted in the *daimyo* sending men to observe the unloading of the *Sea Adventure* and ensure that the crewmen received their due. Cocks was appalled that Adams sided with the crew and was unwilling to support the E.I.C. factory in its complaint to the Matsuura, writing of Adams' 'extraordinary humour' and adding, evidently in some anger 'I take God to witnes I do what I can to keepe in w'th this man.' (Massarella, 1990, 251) Edmund Sayers' journal of this voyage is of interest not least because it inadvertently records the strain of keeping accurate records at a time of danger and stress; Sayers' journal has a mere 30 days for December 1615 and a surprising 31 days in September. There are other oddities but the text describes a journey fraught with danger in suitably unsophisticated Jacobean prose; 'The storme was soo great thatt att mednight wee were fane to poutt all thenges that was beetwext the deckes doane into the hould. This night wee loste our poumpe overbourde, havinge everye seaye cominge in a buthe siedes, as thoughe it would have sounke hure.' (Farrington, 1991, 1075) On the return journey, which Sayers completed aboard a different vessel from that aboard which Adams sailed, things seemed desperate at one point; 'Theine all of ofeceres and mareneres thatt ware Crestyanes mayed a seremoney and bought the roudere of the jounke and promesed to geive it, or the worth of it, to the Mesery Cordeye when theay came to Langasacka.' (Farrington, 1991, 1093) The *Misericordia* Hospital in Nagasaki, located between the churches of Saint Anthony and Saint Paul, would have been familiar to every Christian in Hirado and Nagasaki. The seven demonstrative processions of the Nagasaki Christians on Wednesday, May 14th 1614 passed by the door. The *Misericordia* was, in part, a leprosarium, but it functioned as a general hospital and hospice, too. (Plutschow, 1983, 34)

The return voyage was ghastly; at one point the junk put in at the Wu'ch'iu Hsü islands to collect water, having first exchanged hostages with some fishermen in the neighbourhood. Despite 'haveinge hallfe of our compenye with the skervey, swelled that thay could nott work', Sayers contrived to hire local boatmen to tow their junk to windward, to escape a headland and so escaped to endure fresh perils in what was stormy, very capricious weather; the crew loudly arguing as to where each man believed they were. A month after leaving the Chinese islands, the vessel and its survivors reached Odamari in Satsuma.

THE COCHINCHINA VOYAGE OF 1617

The 1617 voyage was to Cochinchina, the southernmost kingdom of what is now Vietnam. Edmund Sayers sailed as a passenger on the *Gift of God,* a junk belonging to William Adams.

A minor, if disagreeable incident occurred prior to Adams' departure; a number of Yasimon's relatives loudly contended that Adams should have sold them a larger share of the Siamese wood brought back on the previous voyage. At least one assaulted Adams, who responded by holding the *Bakufu*'s *shuinjo* above his head to emphasise that he enjoyed Hidetada's protection. (Rogers, 1956, 98)

The term Cochin-china referred to the Annamite territories of Vietnam, especially the southern provinces centred on Quang-tri with Hué as the capital. In theory, this area was subject to China, but Chinese authority was nominal at best, as in Siam and Burma.

Sayers was instructed to purchase silk, to secure the permission of the local ruler to establish an E.I.C. factory at a later date and to obtain a safe pass to permit trade in the meantime and, not least, to endeavour to establish what had befallen Carwarden and Peacock.

The cargo aboard the junk on which Peacock and Carwarden sailed was worth 2983 taels, approximately £746. Apart from the loss of the two men, the loss of so much money was an inauspicious beginning to the Hirado factory's overseas trade and a disaster which cast a pall of gloom over the factory's early days. The loss of the junk and the two Englishmen deprived the factory of 13% of its opening stock, estimated to have been £5,647 11s in December 1613. (Farrington, 1991, 9)

On this voyage, the Hirado factory sent goods and money to a value of 1,896 taels; broadcloth, India cloth and ivory, copper, Muscovy hides, fowling pieces, table books and assorted other goods. The voyage commenced in late March, arriving at Faifo, now Hoi Ar on the coast of central Vietnam, in late April. One-third of the Hirado factory's lading had to be returned as unsaleable but broadcloth and ivory sold well, copper poorly. Silk and aglaia wood was purchased for the return voyage. So far as Sayers was concerned, the voyage would have been a modest success had he not been neatly cheated out of more than 650 taels in ready money in an awkward encounter involving the promised or pretended sale of silk. Astonishingly, this money was later recovered and given to the custody of the king, who refused to hand it over to Sayer's servant, Melisore, preferring to await the return of the English. (Massarella, 1990, 405)

Adams and Sayers pieced together a credible account of the deaths of Carwarden and Peacock. Peacock had been killed in revenge for his disrespectful behaviour towards the Annamese; Carwarden had fled towards the coast but had perished in a storm. This, which was similar to the version provided by Li Tan, the head of the Chinese community at Hirado, seemed to be as much as could be learned. Adams and Sayers were told unambiguously not to pursue the matter with the monarch, who was evidently ignorant of the whole affair. An alternative version of Peacock's demise was that he had unwittingly become involved in the factional polices of the court, evidently no place for an innocent outsider. Richard Cocks' attempts to recover some, at least, of the cargo of the voyage on which the two men had died were unsuccessful; the Tokugawa *shogunate* declined to interest itself in the matter and attempts to recover half the missing cargo by offering the other half as a reward were, perhaps predictably, unavailing.

Adams sold this junk at the end of the year, not an uncommon practice; frequently merchants would own junks for the duration of one or two voyages only.

Edmund Sayers kept a journal of this voyage, which has survived and is reprinted in full in Anthony Farrington's compendious work. Sayers, although not an excellent chronicler, wrote well although his account is somewhat hard to follow when relating exchanges concerning the demise of Carwarden and Peacock. A court official assured Sayers that the two had died by misadventure; 'drouned by misechance in a small bott'. When requested to make it possible for Sayers and Adams to visit the monarch in an attempt to clarify the matter and, if possible, obtain redress, the official readily countered 'that it was a great jorney and to mouch panes for us to tacke'.

Sayers found this disconcerting, insisting 'wee ware sent to knowe what was beecomne of the 2 Englishemene that was sent to him, and to seck joustes att his handes fore theme which mayed theme awaye, and to secke to recovere the goodes and moneys that thaye loste. . .'

Sayers' account makes it clear that further insistence would be unavailing, possibly even dangerous.

Surprisingly, the monarch accepted the Britons' presents graciously and asked, through his secretary, why they had not come to his court in person. It was quite evident to Sayers and Adams that the king was being kept ignorant of the deaths of Carwarden and Peacock, although he was apparently aware that Englishmen had been to his realm beforehand.

Perhaps the most vivid item in the journal is the lamentable tale of how Sayers was robbed of 656 taels by his interpreter in league with a Chinese merchant. The *modus operandi* was simple; Sayers was induced to enter a house next door to the interpreter's and put his bag of money safely out of sight of various passing traders. Waiting innocently beside the money for a little while, Sayers was unaware that nimble hands were being slipped through the reed wall separating the two houses and furtively abstracting the money; 'And wee siting there an ouere, wee sad, thes mene stayes very longe, lett us goo and see what thaye doo. Soo wee stoupinge doune to tak up the money, but it wase stolne'.

The timing had been exquisite, too; '. . . Captane Adames binge without the rever with his jounke, redey to sett sall, I was fane to leve Melisore to recover it. . .' (Farrington, 1991, 1134)

THE COCHINCHINA VOYAGE OF 1618

The Hirado factory's Cochinchina voyage of 1618 was aboard a junk owned by a Nagasaki merchant, Shiquan. William Adams was the vessel's captain; indeed, his engagement as captain of the voyage was the reason he gave for declining to accept a passage to England aboard the *Advice,* a British ship then at Hirado and due to sail for Bantam. Edmond Sayers and Robert Hawley, later to be Cocks' second-in-command at Hirado, accompanied Adams as factors on the voyage, which left Nagasaki on 17 March.

The voyage proved to be unsuccessful, foul weather in the

East China Sea damaging the rudder and obliging Adams to return to Hirado from the island of Amami Oshima, north of the main Okinawa group of islands, reaching Hirado, *via* Nagasaki on 14 May with an intact cargo.

The voyage began inauspiciously with damage to the vessel's rudder in an inlet in the Goto Islands, sought as a temporary refuge in a squall. The junk was unladen and the rudder repaired after great efforts, 'all hands ware att woork in hewinge of the tembere and poutinge the starne poste in', as Sayers wrote.

The weather continued to be stormy and threatening as the vessel sailed southwards. Eleven days after the first mishap, the rudder was damaged by a wave and, after consultations, the crew 'ware a greed to stand ffor woshma a nielland of the Leuckes to see if wee Could gett a nother Roodere'.

At Amami Oshima, trees were cut but proved to fall short of what was required for adequate repairs, 'soo wee had noo hopes to make any viege this yere'.

Such setbacks were not uncommon in the days of sail; a single mishap of this kind was sufficient to wipe out a year's profits.

THE TONGKING VOYAGE OF 1619

The Tongking Voyage of 1619 was made on Adams' own account aboard a privately-owned junk which left Hirado on 17 March 1619, arrived at Tonkin a month later and sailed for Japan on 16 July, arriving at Hirado in August. (Farrington, 1991, 1588)

Adams' last voyage was delayed somewhat due to a breach of the regulations concerning *shuinjo*. Adams had sold the *Gift of God*, through Cocks, together with its *shuinjo*; all would have been well had not the crew of the vessel on its subsequent voyage created, or been involved in, a disturbance of some kind in Cochin-china. Word of this had reached the *Bakufu*, who were evidently displeased. Adams last voyage, therefore, was not aboard a vessel owed by the E.I.C. factory or himself but aboard a junk owned by Sagawa Shuma of Hirado. (Makino, 1983, 74)

This voyage was evidently a modest success for the English factory. Although sales in Japan were sluggish, and prices disappointingly poor, the fact was that Dutch competition, along with altered conditions of trade in Japan generally, was having a depressing effect on prices.

Cocks persistently complained that a 'ring' of buyers had destroyed the Japanese market by 1620; 'It is strange to see the changes of merchandising so altered since our first arrival in Japan; for heretofore yearly white raw silk was sold at 500, 400 and 300 taies the pico at least and now it is fallen to 130, yea some have sold for 105 taies the pico this year which 3 years past was worth 300 taies pico. The reason is, a company of rich men have got all the trade of Japan into their hands. So they agree all together and will not buy but at what price they think good themselves and it is not to be remedied'. (Thompson, 1883, II, 322-323)

The Hirado factory invested 700 taels in this voyage, the Hirado Dutch 500 taels and Adams himself 950 taels. (Purnell, 1915, 268)

The Hirado factory's investment brought it 4 peculs 20 catties of yellow silk but prices had slumped by almost 30% in the Japanese market. In September 1619, Eaton commented that he was at a loss to know how to generate enough income for the factory to pay its way. Such was the gloom among the Hirado Britons that all talk of profits had ceased. (Massarella, 1991, 264)

This voyage, while neither dangerous nor greatly profitable, produced one of the more famous artefacts associated with Adams; the well-known log of the voyage. Evidently written as an *aide-memoir*, it lacks the vividness and directness of Adams' letters but possesses a period flavour which Victorians like Purnell and William Dalton would have considered charming and quaint:

> 'By the grac of God begoun a voag this yeer 1619 the 15 of March for Tounkin in a new jounk of the toun of Ferando'. (Farrington, 1991, 1153)

Even Adams, with all his experience of trading from Japan, sometimes found the going hard:

> 'Sonday the 25 wee had much ado to get our marchants to agree in dellivering monny afforhand, w'thout w'ch wee could not have his lisshenc to do nothinge, I say from the kinge ssoonn'. (Farrington, 1991, 1160)

XV

THE GREATEST AND POWREFULLEST TERRANY

Richard Cocks had barely been resident in Japan for a year when he described the nature of the Tokugawa régime to Lord Salisbury thus;

> 'This government of Japan may well be accompted the greatest and powrefullest terrany that ever was heard of in the world, for all the rest are as slaves to the Emperour. . . whoe, upon the leaste suspition or jelosie, or being angry w'th any man (be he never soe great a man), will cause hym upon the recepte of his letter to cutt his bellie, w'ch yf he refuse to doe, not only he but all the rest of their rase shall feele the smart thereof'. (Farrington, 1991, 259)

Cocks was not exaggerating in the slightest; the Tokugawa régime was an efficient, spy-ridden despotism which would have excited jealousy in the minds of European absolutist monarchs. The foundations of Tokugawa absolutist power were laid between 1600, the year of Ieyasu's victory at the decisive battle of Sekigahara, and 1616, the year of Ieyasu's death and his succession by Hidetada, his son.

Toyotomi Hideyoshi's death in 1598 left Japan governed by the guardians of his youthful heir, Hideyori. As might have been predicted in so turbulent a feudal society, these soon quarrelled and Ieyasu, by a judicious mixture of guile, blandishments and force, rapidly acquired the authority wielded by his two powerful predecessors. Tokugawa Ieyasu achieved the goal which had eluded Nobunaga and Hideyoshi by establishing a *de facto* dynasty, repeating the accomplishments of the Fujiwara, the Taira, the Minamoto, the Hojo and the Ashikaga. The Tokugawa *shogunate* attained power in 1600 at the decisive battle of Sekigahara, fought between Ieyasu's adherents and those disposed to challenge Tokugawa hegemony.

Writing in 1613, John Saris summarized the situation in Osaka as perceptively as any foreigner might have done;

> 'In this castle did dwell at our beeing there, the sonne of Tiquasamma, who being an infant at the time of his fathers decease, was left to the governement and education of foure, whereof Ogoshosamma (*Ieyasu*), the now Emperour, was one and chiefe. The other three, desirous of soveraigntie each for his particular, and repulsed by Ogoshosamma, were for their own safetie forced to take up armes, wherein fortune favouring Ogoshosamma at the triall in field, two of them beeing slaine, the third was glad to save himselfe by flight'. (Farrington, 1991, 1012-3)

The destruction of the remnants of Toyotomi power in the Winter Campaign and the Summer Campaign of 1614-15 was a struggle in slow motion in two acts, the first ending with a negotiated peace after a cautious siege of Hideyori's Osaka stronghold and the second culminating in the destruction of Hideyori's army and Hideyori's despairing suicide, followed by the remorseless extermination of virtually his entire clan.

Cocks, writing in December 1614, was well aware of the impending conflict, observing:

> 'Hear now is great likelyhood of warrs in Jappann for that the ould Emperor Ogosho Same is com downe in p'son w'th a mightie army as farr as Fuchma (*Fushimi*), to bringe in Fidaia Same, a younge man of som 22 years ould, who hath fortified himselfe in the castell of Osekey but is thought cannott longe prevayle. Yett the Daire, or Pope of Japann, laboreth to make them frends'. (Farrington, 1991, 246)

The impotent and powerless Miyako court was unable to achieve a reconciliation; Ieyasu was determined to annihilate the visible remnant of Toyotomi power at whatever cost. Writing in, or shortly before, 1552, Francis Xavier had observed of the Japanese that 'They have but one king, although they have not obeyed him for more than 150 years, and for this reason these internal wars continue'. The conflict between Ieyasu and Hideyori was to be the last such struggle until the Tokugawa were overthrown by rebellious *daimyo* under the Imperial banner, a struggle to which various Europeans were witnesses, in the late nineteenth century.

Following Sekigahara, Ieyasu's primary concern was to establish military superiority over any possible combination of his adversaries. This superiority was attained by confiscation of the territories of his defeated adversaries, feifdoms carefully distributed to his trusted vassals, the *Fudai* vassals, hereditary lieges of the Tokugawa. Rightly, Ieyasu considered these men more dependable and obedient than the *Tozama*, the 'Outside Lords', with whom Ieyasu had no inherited connection. Elizabeth Tudor of England reduced the wealth of her great nobles by quartering her court upon them for months on end; Tokugawa Ieyasu achieved the same end by obliging the *daimyo* to spend their time and resources on public works commissioned by the *Bakufu*. As Cocks expressed it,

> '. . . all the *Tono* or Kings, have each one their taske set them to doe at their owne proper charge, not without much grudging. . . which angreth them not a little, but they must, will they nill they; in paine of belly-cutting'. (Cooper, 1965, 138)

Arthur Hatch, the preacher aboard the E.I.C. ship *Palsgrave*, wrote a long letter to Samuel Purchas on his return to England. Included therein was a remarkably perceptive description of the way in which the *daimyo* were subject to the Tokugawa;

> 'All each of these severall Princes must alwayes bee either himselfe in person, or his Brother, eldest Sonne, or the chiefe Nobleman within his Realme at the Emperours Court; the reason of it is not well knowne, but it is pretended that it is done to keepe the severall Kingdomes in quiet, and free from tumults, treasons and rebellions.
>
> The Emperour doth ordinarily requite his Princes presents after this manner: hee gives them a Feather for a Goose, some few *kimono* or Coates, for Gold, Silver or other precious and rare commodities; and that they may not grow rich, and of sufficient abilitie to make head against him, he suffers not their Fleeces to grow, but sheares them off, by raising Taxes on them for the building of Castles, and the repairing of Fortifications, and yet they are not suffered to repaire their owne, or any way to fortfie themselves'. (Cooper, 1965, 80)

Ieyasu treated the *Tozama* with formal courtesy but little trust. In addition to obliging them to furnish labour and resources to build, or reconstruct, such castles as Fushimi, Hikone, Edo and Suruga, he imposed limits on the size of their castles and on the capacity of the transport vessels they used. *Fudai* vassals were appointed to neighbouring territories in much the same way that a cautious player of the Japanese board game *Go* ensures that each stone his opponent places on the board is guarded by one of his own. *Fudai* vassals could be, and were, moved from one feudal domain to another at the *Bakufu*'s whim, a practice the *daimyo* detested, just as they detested being unable to marry or travel without express permission.

The system of keeping *daimyos*' families as hostages was perfected under Ieyasu's successors but Ieyasu appears to have begun it. Writing in early 1616, Richard Cocks noted that Ieyasu had ordered 'all the kyngs in Japon to goe for Edo, and there to remaene for the space of 7 yeares, and to carry their wives with them, and live every one in his howse aparte, with a servant of the Emperours to be allwaies in company with them – I meane with each one, to heare and see what passeth. This he doeth to prevent them from insurrections, and will not have sonns nor kynsmen, but the kinges them selves'. (Cooper, 1965, 82) Writing home to England at about the same time, Cocks wittily said '. . . now all the kinges and queenes of Japon are bound prentis to the Emperour', adding that Ieyasu 'aledgeth it is for their goods he doth it, to keepe Japon in quiet, which otherwaies would still be in broyles'. (Cooper, 1965, 89)

As a system of government, the method of rule in early Tokugawa Japan may seem haphazard to modern eyes but it was effective. Ieyasu met problems as they arose, delegating power to dependable subordinates who were responsible for affairs under their immediate control, a system of administration more akin to the affairs of a tribal confederacy than a modern despotism. Later the system became more sophisticated under Hidetada's successors, evolving into a machine so carefully constructed that a child could have managed it, as Ernest Satow was to write. (Satow, 1983, 39)

The Japan in which Adams arrived was a society in transition; had Ieyasu been defeated at Sekigahara it is possible that the nation would have disintegrated into a collection of warring states as it had been at the time of João Rodrigues' arrival in the 1570s. That this did not happen has been considered a matter of good fortune by Japanese historians, especially those of conservative and nationalist inclinations. Whatever else may be said about the Tokugawa *shogunate*, foreign influences were kept at a safe distance for more than two centuries.

Ieyasu was always attentive to matters of finance. Although personally frugal, he was always eager to ensure that the wealth of the Tokugawa family should be commensurate with its political power. The basis of the economy was rice, assessed in *koku*. The Tokugawa were masters of about 1,000,000 *koku* in 1590, when Ieyasu had first established himself in the *Kanto*, the eight eastern provinces. By 1598, the year of Hideyoshi's death, the Tokugawa possessed 2,557,000 *koku*. (Samsom, 1990, III, 3)

These immense revenues, which swelled to over 6 million *koku* after Sekigahara, were not all retained by the Tokugawa. A great proportion was distributed among Ieyasu's vassals and retainers as a reward for services rendered; the process of confiscation and distribution being virtually continuous.

Ieyasu was capable of almost capricious generosity on occasion. When the annual Macau carrack was seized and looted by the Dutch in July 1603 he offered the Jesuits a donation equivalent to 350 cruzados, amazing the entire court. (Boxer, 1951, 182-3). This happened in the honeymoon period of Ieyasu's relations with the Jesuits, who greatly esteemed his mild government of the country and his benign tolerance of Christianity. Some Jesuits considered the discovery of gold mines on Sadogashima to be a direct reward from God, bringing Ieyasu immense wealth, as they did.

Although James I of England disdained to give credence to Cocks' letters about Japan, he had not a little in common with Ieyasu, in his attitudes to the process of rule, if no more, observing that kings were '. . . as God's vice-regents on earth, and so adorned and furnished with some sparkles of the Divinitie'. Ieyasu, deified after his death, could hardly have expressed it better.

While no admirer of 'terrany', Richard Cocks had great respect for Ieyasu's strong character. Shortly after Ieyasu's death in 1616, Cocks wrote 'But I do verely beleeve he will sowne rise again, yf any wars be moved against his soone within these 3 yeares'. (Cooper, 1965, 88)

Unlike Hideyoshi or the despotic Nobunaga, however, Ieyasu was a practising Buddhist, even if the tenets of the faith meant little to him except as a legitimisation of social control. Under the later Tokugawa a form of Confucianism became the state creed although Buddhism, rooted in Japan and adapted to Japanese conditions, was tolerated, if maligned. (Elison, 1973, 253)

It probably never occurred to Cocks to wonder why Ieyasu never chose to invest money in Dutch and British vessels, as he did in the Macau ship's cargo. In the year of Ieyasu's death, 1616, Hasegawa Gonroku, the *bugyo* of Nagasaki after 1615, warned the Dutch and the British 'that they should take heed they did not meddel with the greate ship of Amacon, for that the Emperour had much adventure in her', this in spite of Ieyasu's anti-Christian edicts. Cocks, remarkably, saw fit to write '. . . I wish we might take her and then make the reconying after', a singularly ill-considered thought. (Boxer, 1951, 305)

Rice was the mainstay of the economy but other sources of wealth were of growing importance. Ieyasu confiscated the gold and silver mines of Sado Island (*Sadogashima*) and the silver mines of Iwami, giving orders that all mines were to increase their output. By 1601, a year after the *Liefde* arrived, Ieyasu had begun to mint gold and silver coins in quantity. His interest in mining and metallurgy led him to have great hopes, eventually unrealised, of the assistance of skilled miners and artificers from Mexico.

Further revenues were forthcoming from commercial cities. Ieyasu decreed that the privileges enjoyed by Osaka, Sakai, Fushimi, Nagasaki, Nara and Yamade were to be abolished and their citizens made subject to officers appointed by the *Bakufu*, known as *Shoshi-dai* in Kyushu and *Bugyo* elsewhere. Private enterprise was initially hurt by such draconian measures but a new class of entrepreneurs sprang into being in the form of government contractors who profited greatly from monopolies and near-monopolies in various large-scale commercial activities. Unlike his successors, Ieyasu encouraged merchant shipping and overseas trade. It is probable that Adams was taken into his service in 1601. (Sansom, 1990, III, 5)

The years during which Adams lived in Japan were years of change, sometimes gradual and sometimes abrupt. The anti-Christian persecution which Adams and the other Britons encouraged by their outspoken observations about the *Jessuits and Fryers* was accompanied by a steadily increasing watchfulness and guile on the part of the *Bakufu*.

In 1600 these changes lay in the future; at the time the stricken *Liefde* arrived on the coast of Kyushu, the Jesuits were sufficiently confident of their position to do what they could to demand the execution of the survivors. Herein lies a paradox; Jesuits were strictly forbidden, by their own rules, to involve themselves in political matters. However, the reality of their situation in Japan during the period of civil wars, the *Sengoku Jidai* period, and the years thereafter inescapably involved them in political matters. It was impossible for the Jesuits to pretend neutrality between Christian and anti-Christian *daimyo*, between Christian converts and their persecutors or between those foreigners, mainly Iberian, who aided the Catholic cause in various ways and those, the Dutch and the British, who traduced the Jesuits' mission work at every opportunity. João Rodrigues, the learned Jesuit who wrote the *História da Igreja do Japão* and the *Arte da Lingoa de Japam*, served as interpreter, and probably advisor in an informal capacity, to Hideyoshi and Ieyasu. His expulsion from Japan in 1610 was a bitter blow to the Jesuits and scarcely less of one to such Japanese Christians as Oyuki, Adams' wife, who was later to be suspected of harbouring missionaries.

Ieyasu sought good trading relations with all foreign countries and gave the impression, possibly misleadingly, that he desired still more intimate cultural intercourse; his letter to 'His Highness the Lord of Holland', written after two Dutch vessels had arrived at Hirado, said

> 'If both our countries have the inclination, though separated by a thousand myriad miles of ocean, they may by yearly communications become not dissimilar',

a sentiment which would have appalled his xenophobic successors. (Sadler, 1984, 233)

Ieyasu was well aware that trade possesses its own dynamic, quite distinct from political relations. Cocks recorded, in the letter to Lord Salisbury written in December 1614 and quoted above, that although Ieyasu '*hould the Emp' of China for his Enymie, yet he doth suffer Chinas quietlie to trade into Japan for the greate benefite they bring hym, and doth all that he can to make peace with the China Emperour*'. (Farrington, 1991, 258). This was true, Ieyasu had ordered the execution of *wako* for raiding the Chinese coast and preying upon Chinese shipping, although Ieyasu did not specifically command the Dutch to refrain from piratical attacks on Chinese shipping plying between the Phippines and the Chinese mainland while using Hirado as a base for such attacks. Possibly Ieyasu felt that the Chinese were well able to look after their own affairs; in any case, the *Bakufu* was unwilling to listen to complaints about events which took place in waters distant from Japan, as the Chinese, Iberians and Hirado Britons were to learn over the years.

There was always a degree of ambiguity and ambivalence about Sino-Japanese relations, as educated Chinese and Japanese were well aware. Although Japan was never a tributary state of China *per se*, in the way in which Siam, Annam, Nepal and Korea were, the Japanese had acknowledged the shadow, if no more, of Chinese suizerainty on a number of occasions. In 1403 the *shogun* Ashikaga Yoshimitsu described himself as '*your subject*' in a letter to the Ming emperor. (Massarella, 1990, 32). The context was one in which 'official trade' existed in the guise of tribute-bearing missions to the Imperial court and reciprocal 'presents'; both nations were aware that the Mongol rulers of China had attempted to invade Japan in 1274 and 1281.

That Tokugawa rule brought Japan stability is indisputable. Ieyasu, unlike his predecessors, was able to ensure his succession; in 1605, only two years after having become *shogun*, he resigned the office in favour of his son Hidetada. In reality, power remained largely in Ieyasu's hands; the formal succession of Hidetada was intended to make it plain to all that the office of the *shogun* was henceforth to be hereditary in the Tokugawa family. Formal resignation from office, known as *inkyo*, was by no means uncommon in Japan in this era; not infrequently the supposedly retired office-holder continued to control affairs at one remove. There was certainly no doubt in the mind of Richard Cocks, for example, as to who was the 'Emperour' of Japan, despite Hidetada's formal accession and the necessity of foreigners visiting *both* Edo and Suruga.

Ieyasu sought to legitimise Tokugawa rule by all available means. In distant Hirado, Cocks was told by a mariner: 'Ieyasu *Sama* sues to the *Dairi* to have the name of Kanpaku, which . . . is as the names of Ceasar of Augustus amongst the Emperours of Rome . . . But he denied it till he know Hideyori *Sama* is dead'. (Cooper, 1965, 87).

Ieyasu's edicts against Christianity were undoubtedly political in nature rather than being inspired by religious conviction or bigotry. Nonetheless, the text of the edict promulgated on 27 January 1614 contained elements of Buddhism and Confucianism, having probably been written, in part at least, by Hayashi

Razan, a Confucian scholar, and Soden (or *Suden*), a Zen priest of the Konji-in at Kyoto. (Boxer, 1951, 317-8). The kernel of the edict was secular rather than spiritual; 'the Kirishitan band have come to Japan, not only sending their merchant vessels to exchange commodities, but also longing to disseminate an evil law, to overthrow true doctrine, so that they may change the government of the country, and obtain possession of the land. This is the germ of great disaster, and must be crushed'. Buddhism, available as a convenient means of thought control, was pressed into service; all citizens were to be required to adhere to one or another of the Buddhist sects and were to be supervised by their priests to ensure that there were no backsliders among them. Christianity, of a primitive and furtive kind, survived Tokugawa persecution and was rediscovered, long after all hope had been lost, in 1865. A faith kept by poor peasants is seldom a political threat and the Tokugawa might easily have tolerated the 'hidden Christians', the *Kakure Kirishtan* communities, had not the mechanism of persecution and enforcement developed a life of its own. After 1614 Christianity was on the defensive against state persecution.

There was no central authority within Japanese Buddhism capable of defying, or willing to defy, the *Bakufu*. Quite apart from the fragmented state of Japanese Buddhism, neither the Tokugawa régime nor its predecessors would have tolerated the emergence of such a body. If, as Evelyn Waugh wrote, one of the functions of an aristocracy is to keep the clergy in its place, the *Bakufu* made very sure that no monk or priest interfered with the processes of government.

XVI

EPILOGUE

There is no stranger seventeenth-century romance than that of this plain English pilot, – with only his simple honesty and common-sense to help him, – rising to such extraordinary favour with the greatest and shrewdest of all Japanese rulers.
Lafcadio Hearn (Hearn, 1984, 317)

The supposed site of Adams' residence in Edo is commemorated to this day in Nihonbashi Muromachi; a memorial of modest proportions commemorates the spot and is a Designated Cultural Property of the Tokyo Metropolitan Government, in the contemporary Japanese style. As Japan became steadily more expansionist and xenophobic in the early twentieth century, the commemoration ceased in the 1930s, to be revived in the postwar period. To a minor but significant extent, the commemoration of Adams' life in Japan has been a matter of controversy; those who enthusiastically espouse international connections are keen to see Adams, Xavier and Perry commemorated. The dour nationalists oppose commemoration, with varying degrees of enthusiasm.

The posthumous commemoration of Adams has had three distinct stages. The first followed his death at Hirado in 1620, though how long afterwards remains uncertain. The 'tombs' associated with Adams and his wife, the *Anjin-zuka*, close to the Jodoji temple, not far from Yokosuka station, are popularly believed to have been erected by the couple's son, Joseph. The custom observed by the inhabitants of Anjin-cho contributing a donation of rice to the Jodoji temple to pay for an annual memorial service apparently began in 1626, not long after Adams' death. In 1681 this contribution was established as an annual cash sum and the contribution continued for two centuries thereafter. The residents of Anjin-cho contributed stone lanterns to the *Anjin-zuka* in 1799, long after the memory of Adams had faded. The site was 're-discovered' in 1872 by James Walters, an expatriate resident of Yokohama. Walters paid to have the area round the 'tombs' tidied and published an illustrated article on Adams in a magazine called '*The Far East*'. Evidently Walters' interest had been kindled by reading Richard Hildreth's *Japan as it was and is*, a book then justly esteemed among European residents in Japan with an interest in the first European period in Japanese history. A Hemi native, Zenroku Anzai, the owner of the Fujiyama Hotel in Yokosuka, provided a stone plinth for the 'tombs'. In 1887 the Duke of Connaught, one of Queen Victoria's sons, contributed a sum to their upkeep and, after some controversy as to whether to 'tombs' ought to be moved to the foreigners' cemetery in Yokohama, an Anglo-Japanese committee provided funds to pave the area around the 'tombs' and the lanterns and to provide railings and steps. (Makino, 1983, 120).

In 1905 an excavation established that no human remains were to be found and it was accepted that the 'tombs' were, in all probability, memorials erected by Joseph Adams.

During this period of Adams' 'rediscovery', which coincided with the halcyon days of the Anglo-Japanese Treaty, such luminaries as Prince Arisugawa Takehito were graciously pleased to extend their patronage to such causes as the renovation of the Hemi 'tombs'. (Rogers, 1956, 117)

Commemoration ceased temporarily in 1935, for political reasons, but was resumed in 1947. According to the priests of Jodoji, Adams' posthumous Buddhist name was Juryomaninzenzui Koji and that of his wife Kaikaoinman Bikuni. (Makino, 1983, 120). Another version of the Romanisation of the two names renders them thus: Juryo Manin Genzui Koji and Kaikwa Oin Myoman Biku. (Rogers, 1956, 119)

It has been claimed, somewhat implausibly, that Adams was a regular visitor to Jodoji, though whether as a respectful visitor or as a parishioner remains open to question, as does the affiliation of Adams' wife with the temple. Regular attendance at Buddhist services was one way of making certain than the taint of Christianity was dispelled, although the similarity of the trappings and rituals of Buddhism are, and were, so similar to Catholicism that the acceptance of the former might well suffice to assuage the loss of the latter.

The commemoration of Adams in England dates from 1934, when a clock tower of great ugliness was erected in Gillingham. By an irony which Adams would have appreciated, his commemoration in England, which continues to this day, commenced at a time when increasing tension in the Far East led to suspension of his commemoration in his adopted country, Japan.

The third period of Adams' commemoration in Japan dates from the period of Allied occupation following the end of the Pacific War. The Ito Tourist Association is the body responsible for the Anjin Festival at Ito, commemorating Adams' construction of Ieyasu's two ships there. With the enthusiastic participation of Lieutenant-General H.C.H. Robertson, the Commander-in-Chief of the British Commonwealth Occupation Force in Japan, the first Anjin Festival at Ito was held in August 1947. The British poet Edmund Blunden, then teaching at Tokyo University, contributed a poem of singular dreadfulness, still to be seen carved in stone at Ito:

> To the Citizens of Ito:
> Here then while Shakespeare yet was with us came
> An Englishman to win a different fame. . .
> I know his home in England, and I know
> At last his home by the Pacific's flow,
> And am most happy, thinking of that man,
> Who first united England and Japan;
> Happy to find that spirit flowering still
> Which set your garland on the brow of Kentish Will

There are no celebrations of a similar nature at Hirado, now a quiet backwater once again after the rowdy boom years. The sites of the V.O.C. and E.I.C. factories are marked; there are excellent museums commemorating the Matsuura and the early Christian period in Hirado's long and eventful history. One Jinzaburo Osato of Hirado brought two small stones to Japan from the cemetery of the Church of St Mary Magdalen at Gillingham and, having buried these, erected a stone above them to commemorate Adams and his English wife, Mary Hyn. (Makino, 1983, 123)

Adams' life has inspired a number of novels, the best of which remain those written by Richard Blaker, *The Needle-Watcher,* and Christopher Nichole, *Lord of the Golden Fan*. Published first in

1932 and 1973 respectively, both strive for accuracy and period detail. The far better-known work of fiction, James Clavell's *Shogun,* is appalling nonsense. It has, however, sold over 6 million copies in various languages and has served as a introduction of sorts to early seventeenth century Japanese culture to many readers. Some few of these are then led to further studies, so not all is loss.

FINIS
LAUS DEO

APPENDIX 1

Giving precise dates for events in Japan during Adams' residence there presents a number of difficulties. The English, whether at home or abroad, used the Julian calendar (Old Style) until 1752; most of continental Europe had adopted the Gregorian calendar (New Style) in 1582. Under the Old Style of reckoning years, the year ended on 24th March, the new year began on 25th March, hence the puzzling use of such dates as 1616/17 in some histories.

The Spaniards came to East Asia from the Americas, the Portuguese sailed via the Cape of Good Hope, Portuguese India and Malaya; there was usually a day's difference in their calendars, the Portuguese being one day 'ahead'. The Japanese still used the lunar calendar, which had a regulating feature. As Bernardino de Avila Girón explained, 'Every four years they have the custom of inserting a month, which they call *uru-tsuki*, so that three years each have twelve months, while the fourth has thirteen, for the month is added in the fourth year. But it is not always inserted at the same time; sometimes they put it in after the third month (or *sangatsu*), which they then count twice, and at other times they insert it at the end of the eighth month, which is then counted twice over.' (Cooper, 1965, 231). The Japanese government adopted the Gregorian calendar in 1873.

Spelling of Elizabethan and Jacobean English presents a particular difficulty. Adams, or *Addames*, used such spellings as Jellingham, Chattam, Javo, Puttan and Jor in his letters. Contemporary writers spelled words as they felt they should be spelled, often changing the spelling in the course of a single page. As in the twentieth century, there were very obvious gradations of literacy among the Britons in Japan. Saris spelled more consistently than the erratic Richard Cocks. William Adams, who left school to be apprenticed at the age of twelve, was a highly idiosyncratic speller even by the standards of his day. Before the age of dictionaries there were few rules governing spelling in English.

The tael or liang was the Chinese money of weight and account and divided into 10 mace or 100 condorins or 1,000 *cash*. Two taels equalled 15 silver tangas or three cruzados. In Japan in 1604, according to João Rodriguez, the cruzado and the tael stood at parity.

'In 1594 I saw in the kingdom of Satsuma a peasant, his wife and two children put to death on account of two bales of *momi* (that is, rice before it is threshed and cleaned), which at that time must have been worth about three mace', the Spanish traveller Bernardino de Avila Girón wrote. These hapless peasants had failed to pay sufficient money to the *daikan,* or steward, of the *daimyo*. Lilliputian though the sums involved were, failure to pay them could have hideous consequences.

The Portuguese expression '*um conto de ouro*' literally meant a million cruzados but was often used as figure of speech to describe any huge sum.

The tael was also a unit of weight; 16 taels amounted to a catty or kin and 100 catties made a picul or 133. 3 pounds English (avoirdupois) weight (61.1999 kg).

The Iberian quintal, a unit of weight, was of 100 pounds, like the English hundredweight of the period. The later hundredweight of 112 pounds included an allowance for the container.

A *koku* of rice was equivalent to 4.96 bushels or 180 litres. Revenues of *daimyo* and official salaries were reckoned in *koku*.

According to Ralph Coppindale, a *koku* of rice in October 1615 was valued at 2 taels 6 mace, double the usual price because due to Ieyasu's summer campaign against Toyotomi Hideyori in Osaka. In 1617 Richard Cocks observed that the real of eight was worth eight *mas* or four shillings sterling. João Rodrigues, writing between 1604 and 1608, equated 10 Japanese momme with one Chinese silver tael or one Portuguese cruzado, roughly four shillings in English money.

Other currencies were occasionally used in Japan or referred to in journals or correspondence; there were four crowns to one pound, a mark was worth 12s 6d. A ducat was worth 9s 4d.

Currencies fluctuated in relative value, often dramatically. Silver was relatively 'cheap' in Japan in terms of its value in gold. Lucky and far-sighted traders could profit greatly from this.

The Dutch at Hirado and elsewhere in the Indies used florins, or guilders (*f*), in their records. Twenty guilders were worth 21s 4d in English money during Adams' residence in Japan.

The higher money in Japan during the period of the E.I.C.; factory was in the form of oblong gold 'coins' called obang (2564 grs troy) and kobang (222 grs troy), issued from 1580 onwards. The itzebo was a smaller gold piece of oblong shape. There were four itzebo to a kobang and a kobang was worth '5 tais 4 mas', according to Cocks. (Thompson, 1883, I, 165)

A league, now virtually obsolete, was three miles in length.

Comprehensive comparisons of weights, measures and currencies will be found in C.R. Boxer's *The Great Ship from Amacon,* Derek Massarella's *A World Elsewhere* and Anthony Farrington's *The English Factory in Japan*.

APPENDIX 2

Adams' letters and other surviving writings have recently been published in full, in what is believed to be their most accurate extant versions, in Anthony Farrington's *The English Factory in Japan 1613-1623*.

1. To Adams' wife in England c 1605
2. To Adams 'unknown friends and countrymen' at Bantam October 1611
3. To Augustine Spalding at Bantam January 1613
4. To the East India Company in London December 1613
5. To Thomas Best at Bantam December 1613
6. To Richard Wickham at Edo July 1614
7. To Richard Wickham at Edo, from Sumpu (*Suruga*) October 1615
8. To Jacques Specx at Hirado October 1616
9. To Sir Thomas Smythe in London January 1617
10. To Richard Wickham at Hirado, from Sakai November 1617
11. To Richard Wickham at Hirado, from Osaka November 1617

The first, the most famous and the most-quoted, exists in an abbreviated copy, the remainder having supposedly been suppressed 'by the malice of the bearers', the Dutch. Like the second, it is autobiographic in nature and describes the voyage to Japan and Ieyasu's reception of Adams in Osaka Castle. That to Spalding in Bantam, describes contemporary conditions of trade in Japan and observes his letters were 'intercepted allwayes'. Although written in Hirado, as were most of Adams' letters, it urges Spalding to ensure that an E.I.C. ship be sent to the Edo area rather than to Hirado, Hirado being '. . . farr to the courte, about 230 (*leagues*), a werysoum way and fare.' Adams' fourth surviving letter describes the reception of Captain (or *General*) John Saris of the *Clove* by Ieyasu and refers, at some length, to Adams' shipbuilding experience and the prospects of 'the discoveri to the northward' as well as recounting the negotiations relating to Adams' acceptance of employment in the service of the E.I.C., the letter to Best covers much the same ground. That written to Wickham relates the death of Peacock and the disappearance of Walter Carwarden, the one immediately thereafter informs Wickham that Adams will endeavour to seek the release of a Spaniard and an Italian held '*in irrons*' aboard the Macau carrack. The letter written to Specx survives in a translation entered in Specx's copy-book and relates the sad news that foreigners were to trade at Hirado and Nagasaki only. The remaining letters to Wickham concern trade, spiced with gossip and salutations to mutual friends.

Adams' other surviving writings, as collated by Farrington, are four journals of voyages; that to the Ryukyus, with miscellaneous additions and jottings entered between November 1614 and November 1616, that relating to the Cochin-China voyage Adams commanded between March and August 1617, that of Adams' voyage to the Ryukyus of March-May 1618 and that of the Tonking voyage between March and August 1619.

It is presumed that Adams' will was penned by another, better-schooled, hand at Adams' dictation.

BIBLIOGRAPHICAL NOTE

Richard Cocks' *Diary*, edited by various scholars, and Saris' *Journal* are essential reading for those interested in the *minutiae* of the East India Company's endeavour in Japan. Regrettably, both works are far from being readily accessible. Sir Ernest Satow's edition of Saris' *Journal,* published under the title *The Voyage of John Saris to Japan,* was published by the Hakluyt Society in 1900. Edward Maunde Thompson's edition of Cocks' *Diary* was published by the Hakluyt Society in 1883 and in a Japanese edition with additional notes by Murakami Naojiro in 1899. More recent editions have been published in Tokyo in both English editions in three volumes in 1978-80 and in Japanese in three volumes with an appendix (1979-82). The original 1883 Hakluyt Society edition was reprinted in a facsimile edition by Burt Franklin, a New York publisher, but undated. Professors Murakami and Murakawa published *Letters written by the English Residents in Japan in Tokyo* in 1900. A limited facsimile edition was published by Tenri Central Library in 1973; an edition of a mere 200 copies.

More recent scholarly work on the period includes two works likely to prove definitive; Derek Massarella's magisterial *A World Elsewhere: Europe's Encounter with Japan in the Sixteenth and Seventeenth Centuries* (1990) and Anthony Farrington's *The English Factory in Japan* (1991). It is indicative of the difficulties faced by publishers of serious work on this period of European-Japanese history that both of these publishing ventures were underwritten by assistance from Japanese sources; *A World Elsewhere* by the Japan Foundation, *The English Factory* by the Great Britain-Sasakawa Foundation. The latter exists in an edition of 300.

The work of Charles Ralph Boxer, especially the vivid book *The Christian Century in Japan 1549-1636,* is outstanding. Much of Boxer's work is difficult of access; however, this is beginning to change gradually as reprints appear in the U.K., the U.S.A. and Macau.

Michael Cooper's books and articles concerning João Rodrigues, Richard Cocks and much else besides provide valuable, and sympathetic insight into the Christian period in Japan. The outstanding illustrated book *The Southern Barbarians* deserves to be reissued at the earliest opportunity.

The intriguing minor work on William Adams, *The Blue-eyed Samurai: William Adams,* by Makino Tadashi, himself a former sailor, was published by the Ito Tourist Association in 1983. The present author's text *Miura Anjin: The Story of Captain William Adams* owed much to it.

BIBLIOGRAPHY

Masaharu, Anesaki *History of Japanese Religion* London: Kegan Paul 1930

Anon. (Presumed to be V.O.C.) *The Hollanders Declaration of the Affaires of the East Indies (1622)* Amsterdam: Theatrum Orbis Terrarum, 1971

Anon. (Presumed to be E.I.C.) *An Answere to the Hollanders Declaration of the East-India (1622)* Amsterdam: Theatrum Orbis Terrarum 1971

Anon. (Presumed to be E.I.C.) *A Courante of Newes from the East India (1622)* Amsterdam: Theatrum Orbis Terrarum, 1975

Anon. (Presumed to be E.I.C.) *A Second Courante of Newes from the East-India (1622)* Amsterdam: Theatrum Orbis Terrarum, 1975

Richard Blaker *The Needle-Watcher* Tokyo: Charles E. Tuttle, 1986

Harold Bolitho *Treasures Among Men: The* Fudai Daimyo *in Tokagawa Japan* New Haven, Conn.: Yale University Press, 1974

Nicholas Bourne and Thomas Archer *Newes Out of Holland of the East Indie Trade There (1622)* Amsterdam: Theatrum Orbis Terrarum, 1973

C. R. Boxer 'The Affair of the Madre de Deus' *Transactions of the Japan Society Vol. XXVI* London: 1929

C.R. Boxer 'Notes on European Military Influence in Japan' *Transactions, Asiatic Society of Japan 2nd Series Vol. VIII* Tokyo: 1931

C.R. Boxer 'Portuguese Commercial Voyages to Japan Three Hundred Years Ago (1630-1639)' *Transactions of the Japan Society XXXI* London: 1934

C.R. Boxer 'Some Aspects of Portuguese Influence in Japan, 1542-1640', *Transactions of the Japan Society Vol. XXXIII* London: 1936

C.R. Boxer 'The Rise and Fall of Nicholas Iquan' *T'ien Hsia Monthly Vol. XI No. 5* Shanghai: 1941

C.R. Boxer *Fidalgoes in the Far East* The Hague: Martinus Nijhoff, 1948

C.R. Boxer *The Christian Century in Japan 1549–1650* Los Angeles, Berkeley: University of California Press, 1951

C.R. Boxer (ed) *The Tragic History of the Sea 1589-1622* Cambridge: Cambridge University Press, 1959

C.R. Boxer *The Dutch Seaborne Empire* London: Hutchinson, 1965

C.R. Boxer (ed) *Further Selections from the Tragic History of the Sea* Cambridge: Cambridge University Press, 1968

C.R. Boxer *Jan Compagnie in Japan, 1600-1817* Oxford: Oxford University Press, 1968

C.R. Boxer *Seventeenth Century Macau in Contemporary Documents and Illustrations* Hong Kong: Hutchinson, 1969

C.R. Boxer *Portuguese Conquest and Commerce in Southern Asia: 1500-1750* London: Variorium Reprints, 1985

C.R. Boxer *The Great Ship from Amacon* Macau: Instituto Cultural de Macau: Centro de Estudos Marítimos de Macau, 1988 (a)

C.R. Boxer *Ásia Sinica e Japónica* Macau: Instituto Cultural de Macau: Centro de Estudos Marítimos de Macau, 1988 (b)

C.R. Boxer *Dutch Merchants and Mariners in Asia* London: Variorum Reprints, 1988 (c)

C.R. Boxer *Número Especial dedicado a Charles R. Boxer; Boletim do Centro Estudos Marítimos de de Macau* Macau: Centro de Estudos Marítimos de Macau ,1989

Arthur Coke Burnell (ed. Vol. 1) P.A. Tiele (ed. Vol. 2) *The Voyage of John Huyghen van Linschoten to the East Indies (2 Vols.)* London: Hakluyt Society, 1885

Otis Cary *A History of Christianity in Japan* Tokyo: Charles E. Tuttle, 1987

Basil Hall Chamberlain *Japanese Things* Tokyo: Charles E. Tuttle, 1984

Austin Coates *A Macao Narrative* Hong Kong: Oxford University Press, 1978

Austin Coates *Macao and the British, 1637-1842: Prelude to Hong Kong* Hong Kong: Oxford University Press, 1989

Michael Cooper (ed.) *They Came to Japan: An Anthology of European Reports on Japan 1543-1640* Los Angeles, Berkeley: University of California Press, 1965

Michael Cooper (ed.) *The Southern Barbarians* Tokyo: Kodansha International, 1971

Michael Cooper *Rodrigues the Interpreter* New York and Tokyo: Weatherhill, 1974

Michael Cooper 'The Second Englishman in Japan' *Transactions of the Asiatic Society of Japan 3rd Series vol. XVII* Tokyo: 1982

Michael Cooper 'The Brits in Japan', *Monumenta Nipponica Vol. 47, No. 2* Tokyo: Sophia University, 1992

Bolton Corney *The Voyages of Sir Henry Middleton to Bantam and the Maluco Islands* London: Hakluyt Society, 1860

William Corr *Miura Anjin: The Story of Captain William Adams* Nara: Dawn Press, 1989

William Corr 'Maritime War and Trade before *Sakoku*' *Osaka International University Journal of International Studies* Osaka: 1990 (a)

William Corr 'The Failure of the English Factory at Hirado' *Keizai Keiei Ronshu, Kobe International University* Kobe: 1990 (b)

William Corr 'The Iland of Iapan described in Jan Huygen van Linschoten's Itinerario of 1596' *Himejigakuin Review* Himeji: 1990 (c)

William Corr 'The Crew and Cargo of the Liefde' *Himejigakuin Review* Himeji: 1991 (a)

William Corr 'The Japanese and the British: The Earliest Encounters' *Himejigakuin Journal* Himeji: 1991 (b)

William Corr 'The Iland Japan and the way thither in Richard Hakluyt's Principal Navigations' *Himejigakuin Journal* Himeji: 1992

Sir Hugh Cortazzi *Isles of Gold: Antique Maps of Japan* Tokyo & New York: Weatherhill International, 1983

Armando Cortesão (ed.) *The Suma Oriental of Tomé Pires and the book of Francisco Rodrigues* London: Hakluyt Society, 1944

R.D. Cremer (ed.) *Macau, City of Commerce and Culture* Hong Kong: U.E.A. Press, 1987

Shann Davies *Chronicles in Stone* Macau: Department of Tourism, 1985

Pierre F.X. de Charlevoix *Histoire du Japon (t.2)* Paris: Ganeau, Bauche et D'Houry, 1754

Horacio de la Costa *The Jesuits in the Philippines: 1581-1768* Cambridge, Mass.: Harvard University Press, 1961

Fernao de Queyroz S.J. *The Temporal and Spiritual Conquest of Ceylon (tr. by S.G. Perera S.J.)* Colombo: Government Press, 1930

Arthur Diósy 'In memory of Will Adams, the first Englishman in Japan' *Transactions of the Japan Society VI* London: 1906

East India Company *A True Relation of the Unjust, Cruell, and Barbarous Proceedings against the English at Amboyna (1624)* Amsterdam: Theatrum Orbis Terrarum,1971

George Elison *Deus Destroyed* Cambridge, Mass.: Harvard University Press, 1973

George Elison & Bardwell L Smith (eds.) *Warlords, Artist and Commoners: Japan in the Sixteenth Century* Honolulu: University of Hawaii Press, 1981

William Ellis *Journal of William Ellis: Narrative of a Tour of Hawaii, or Owhyhee: with Remarks on the History, Traditions, Manners, Customs and Language of the Inhabitants of the Sandwich Islands* Honolulu: Honolulu Advertiser, 1953

Anthony Farrington *The English Factory in Japan, 1613-1623 (2 vols.)* London: British Library, 1991

Donald Ferguson (ed.) *The Travels of Pedro Teixeira* London: Hakluyt Society, 1902

Grant Goodman *Japan: The Dutch Experience* London: Athlone Press, 1986

Jorge Graça *The Fortifications of Macau* Macau: Direcçao dos Serviços de Turismo de Macau,1984

Gerald Hammond (ed.) *Sir Walter Ralegh: Selected Writings* Harmondsworth: Penguin Books, 1984

Lafcadio Hearn *Japan: An Interpretation* Tokyo: Charles E. Tuttle, 1984

Richard Hildreth *Japan as it was and is* Tokyo: The Sanshusa, 1905

J.W. Ijzerman *Dirck Gerritsz Pomp alias Dirck Gerritsz China, de eerste Nederlander die China en Japan bezocht (1544-1604)* The Hague: Linschoten Society, 1915

Joseph Jennes *A History of the Catholic Church in Japan* Tokyo: Oriens Institute for Religious Research, 1973

George H. Kerr *Okinawa: The History of an Island People* Tokyo: Charles E. Tuttle, 1984

Johannes Laures 'Takayama Ukon: A Critical Essay' *Monumenta Nipponica Vol. V.* Tokyo: Sophia University, 1942

Johannes Laures *The Catholic Church in Japan* Tokyo: Charles E. Tuttle, 1954

Thomas Babington Macauley *History of England (4 Vols.)* London: J.M. Dent, 1966

R.H. Major (ed.) *Early Voyages to Terra Australis, now called Australia* London: Hakluyt Society, 1859

Tadashi Makino *The Blue-Eyed Samurai: William Adams* Ito: Ito Tourist Association, 1983

Albert Hastings Markham (ed.) *Voyages and Works of John Davis, the Navigator* London: Hakluyt Society, 1880

Clements R. Markham (ed.) *Voyages and Works of Pedro Sarmento de Gamboa* London: Hakluyt Society, 1895

Colin Martin and Geoffrey Parker *The Spanish Armada* Harmondsworth: Penguin Books, 1988

R.H.P. Mason and J.G. Caiger *A History of Japan* Tokyo: Charles E. Tuttle, 1989

Derek Massarella 'The Early Career of Richard Cocks (1566-1624), Head of the English East India Company's Factory in Japan' *Transactions of the Asiatic Society of Japan 3rd Series, Vol. 20.* Tokyo: 1985

Derek Massarella *A World Elsewhere: Europe's Encounter with Japan in the Sixteenth and Seventeenth Centuries* New Haven, Conn.: Yale University Press, 1990

Derek Massarella and Izumi K. Tytler 'The Japonian Charters' *Monumenta Nipponica Vol. 45, No. 2.* Tokyo: Sophia University, 1990

G. Masselman *The Cradle of Colonialism* New Haven, Conn.: Yale University Press, 1963

Kiichi Matsuda 'The Chronological Table of the Intercourse between Japan and Europe in the Sixteenth and Seventeenth Centuries *Academic Bulletin, Kyoto University of Foreign Studies, Vol. XXXVII* Kyoto: 1991

Kenneth Gordon McIntyre *A Descoberta Secreta da Austrália* Macau: Fundaçáo Oriente, Centro de Estudos Marítimos, 1989

M.A.P. Meilink-Roelofsz (ed.) *Dutch Authors on Asian History* Dordrecht: Foris Publishers, 1988

Yoshio Moriya (ed.) *Teikoku's Complete Atlas of Japan* Tokyo: Teikoku-Shoin, 1987

Pedro Morejón *A Briefe Relation of the Persecution lately made against the Catholike Christians in the Kingdome of Iaponia* Amsterdam: Theatrum Orbis Terrarum, 1975

N. Murakami and K. Murakawa (eds.) *Letters written by the English residents in Japan* Tokyo: The Sankosha, 1900

James Murdoch and Isoh Yamagata *A History of Japan* London: Routledge & Kegan Paul Ltd., 1949

Stephen Neill *A History of Christian Missions* Harmondsworth: Penguin Books, 1990

Zelia Nuttall 'The Earliest Historical Relations Between Mexico and

Japan *University of California Publications in American Archaeology and Ethnology 4* Berkeley, 1906

Yoshito Okamoto *The Namban Art of Japan* Tokyo: Heibonsha, 1972

Edouard Papinot *Historical and Geographical Dictionary of Japan* Tokyo: Charles E. Tuttle, 1988

Montague Paske-Smith *A Glympse of the 'English House' and English Life at Hirado, 1613-1623* Kobe: J.L. Thompson, 1927

M.N. Pearson *The New Cambridge History of India: The Portuguese in India* Cambridge: Cambridge University Press, 1990

P.E. Pieris *Portugal in Ceylon* Colombo: C.A.C. Press, 1944

Benjamin Videira Pires *A Viagem de Comércio Macau-Manila nos Séculos XVI a XIX* Macau: Centro de Estudos Marítimos de Macau, 1987

Herbert E. Plutschow *Historical Nagasaki* Tokyo: Japan Times, 1983

F.P. Purvis 'Japanese Ships of Past and Present' *Transactions of the Japan Society Vol. XXIII* London: 1926

F.W. Putzger *Historischer Schulatlas* Bielefeld: Velhagen & Klasing, 1960

John Reader *Man on Earth* Harmondsworth: Penguin Books, 1990

Reinaldo Riosexa H., Maria Henriques R. and Ana Maria Errazuriz K. 'Primeras Fases del Reconocimiento del Territorio Nacional' *Atlas del la Republica de Chile* Santiago de Chile: Instituto Geographico Militar, 1983

Philip George Rogers *The First Englishman in Japan: The Story of Will Adams* London: Harvill Press, 1956

Thomas Rundall *Voyages towards the North-West in Search of Passage to Cathay and India, 1496-1631* London: Hakluyt Society, 1849

Thomas Rundall *Memorials of the Empire of Japon in the XVI and XVII Centuries* London: Hakluyt Society, 1850

José Ruy *História de Macau* Macau: Ediçoes Asa, 1989

Arthur Lindsay Sadler 'The Naval Campaign in the Korean War of Hideyoshi' *Transactions of the Asiatic Society of Japan 2nd Series Vol. XIV* Tokyo: 1937

Arthur Lindsay Sadler *The Maker of Modern Japan: The Life of Tokugawa Ieyasu* Tokyo: Charles E. Tuttle, 1984

Sir George Sansom *Japan: A Short Cultural History* Tokyo: Charles E. Tuttle, 1985

Sir George Sansom *The Western World and Japan* Tokyo: Charles E. Tuttle, 1987

Sir George Sansom *A History of Japan (3 Vols.)* Tokyo: Charles E. Tuttle, 1990

Sir Ernest M. Satow (ed.) *The Voyage of Captain John Saris to Japan, 1613* London: Hakluyt Society, 1900

Sir Ernest M. Satow *A Diplomat in Japan* Tokyo: Charles E. Tuttle, 1983

Iwao Seiichi 'Jan Joosten: The Forerunner of the Dutch-Japanese Relation' *Bulletin of the Japan-Netherlands Society 1* Tokyo: 1958

G.V. Scammell *The World Encompassed* London: Methuen, 1981

Sir Anthony Sherley *Relations of Travels into Persia* Amsterdam: Theatrum Orbis Terrarum, 1974

Shiba Ryotaro *Osaka as Precipitate of History* Osaka: Osaka Municipal History Association, 1987

William F. Sinclair (ed.) and Donald Ferguson *The Travels of Pedro Teixeira* London: Hakluyt Society, 1892

J.B. Snellen 'The Image of Erasmus in Japan' *Transactions of the Asiatic Society of Japan 2nd Series, vol. XI* Tokyo: 1934

Henry N. Stevens (ed.) *New Light on the Discovery of Australia* London: Hakluyt Society, 1930

Richard Storry *A History of Modern Japan* Harmondsworth: Penguin Books, 1985

Richard Tames *Will Adams* Aylesbury: Shire Publications, 1973

Ivan E. Taylor *Samuel Pepys* New York: Twayne Publishers, 1967

Manuel Teixeira *IV Centenário dos Dominicanos am Macau: 1587-1987* Macau: Fundaçao Macau, 1987

Manuel Teixeira 'Primeiros contactos dos Portugueses a Espanhóis com a Ilha de Bornéu' *Boletim do Centro de Estudos Marítimos de Macau No. 1* Macau: Museu Marítimos de Macau, 1988

Edward Maunde Thompson (ed.) *The Diary of Richard Cocks (2 Vols.)* London: Hakluyt Society, 1883

G.M. Trevelyan *A History of England* London: Longman, 1973

Thomas Uyttenbroek *Early Franciscans in Japan (Missionary Bulletin Series 6)* Himeji: Committee of the Apostolate, 1958

Jan Huygen van Linschoten *Voyages into ye East and West Indies* Amsterdam: Theatrum Orbis Terrarum, 1974

Ilza Vieth *'Englishman or Samurai: The Story of Will Adams' Far Eastern Quarterly 5* Menasha, Wisconsin: 1945

Tennakoon Vimalananda *Buddhism in Ceylon under the Christian Powers* Colombo: M.D. Gunasena & Co., 1963

C.G. von Brandestein 'The First Europeans on Australia's West Coast' *Boletim do Museo e Centro de Estudos Marítimos de Macau* Macau: Museo e Centro de Estudos Marítimos de Macau, 1989

F.C. Wieder (ed.) *De reis van Mahu en De Cordes Door Straat van Magalhães Naar Zuid-Amerika en Japan, 1598-1600* The Hague: Linschoten Society 1923-5

Cyril Wilde (ed.) *Purchas His Pilgrims in Japan* Kobe: J.L. Thompson & Co., 1938

Yang Dan (ed. English Text) *Atlas of the People's Republic of China* Beijing: Foreign Languages Press and China Cartographic Publishing House, 1989

Henry Yule and A.C. Burnell *Hobson-Jobson: A Glossary of Colloquial Anglo-Indian Words and Phrases* London & New York: Routledge & Kegan Paul, 1986

Diego Pacheco Yuuki *The Martyrs' Hill, Nagasaki* Nagasaki: Twenty-Six Martyrs Museum, 1986

Diego Pacheco Yuuki *The Founding of the Port of Nagasaki* Macau: Centro de Estudos Marítimos de Macau, 1989 (a)

Diego Pacheco Yuuki *Twenty-Six Martyrs Museum Catalogue* Nagasaki: Twenty-Six Martyrs Museum, 1989 (b)

GLOSSARY

Bakufu	lit. *Tent, or armed camp, government;* the Tokugawa government apparatus
bonze	(*Bonzo*, Morejón) Buddhist priest or monk
bugyo	special commissioner or governor appointed by the *Bakufu*
cofradía	mutually supporting lay Christian groups, especially valuable during the era of persecution
daikan	deputy. The Nagasaki *daikan* was appointed by the *Bakufu* and governed Nagasaki
daimyo	(*tono*) Petty feudal lord. Under the *Bakufu*, daimyo could be created, dispossessed or transferred at will
Nanban	South Barbary; those parts of Asia ruled or controlled by the Iberians. During the *Sakoku* period, knowledge of the world beyond Japan declined to the point where official Japanese sources referred to a 'King of South Barbary'
Nambanjin	South Barbarian, a Catholic European or Goan
Nihonmachi	settlement of Japanese traders and permanent residents outside Japan; e.g. in Korea, Philippines, Siam
jurabasso	interpreter, from the Malay *jurubahasa*; language master
rutter, roteiro	written sailing instructions giving directions and advice to mariners sailing on established routes. Several were published in Linschoten's *Itinerario*
saker	a small swivel-gun mounted aboard a ship
Sakoku	Lit. *Closed Country*, a later literary term invented to describe the period of Japan's virtual isolation from the world. Although not contemporary, it is too useful to avoid
Sengoku Jidai	the lawless period preceding the *de facto* hegemony of Oda Nobunaga over much of Japan
seppuku	(*hara kiri*) ritual suicide committed by insertion of a sword or dagger into the intestines; a 'second' might

	thereafter decapitate the suicidee. Women committed *seppuku* by thrusting a dagger into the jugular vein and carotid artery
shogun	Lit. *Barbarian-conquering Marshal*, a title in the gift of the Emperor in Miyako. Tokugawa Ieyasu was the founder of the Tokugawa *shogunate* (1603-1868)
shuinjo	vermilion-seal passport authorising foreign trade
shuinsen	ship(s) with valid *shuinjo*
Taiko	*de facto* hegemon, a title stopping short of shogun
wako	(Chinese; *wo'k'uo*) pirates operating from Japan, especially from Kyushu and neighbouring islands. They engaged mainly in piracy in Chinese waters

INDEX

INDEX OF SHIPPING